EDINBURGH CURIOSITIES

EDINBURGH CURIOSITIES

James U. Thomson

Revised by
Hamish Coghill

JOHN DONALD

This edition published in 2004 by
John Donald Publishers,
an imprint of
Birlinn Limited
West Newington House
10 Newington Road
Edinburgh EH9 1QS

www.birlinn.co.uk

First published as *Edinburgh Curiosities 1* and *2* in 1996 and 1997
by John Donald Publishers, Edinburgh

ISBN 0 85976 593 8

British Library Cataloguing-in-Publication Data
A catalogue record for this book is available from the British Library

Typeset by Textype, Cambridge
Printed and bound by GraphyCems, Spain

Contents

ACKNOWLEDGEMENTS

A city as rich in history as Edinburgh has a multitude of stories to tell. Many of the characters involved are very much part of the city's folklore. People like the handsome Young Pretender Prince Charles Edward Stewart who was dubbed 'Bonnie' by a housewife after his highlanders had slipped into Edinburgh when a gate in the city wall was opened; Deacon William Brodie, the on-the-face-of-it prosperous cabinetmaker who ran a gang of housebreakers – and paid the ultimate penalty for his crimes; Professor Sir James Simpson whose discovery of the anaesthetic use of chloroform brought an end to much of the suffering in surgical operating rooms; Queen Victoria whose statues abound, but who took time to pay homage at the graves of two loyal servants in a quiet city graveyard. And why should the royal cypher of one of her successors cause an explosive protest in the 1950s?

They all add to the curiosities of this old town in which so many of the ordinary men and women have also written a little chapter through their infamy or heroics. A brutal child murderer; a scheming philanderer who poisoned his wife; a woman who killed the babies she bought for a few pounds; a young lad who cheerfully encouraged the rescuers digging him out of the rubble of a collapsed tenement; the struggle of the poorest citizens to survive in appalling slums while the well-to-do enjoyed the spacious comfort of the New Town.

One definition of the word 'curious' is inquisitiveness and James U. Thomson certainly had a strong streak of inquisitiveness. *Edinburgh Curiosities* had its conception in a series of articles written for Edinburgh newspapers and other magazines. They were later gathered into two volumes published in 1996 and 1997.

I well recall Jimmy's pride when he told me his first book manuscript had been accepted for publication. I also well remember the hours he spent digging through the bound newspaper files in the *Evening News* offices in Market Street and North Bridge trying to track down some elusive report to settle his own curiosity. He delved assiduously through many sources looking for those extra details on the prominent and ordinary folk involved in whatever story he wanted to tell.

The curiosities cover a wide range of events in the city's life, but this is a book not purely for Edinburghers. It fleshes out for every reader, local or visitor, the flavour of the city where beneath the surface good and evil lie side by side. Deacon Brodie was the inspiration for Robert Louis Stevenson's unforgettable character Dr Jekyll and Mr Hyde. Edinburgh is in many respects a 'Jekyll and Hyde' city and Jimmy Thomson's curiosity takes us above and below that surface.

In editing and slightly abridging the two volumes and providing extra illustrations, I have been conscious of the immense work Jimmy put into his research to find the unusual detail which adds to our knowledge and entertainment.

Hamish Coghill
Edinburgh
March 2004

1

EDINBURGH THROUGH EIGHTEENTH-CENTURY EYES

Hundreds of thousands of tourists come to Edinburgh every year and an essential for visitors getting to grips with the city is a good guidebook. The choice is wide and varied and now most are highly illustrated with colour photographs.

Guidebooks, of course, are not a product of the modern era; they have been around for centuries, and many years ago I had occasion to consult one such publication which had been produced by T. Brown, North Bridge Street, Edinburgh, in 1792. This 118-page book contained a brief history of the town, a description of the buildings and general information on transport and postal services.

In 1621, the book records, a law was passed whereby houses which previously had been roofed with straw or boards were required to be covered with slates, tiles or lead. Seventy-seven years later a further regulation was introduced to restrict the height of buildings to five storeys. Street lighting also received the attention of the magistrates who, in 1684, directed that candles were to be hung from the first floor window of every house.

Also in that year it was agreed that two coaches and eight horses be purchased for the use of the magistrates; and women were forbidden to wear shawls over their heads. The penalty for defying this law was a fine of £5 and forfeiture of the shawl. A third offence of this nature could be punished with banishment from the town.

The list of places worthy of a visit is surprisingly familiar and included the Castle, St Giles' Cathedral, Parliament House, Register House, Canongate Church, the High School and Holyrood. Also included were Heriot's Hospital, Watson's Hospital, the Merchant Maiden Hospital, Trades Maiden Hospital and the Orphan Hospital (which stood roughly in the vicinity of the former GPO building).

Visitors were informed that the Infirmary was attended by two physicians chosen by the managers. They visited the hos-

pital daily, but all members of the College of Surgeons attended in
rotation. Statistics were obviously not issued too frequently as those
quoted related to the year 1782 when 6,370 patients were admitted.
Of those who crossed the hospital portals, 4,395 were cured, 358 died,
and the others either were relieved of their ailments, dismissed as
incurable, left of their own accord or remained in the Infirmary.

The Assembly Rooms, then not long open in George Street, were
recommended as a meeting place, and here, for a fee of five shillings,
visitors could play cards or dance under the direction of a master of
ceremonies. It was proudly boasted that the largest room in the suite,
which was 100 feet long and 40 feet broad, was the second largest of
its kind in Britain.

On the road to the Port of Leith, Edinburgh's harbour for centuries, stood the Amphitheatre, which had been opened in 1790 for
equestrian exhibitions, pantomimes and dancing. The entertainment
provided at this establishment was described as being on a par with
that seen in London. It also served as a riding school.

The theatre would be found in Shakespeare Square at the east end
of Princes Street and, although described as a plain building on the
outside, it was elegantly fitted within. These premises were open on
three evenings a week.

In the High Street, visitors could see the Tolbooth, which was
erected in 1561 and housed the prison, parliament offices and the
courts. It was delicately pointed out, however, that this building had
become unfit for habitation and was to be demolished. It stood a few
years more until it was taken down in 1817.

The Lord Provost was Captain of the Tolbooth, although it was
administered by a jailer. The latter had sole responsibility for obtaining all provisions for the prisoners, 'a circumstance,' the guidebook
pointed out, 'which must certainly be considered as a grievous
oppression, those who are least able to purchase them being thus
obliged to do so at the highest price.'

Forrest Road now passes through what was the Charity
Workhouse site. The institution was built in 1743 and housed 700
residents and 300 outworkers. Each was allowed to retain two pence
of every shilling earned. The authorities had one problem – the
expenditure for running the establishment had been set at £4,000
per annum, but they found that it required £4 10s. a head to provide
the necessities of life!

Edinburgh had a population of 100,000 in 1792, but the Town Guard comprised only three officers and ninety other ranks. They were dressed in similar fashion to soldiers and when called to quell a mob they were provided with Lochaber axes.

The officers received the same pay as an army lieutenant and the rank-and-file were paid in accordance with their equivalent army rank. The upkeep of this organisation was met from a tax levied on the tradesmen. This, however, produced only £1,250 and the balance had to be provided by the magistrates.

Letters to England left the town each day except Thursday at 3.30 p.m. and arrived three days later. The charge was sevenpence. Mail to North America and the West Indies was made up on the Saturday preceding the first Wednesday of every month. The cost was one shilling and sevenpence; this had to be paid in advance if addressed to a North American resident, but letters to the West Indies were accepted COD.

Public transport consisted of a half-hourly horse-drawn vehicle service which operated between the Mercat Cross in the High Street and Leith Shore; the fare was 4½d. Four coaches a day, except Sunday, operated between the town and Dalkeith at a cost of 1s. 3d. Other fares were Musselburgh 1s., Haddington 4s., Peebles 5s., Glasgow between 8s. and 12s. 6d., Perth 11s. 6d., Aberdeen £2.2s., Jedburgh 11s. 6d., Kelso 13s., Linlithgow 3s. 6d. and Falkirk 5s. (An old shilling (s.) was the equivalent of 5p, and there were 12 pennies (d.) to a shilling.)

The Edinburgh–London Royal Mail set out from St Andrew Street each afternoon at 3.30 and was at Newcastle by nine o'clock next morning.

It was due in York at 4 p.m. the same day and was in London by 5 a.m. on the third day after leaving the Scottish capital. The fare was £1.16s. to Newcastle and £6.6s. to London.

Hackney carriages were available in the town at a cost of sixpence for a local journey, but to Leith the charge was 2s. 6d. An extra sixpence was asked for a night journey. A weekly 'runabout' hire was 25s.

Porters could be hired very readily, and charged three shillings to transport 12 cwt of coal to the fourth floor or above, two shillings and twopence to the third level and two shillings below this point. They would carry articles (except wine and furniture) to any part of the town for one shilling.

And this guide to Edinburgh had one final word of assurance for the visitor, claiming that 'no city in the world can afford greater security to the inhabitants in their person and properties than Edinburgh'.

What a Glaswegian saw

The journey between Glasgow and Edinburgh is today not too harrowing an experience. There is an adequate train service and, traffic congestion and roadworks permitting, the trip by road can usually be completed in a reasonable time. Yes, there are problems, but nothing compared with the nightmare which one Glasgow man was subjected to in 1784: he was thirteen hours on the road!

Our visitor, who was making his first trip to Edinburgh as a guest of a minister friend, had an early start from his home in order to reach the Saracen's Head Inn in the Gallowgate, where the chaise and pair to Edinburgh departed daily at 7 a.m. The journey to join the coach was made on foot, and on the way he passed Gabriel Watson's quarters, where a great six-wheeled coach drawn by eight horses was already being unloaded. It was the London to Glasgow stage which had just arrived after an arduous journey.

The two horses on the Edinburgh-bound coach were harnessed and it left on time. It was a slow journey, however; the speed never exceeded six miles an hour, but even this pace dropped on the slightest hill. Cumbernauld was reached in two hours and at this point a stop was made, lasting one-and-a-half hours, for the passengers to have breakfast and to allow the horses to be rested. The next stop was Linlithgow at 2 p.m., with time for a late lunch and a look around the town before departing at 3.30 p.m.

Although the horses had been replaced, the tempo did not increase and, after a further two hours, yet another halt was made, this time at a wayside inn where tea was taken and the animals rested. At approximately 8 p.m. the horses pulled to a stop in the Grassmarket in Edinburgh. The ordeal was over.

Whenever Edinburgh and Glasgow people meet, sooner or later discussion will turn to the merits of the respective towns. But this is nothing new and the eighteenth-century Glaswegian made no secret of his opinion of Edinburgh. He deplored the attitude that Edinburgh people considered themselves better bred than their Glasgow cousins and there was no doubt in his mind that Glasgow was the better town.

'Our Trongate,' he wrote, 'beat the High Street; our High Church was grander by thousands than their Holyrood; our St Andrew's Church was better than their St Giles' . . . and, as for their college, it was a poor shabby affair and our college beat it to atoms.'

Even Parliament House did not escape the caustic words of the writer, who described it as little better than Glasgow's Tontine. It was conceded that Glasgow did not have long streets which were as new as Princes Street or George Street.

A castle Glasgow did not have, but, not to be outdone, our visitor was firm in his belief that if a large house was constructed in Craig's Park 'it would look as pretty a place as the castle'. The Mound was a 'shapeless mass and scarcely passable for glaur and nastiness', while the Nor' Loch was nothing but a swamp, full of the waste from Castlehill, Lawnmarket, High Street and the Luckenbooths. The dirty Meadows was a most atrocious place, smelling of stagnant water and other filth collected from Bristo Street, Potter Row, George Square, Lauriston and Sciennes. Indeed they were quite incomparable with the beautiful Clyde or noble Glasgow Green.

The Cowgate, Potter Row and Candlemakers' Row were acceptable, but certainly no better than Glasgow's Bridgegate, or its wynds and vennels.

The Calton Hill was not a match for Ratten Raw, while a walk along Princes Street, although impressive, was not as grand as the walks along Trongate and Saltmarket. The West Bow and Nether Bow were, he thought, curious but twenty times better was Deanside Brae or Bell o' the Brae in Glasgow. And how troublesome to climb the steep slopes of Arthur's Seat to see the panoramic view of the town which, after all, did not surpass the sight from Cathkin Braes, 'and we make no brag about the matter'.

Was this Glaswegian poking fun or did he honestly believe that his town was superior to the Scottish capital? That we will never know, but perhaps it was a good thing that Edinburgh and Glasgow were a thirteen-hour journey apart!

And as an Englishman saw the town

Two hundred years ago a trip from the south of England was a venture not undertaken lightly, but some adventurers took the right decision, boarded a stagecoach for Edinburgh and were suitably impressed.

Writing of such a visit in 1771, one southerner, seeing the town for the first time, described it as: 'A city that possesses a boldness and grandeur of situation beyond any that I have ever seen . . . the view of the houses at a distance strikes the traveller with wonder; their own loftiness, improved by their almost aerial situation, gives them a look of magnificence not to be found in any other part of Great Britain.'

Despite the awe-inspiring height of some of the houses (the back of one tenement built on a slope was twelve or thirteen storeys), the practice of several families sharing a common stair did not impress our visitor. Nevertheless, he confessed, the cleanliness within these stairways was, generally speaking, fairly high. The streets were cleaned early each morning, but the inhabitants of some closes and alleys had not yet been convinced that it was not in the interest of public health to deposit filth in the streets. With the familiar phrase, 'gardez-l'eau' (literally, watch out for the water), they would show little respect for the unsuspecting passer-by as the rubbish was thrown from the upper windows. It was little comfort for the unfortunate victim that 'the sufferer may call every inhabitant of the house it came from to account and make them prove the delinquent.' The magistrates dealt severely with any culprits.

Edinburgh Castle, St Giles', Parliament House and Holyrood were, as they are today, great attractions for visitors, but there was much to be seen which can no longer be viewed by the present-day tourist. The Luckenbooths, Tolbooth and the guard house in the High Street were popular attractions, although the writer thought the location of the last two buildings served only to spoil 'as fine a street as most in Europe'. The High Street generally was finely built, he admitted, and its width (80 ft in some places) left a lasting impression. And the English traveller was surprised to find on a church visit that there was no music.

The Royal Exchange (now the City Chambers) was a source of great amusement. It was built between 1753 and 1761 mainly for the benefit of the city merchants, but they clung to their old ways and continued to conduct their business in the open. Even the huge cistern on the Castlehill was considered to be something worth seeing. This container held about 230 tons of water, which was conveyed from the Comiston springs and formed the main water supply for the town. In the Grassmarket, visitors were shown where cattle were sold – and criminals hanged!

The university was a modest building and accommodated 600 students. They were subjected to no regulations yet proved to be most conscientious and few let the college down. Classes were conducted by 22 professors, who were most able men, particularly those in the medical field. The Infirmary had beds for 200 patients and was equipped with an operating theatre.

In close proximity, an area of 27 acres had been earmarked for the building of George Square. It was partly developed, with small commodious houses built in the English style. Such was the spirit of development at this period that in three years, £80,000 had been spent on house-building. On the north side of the city, the New Town was under construction and was a great attraction.

The houses in St Andrew Square were selling at a price of between £1,800 and £2,000. Some of the grander accommodation, however, was also available, and these exclusive properties were on the market at between £4,000 and £5,000. This project, the Englishman admitted, 'is planned with great judgement and will prove a great and magnificent addition to Edinburgh'.

In the markets, pigeons were on sale at between eightpence and five shillings a dozen, chickens cost between eightpence and one shilling a pair, a fowl one shilling and twopence, a large turkey was four or five shillings and a pig the princely sum of two shillings. Coal was available at between five- and sixpence a hundredweight – delivered.

Excursions within easy reach of the town included Craigmillar Castle, Newbattle, Dalkeith and Leith. The latter was described as 'dirty, ill-built and chiefly inhabited by sailors'. Our English visitor had at least some respect for the inhabitants of the port, however, for he noticed that the Leith races, which were held on the sands near low water mark, were poorly attended, 'a proof that dissipation has not generally infected the manners of the North Britons'.

Captain Topham: temporary resident

It is wrong for anyone to pass judgement on a city purely on the basis of an excursion visit.

Perhaps one of the best impressions of eighteenth-century Edinburgh can be gleaned from the letters of Captain Edward Topham, which were written between 1774 and 1775. A seasoned traveller with a wide experience of conditions in many parts of Europe, his immediate reaction on arriving in the Scottish capital was one of shock: 'One can scarcely form in imagination the distress of a miserable stranger on his first entrance into the city as there is no inn that is better than an alehouse, nor any accommodation that is decent, clean or fit to receive a gentleman.'

Topham, an Englishman, had arrived in the Pleasance, accompanied by his travelling companion. They were received by a poorly clad girl without shoes or stockings, and taken to a room where about twenty drovers were devouring a meal of whisky and potatoes. No beds were available, but the visitors were told that they were welcome to share a room with a group of passengers who had arrived by stagecoach. They were not impressed to be told that 'this was the best inn in the metropolis'.

The tired and disillusioned travellers left and made their way to the Cross in search of a coffee-house where, they were assured, there was a woman who let accommodation. Courteously, the pair were conducted to the sixth-floor landing of a tenement where the apartments were 'so infernal in appearance that you would have thought yourself in the regions of Erebus.' (Erebus is, in Greek mythology, the god of darkness and the intermediate region between Earth and Hades!) The accommodation was served by only two windows, which looked out into a five-foot-wide passageway, so dark that even on the brightest day the sun did not penetrate.

'It is extremely strange,' reflected the Captain, 'that a city which is a thoroughfare into all Scotland and now little inferior in politeness to London in many respects, should not be better furnished with conveniences to strangers, or have a public lodging house where you can find tolerable entertainment.'

But not everything met with Topham's displeasure and he noted 'a thousand instances' of resemblances between Scotland and France. The air of mirth and vivacity, the quick and penetrating look, the spirit of gaiety which distinguished the French was equally visible in the Scots.

And our visitor was impressed with the manners of local residents when they met strangers. They did not appear as if they had never seen each other before, or wished never to see each other again. They did not sit in sullen silence, looking at the ground, biting their nails and at a loss what to do with themselves, he observed, adding: 'They appear to be satisfied with each other, or at least if they are really not so, they have the prudence to conceal their dislike. I never met with a more agreeable people, with more pleasing or more insinuating manners in my life.'

Among the upper classes, small dinner parties were popular and it was considered an honour to be invited. The guests usually numbered about eight and the occasion was quite informal. Topham noticed, however, that women tended to consume more wine than their English counterparts but, as he tactfully explained 'the climate requires it'. The evening usually ended with a recital of Scottish songs.

Fashionwise, Edinburgh ladies were not influenced by London, preferring the Paris styles. These women, Captain Topham noted, dressed in general with more elegance and in a way better accommodated to their persons, size and shape than most of the European nations. Their complexion, too, was generally admired. The ladies used no make-up and Topham pointed out that: 'neither their colour or complexion stand in need of it for I know not where they will find their equals in either.' Edinburgh men, on the other hand, had the worst tailors perhaps in the world.

The present Theatre (i.e. the Theatre Royal, which stood in Shakespeare Square, opposite Register House and opened in 1769 at a cost of £5,000) Topham described as 'a plain structure'. Admission charges to the pit and boxes were three shillings. The pit was usually occupied by gentlemen who were not sufficiently dressed for the boxes. On busy nights, however, ladies were also accommodated there, although the management very considerately provided a partition.

Although the theatre had few ornaments it had an elegant appearance. The performances did not impress the southerner. Although murmurs of displeasure were heard from the audience 'they never rain down oranges, apples etc. on the heads of the unfortunate actors. They were suffered quietly for an hour, and if they displeased they were literally heard no more.'

Whereas in England it was usual to drive the unfortunate actors from the stage, in Edinburgh the audience merely refrained from applauding. 'In such circumstances you discover the real manners of the people,' commented the good Captain, who was suitably impressed with the behaviour of the town's residents.

The dances of Scotland he described as being entirely void of grace, and it was a mystery to him how Edinburgh women could sit quite unmoved at the sprightly airs of an English country dance, but on hearing a Scottish air would move as if bitten by a tarantula. How was it, he questioned, that such a drowsy instrument as the bagpipes should be capable of inspiring such uncommon ardour? Dancing assemblies were fashionable modes of entertainment, and were conducted in an orderly manner. Those present were divided into sets and took their turn on the floor in strict rotation.

Oyster Cellars, described by Topham as 'high life below stairs', attracted both sexes of the upper classes. Invited to supper in such a place, one was ushered into a room where the guests were seated around a large table covered with dishes of oysters and pots of porter. Subsequently the tables were cleared, brandy punch was produced, and a jovial evening followed.

The women, it was noted, joined in the repartee to a much greater degree than would have been expected in England. Dancing formed a part of the evening's entertainment and at the end of a happy and enjoyable occasion, carriages were called. The cost of the evening had been two shillings for each guest.

Captain Topham, who hailed from Yorkshire, was educated at Eton and Trinity College, Cambridge, and was a journalist who had travelled extensively on the Continent. He was therefore well qualified to make critical observations on conditions as he found them in Edinburgh. His residence of six months was sufficiently long to make a balanced judgement, and, apart from his initial problems in finding acceptable accommodation he was generally impressed.

Above all, however, Topham's letters are extremely important for the valuable contribution they make to the social history of Edinburgh.

2

A MOST ELEGANT SQUARE

The second half of the eighteenth century saw an explosion of growth in what was basically an overcrowded, dirty, smelly, still-walled town. Buildings were falling down or being demolished because of their ruinous state, pavements were uneven and danger-ous underfoot, and filth was still flung from tenement windows onto the narrow closes below.

So those citizens who started to desert the Old Town and cross the North Bridge to take up residence in the fine houses and wide streets to the north could not have failed to be impressed. One of the most prestigious developments was Charlotte Square, still today a classic of Georgian architecture.

With St Andrew Square at the east end of George Street (named after George III), St George's Square was considered to be an appro-priate address for the dwellings to be erected in the balancing square to the west. But it was too late. George Square was already laid out on the south side of the town and so the name Charlotte was adopted, in recognition of George III's queen.

Robert Adam completed his plans for the square in 1791, but he did not live to see his masterpiece completed. He died in March of the following year, at the age of sixty-four and was buried at Westminster. At the time of his death it is believed that Adam was actively engaged in eight public works and twenty-five private buildings.

The bulk of the former church on the west side of Charlotte Square tends to catch the eye, but very quickly the attention turns to the north side, a lasting memorial to the Kirkcaldy-born genius. He was paid £200 for the layout plan for the square and five guineas for each house he designed in detail. The feuing conditions required that the houses to be built on the north side should be constructed 'on a regular plan to conform to an elevation by the late Mr Robert Adam, Architect, and the ornamental parts of the fronts to be finished in the manner there-in set furth'.

Residents

Charlotte Square immediately became a prestigious address and over the years provided homes for some of the town's wealthiest families.

In 1806, Sir John Sinclair of Ulbster occupied no.6. Sinclair was educated at Edinburgh, Glasgow and Oxford universities and he qualified as a lawyer. While in the south of England he met Sarah, daughter of Alexander Maitland, who was of Scottish descent. The young Scot proposed and was accepted, but a hitch developed – his future mother-in-law!

This lady, reluctant to lose her daughter, insisted on a promise from Sinclair that he would live permanently in England. This ultimatum he could not meet, and he set off for a Continental holiday, believing that the marriage would not take place. He returned to learn that Sarah had prevailed upon her mother and that the wedding could now go ahead.

Following their marriage on 26 March 1776, the couple departed to live in Thurso! In 1780 Sinclair was elected Member of Parliament

Sir John Sinclair (from Kay's *Original Portraits*)

for Caithness. He lost the seat in 1784 but was later returned for Lostwithiel in Cornwall. Sarah died in 1785, leaving two young daughters.

The following year Sinclair was created a baronet and three years after the death of his wife he remarried. His bride was the Honourable Diana, the only daughter of Lord Macdonald. Soon afterwards they settled in Edinburgh, first in the Canongate, before moving to 6 Charlotte Square, and subsequently George Street. It is said that as a form of exercise he regularly walked to Leith.

In 1791 Sinclair embarked on the compilation of *The Statistical Account of Scotland*, a task which took between seven and eight years and consisted of twenty-one volumes. The Account is a collection of reports on the parishes of Scotland and is an invaluable guide to the state of the country at that time.

Sinclair was a great supporter of the celebrated writer Malachi Malagrowther. Who? Malachi Malagrowther was the nom-de-plume adopted by Sir Walter Scott in 1826, when the government proposed to limit the issue of banknotes. This would have had a serious effect in Scotland, and Scott, under his nom-de-plume, expressed his views on the matter with a number of letters published in the *Edinburgh Weekly Journal*.

Sinclair was an internationally known figure corresponding with, among others, George Washington, John Adams and Thomas Jefferson, the first three Presidents of the USA. Any person of note who visited Scotland would almost certainly have carried a letter of introduction to John Sinclair. He died at his George Street home in December 1835, and according to the nineteenth-century writer James Paterson 'was buried on the 30th in the Royal Chapel of Holyrood'.

There were thirteen children from Sinclair's two marriages, but without doubt it is to his daughter Catherine that Edinburgh is most indebted.

Born into a well-to-do family, she could have spent her time, as so many of her class did, enjoying a life of leisure. But this public-spirited woman chose to devote her life to caring for the less fortunate citizens of Edinburgh.

It was Catherine Sinclair, an author with thirty-seven titles to her credit, who introduced public seats to the busy streets of Edinburgh, a feature which remains popular to this day. She founded and

The Catherine Sinclair monument

financed the Volunteer Brigade for the boys of Leith, opened a school where girls from working-class homes were taught domestic work, and provided shelters where cabmen could relax while waiting for fares.

Cooking centres were also provided by this great benefactress. The first, opened at 60 Queensferry Street, proved to be so popular that a second followed shortly afterwards at 33 George IV Bridge. These premises consisted of a kitchen with separate dining rooms for students and families. For as little as 4½d. it was possible to have a meal of soup, meat, potatoes and bread.

Nothing, however, perpetuated the name of Catherine Sinclair more than her drinking fountain, which stood at the junction of

Lothian Road and Princes Street. The Sinclair Fountain was presented to the city in 1859 and was the first in Edinburgh.

For fourteen years it was a popular amenity, where the thirst of man and beast alike could be slaked on warm summer days. But it could be put to other uses. In those far-off days of the horse-drawn tram, when public houses were open all day, many of our policemen were from the north and were not averse to a drop of whisky. Working on points duty at the West End, it was no easy matter for the 'bobby' to get a drop of the 'cratur' without being seen.

There was a way of overcoming this problem: a signal was passed to the local news-vendor, who obligingly ran to the nearest public house to purchase a gill which, at that time, cost between six- and sevenpence. The vendor then went to the well, emptied the whisky into one of the chained cups and signalled to the constable – who sauntered over and drank with pleasure what was of course ostensibly water!

Alas, on 4 June 1873, on the casting vote of Lord Provost James Cowan, it was decided that, because of the increase in traffic, the fountain was causing congestion and would have to be removed. There was an immediate outcry. Letters appeared in the newspapers, and all but one opposed the Council's decision. It was pointed out that this was the only fountain in the area; a survey carried out a short time previously had established that during a three-hour period 273 horses had been watered at the well – proof surely that it should be retained.

The Catherine Sinclair drinking fountain at the junction of
Princes Street and Lothian Road.

The controversy was by no means a local dispute. There was a letter from a correspondent in Tunbridge Wells, part of which read:

> I have just seen – with more sorrow than I can well express – in a late number of your paper, that the Sinclair Fountain, which held its ground successfully through so many onslaughts, has at last been a victim to that great juggernaut the tramway. Forbid it, shade of kind Miss Sinclair. Forbid it in all humanity . . .

The writer went on to explain that for many years he had driven past the fountain four times a day and had derived much pleasure from watching the horses drinking at it. Never once had he witnessed them causing any delay. He enclosed £10 towards a fund to fight the Council decision.

There was one citizen who supported the Council's views, but he chose to hide under the nom-de-plume 'Civus'. This writer pointed out that no correspondent seemed to be aware that a pillar well was placed at each cab stance in the city and that a pail was provided so that the horses might also drink. They were never used, he claimed, and he went on to accuse the cabmen of adjourning to nearby public houses 'for something stronger than water', leaving one boy to attend to the horses; hence the reason for it being necessary to use the fountain. It was evident that 'Civus' was set on having the fountain removed, for he concluded:

> I have seen all the principal towns in the Empire, as well as those of Rome, Naples and many other of the chief towns of the Continent, but never in my experience, either as a professional man or a citizen of the world, have I seen anything to compare, in utter contemptibility, with the ugliness of the Sinclair Fountain, and this aggravated one hundredfold from the fact it occupies a site, the finest in the city and in a street whose beauty cannot be matched.

The campaign for its retention was successful, and at a meeting of the Town Council on 26 June the decision to remove the fountain was reversed. For more than seventy years the landmark remained on its familiar site, but on 2 February 1932 the matter was again raised at a Council meeting.

Once more the decision was taken to remove the fountain, but this time Council officials acted swiftly, and less than two weeks later the work of dismantling had been completed. Curiously, about the same time the City Architect and Burgh Engineer had reported that the fountain was in need of repair and the cost was estimated at £390.

There was a general belief among Edinburgh's citizens that every effort would be made to find an alternative site. But two years on, with no evidence of any progress, a newspaper reporter began to ask questions. He eventually traced the fountain to the Burgh Engineer's yard in the Cowgate. Requests for information about the re-siting of the well were met with silence.

The fight went on, and in 1935 there was some hope that a permanent location might be found near the bandstand in West Princes Street Gardens. No further action was taken.

But not even the Second World War years allowed the subject of this now famous fountain to be forgotten, and in 1941 the newspaper again reminded the Council of their promise to relocate this former prominent city landmark. This time the local authority had a ready-made answer, and a spokesman was quick to point out that no action could be taken for the duration of the war. To strengthen this argument he went on to explain that other cities, far from replacing structures, were removing public monuments to places of safety.

In 1950 an observant citizen noted that a tram island now occupied the site; surely space could be found to reinstate Catherine Sinclair's gift to the town. This plea was also met with indifference.

The years passed, and then in 1964 I decided to investigate. With reluctance, a Council official suggested that the fountain 'might' be in the yard at Russell Road. It was, placed neatly in a corner. Unfortunately, more than thirty years had elapsed since the Council's controversial act; most of the councillors and officials involved in the decision were no longer in the Chambers and there was little enthusiasm to raise the embarrassing subject.

At some point over the ensuing years, this once-familiar piece of street furniture which had been appreciated by man and animal alike, was removed from Russell Road; it was rediscovered quite by chance.

The Council premises at Stanwell Street were known to hold a number of ornamental stones, which had been accumulated over the years, and a decision was taken to identify the stones and compile an inventory. In the course of this work a stone was discovered bearing the inscriptions:

The remains of the Catherine Sinclair fountain,
remind humans that 'water is not for man alone'.

WATER IS NOT FOR MAN ALONE:
A BLESSING UPON THE GIVER:
and DRINK AND BE THANKFUL

This was enough to identify the missing Catherine Sinclair drinking
fountain.

What has survived is again on public display and can be seen on
the cycleway/walkway beside Gosford Place, Leith. It was placed
there in 1983, at the section named Stedfastgate, to mark the centenary of the Boys' Brigade.

Catherine Sinclair died suddenly, aged sixty-four, at the Vicarage,
Kensington, the home of her brother. In recognition of her work for
Edinburgh's needy families, a fine statue was erected at the corner of
North Charlotte Street and St Colme Street, not far from her father's
house in Charlotte Square. Included in the inscription cut into the
stone are the words: 'She was a friend of all children and through her
book *Holiday House* speaks to them still.'

Miss Sinclair lived at 133 George Street and despite her vast phil-
anthropic work which must have occupied a considerable amount of

her time, she was also a prolific writer. The sales of her book *Beatrice* are believed to have exceeded 100,000 copies within a few months of publication.

The Sinclair family were renowned for their height and the pavement outside their Charlotte Square property was known as 'The Giants' Causeway'.

Number 9 might well be known as the doctors' house for here resided two distinguished medical men, James Syme and the future Lord Lister of antiseptics fame.

Syme was educated at Edinburgh's High School and later at the University of Edinburgh. He was appointed professor of surgery at Edinburgh in 1833 and was recognised as the greatest living authority in his speciality. Syme accumulated one achievement outwith medicine to his credit when, in 1818, he revealed a method of making waterproofing. He died in 1870.

Joseph Lister arrived in the city in 1853 to spend a month of postgraduate study with the celebrated Syme. He remained until 1860 (having married Professor Syme's daughter Agnes in 1856), when he was appointed professor of surgery at Glasgow. Lister returned to Edinburgh in 1869 to succeed his father-in-law in the Chair of Clinical Surgery and took up residence at no. 9.

A few doors away at no. 12 lived Sir John Marjoribanks. It was during the provost-ship of Marjoribanks that the Regent Bridge and Calton Jail projects went ahead. Next door, no. 13, was for many years the home of Sir William Fettes, probably Edinburgh's best-known early nineteenth-century Lord Provost, remembered as the benefactor of the world-famous college which bears his name.

Fettes was born on 25 June 1750, and was educated at the High School. In an eighteenth-century directory there is an entry: 'William Fettes, grocer, head of Bailie Fyfe's Close; house 57 Princes Street.' He was twice elected Lord Provost (1800–02 and 1804–06). And one important duty he fulfilled was to serve on the jury at the trial of Deacon William Brodie in 1788. Both were businessmen and must have known each other; nevertheless, Brodie went to the gallows. Justice had to be done and to be seen to be done.

Fettes married Maria Malcolm, daughter of Dr John Malcolm of Ayr, in March 1787. They had only one child, also named William, who was admitted to the Faculty of Advocates in 1810, but died in Berlin five years later.

William Fettes senior was a very successful businessman and accumulated a large fortune. He retired from business in 1800 and devoted the remainder of his time to administering his various estates. In 1804 he was honoured with a baronetcy.

Sir William died on 27 May 1836 – only twenty days after the death of his wife – and was buried in the Canongate graveyard close to where his father had been interred. The college was built between 1864 and 1870 with the legacy of £166,000 Fettes left for it.

Lord Cockburn, judge and writer of the famous *Memorials*, occupied no. 14, and is remembered for the great interest he had in the preservation of Edinburgh.

No fewer than three people of note occupied no. 17 at one time or another, among them James Wolfe Murray who appeared for the prosecution at the trial of Deacon Brodie; he later became a judge. Wolfe Murray was the householder in 1811.

Nineteen years later the Rt Hon. David Boyle, Lord Justice-General, was resident. And here, in 1856, was born the future Viscount Haldane. Educated at the Edinburgh Academy and at the University of Edinburgh, he was Liberal MP for East Lothian (1885–1911), Lord Chancellor (1912–15), and was closely involved in restructuring the army. He died in 1928.

Dr Elsie Maud Inglis, of the Elsie Inglis Maternity Hospital renown, obtained part of her education in a small school at no. 23. This lady, whose services were declined by the War Office during the 1914–18 campaign, worked tirelessly for the Serbs with her field hospitals and died in 1917.

Elsie Inglis was born in India in 1864 and studied at Edinburgh, Glasgow and Dublin. She was surgeon at Bruntsfield Hospital, established a hospice at 219 High Street, and between 1898 and 1914 practised medicine at 8 Walker Street.

At no. 24 Charlotte Square was born on 19 June 1861 Douglas, Earl Haig, Commander-in-Chief of the British Army during the First World War.

St George's Church (West Register House)

Robert Adam did design a church for Charlotte Square but it was never constructed, probably because of cost. The task was given instead to Robert Reid. His revised design did not meet with general

The Earl Haig statue on the Castle Esplanade

approval, and, as one nineteenth-century critic wrote:

> Had the civic authorities adhered as closely to the designs of Mr
> Adam in the erection of St George's Church, as in the other buildings
> of the Square, they would not, from a mistaken notion of economy,
> have erected an edifice, which, although it may be considered by a
> superficial observer as highly ornamental to the place where it is situ-
> ated, is, when minutely and critically examined, found to be destitute
> of all architectural proportions, and an object of general disapproba-
> tion.

At 2 p.m. on Tuesday 14 May 1811, Lord Provost William Calder,
Magistrates and Town Councillors met in St Andrew's Church,
George Street, and walked to the west side of Charlotte Square,
where the foundation stone of St George's Church was laid by the
Lord Provost. This is an historic date in local government history,
for, immediately after the stone-laying ceremony, the Lord Provost
and Councillors again lined up and made their way in procession to
the High Street, where they formally took over the Royal Exchange
(built 1753–61) as the City Chambers.

The church was three years in construction and served this

wealthy congregation for 147 years. In 1959 dry rot was discovered; an appeal for funds was successful, but other faults were found and the cost of repairs proved to be very substantial. Sadly, in 1961, the church closed, and for some time the future of the building was in doubt.

At the same time Register House was facing storage problems, and in 1964 the decision was taken to convert St George's Church into West Register House as a repository for public records. Work began in 1968 and West Register House was opened by the Secretary of State for Scotland on 2 April 1971. A sum of £450,000 had been spent – but the former St George's Church had been saved.

Andrew Thomson, the first minister at St George's, died suddenly on 9 February 1831, but he is remembered to this day as the composer of the tune 'St George's Edinburgh' ('Ye Gates, lift up your heads').

The Albert Memorial

Did Queen Victoria unveil the Albert Memorial in Charlotte Square Garden? It is a question that is often asked, and the answer is that the circumstances are open to interpretation although the Queen was present at that memorable and moving occasion.

Prince Albert died on Saturday 14 December 1861, and most Edinburgh citizens heard the news from church pulpits the following morning. It was received with shock; Prince Albert was only forty-two years old and had been in Edinburgh less than three months previously, when he had laid the foundation stones of the General Post Office and of the museum in Chambers Street.

Edinburgh took the initiative, and in February 1862 it was suggested that a national monument should be erected in memory of the late Prince Consort. But before long it was evident that Glasgow, Aberdeen, Dundee and Perth were not in favour of this proposal.

The capital, in conjunction with the other areas of Scotland (but excluding these cities) launched an appeal which realised £13,400. Subsequently, competitive designs were invited and it was announced that £12,000 would be available for a monument.

The queen was consulted on the design and location, and she nominated a Committee of Advice, whose members were the Duke of Buccleuch, Lord Provost Charles Lawson, Sir William Gibson-Craig, Sir John McNeill, Dr Lyon Playfair (Professor of Chemistry,

Edinburgh, 1858–69; MP for the Universities of Edinburgh and St Andrews, 1868–85; Postmaster-General 1873 and first Baron Playfair), and Sir George Harvey, President of the Royal Scottish Academy. Not surprisingly, this prestigious work attracted the country's top artists.

A shortlist of six designs was drawn up and submitted to Queen Victoria for her approval. She in turn consulted Sir Charles Eastlake, President of the Royal Academy, but without indicating her preference. The two were in agreement and their choice was one of three submitted by Edinburgh-based John Steell showing the prince in the uniform of a field-marshal and mounted on a horse. Steell's other proposals were a drawing of a pedestrian Prince Albert contemplating a globe, and the other, intended for a site on Arthur's Seat, was a clay equestrian model of the consort on the summit of an arched

The Prince Albert Memorial with
West Register House behind

Gothic structure, intended to be viewed from a distance.

The 32-foot-high design was completed as submitted, with only a few minor alterations. At the request of Steell, sculptors William Brodie RSA, Clark Stanton RSA and George McCallum were invited to carry out some of the work, although Steell undertook the equestrian statue and bas-reliefs. He was in overall charge of the commission. McCallum died at an early stage in the work and D.W. Stevenson joined the team.

The Albert Memorial was unveiled on 17 August 1876 (fifteen years after the death of the prince) in the presence of Queen Victoria, Prince Leopold and Princess Beatrice, on a site 'which was loyally offered by the proprietors of Charlotte Square'. Just before 4 p.m. the queen took her place on the dais. During the ceremony, and in a touching moment, music composed by Albert was played by the 79th Highlanders, the Camerons.

In welcoming the Queen to Edinburgh, the Duke of Buccleuch said:

> The Executive Committee for the erection of the Scottish National Memorial to His Royal Highness the Prince Consort have today the high honour and gratification of presenting that memorial in its completed form to your Majesty and to the people of Scotland.
>
> The subscribers to the memorial numbered very many thousands of your Majesty's Scottish subjects. Contributions were received from every county and nearly every parish in Scotland. All classes of society from the highest and the wealthiest, to the lowliest and poorest, willingly combined, according to their respective ability, to render this memorial a monument worthy of the occasion . . .
>
> It is an auspicious coincidence that this day the 17th August is the anniversary of the birth of Her Royal Highness the Duchess of Kent, your Majesty's beloved mother. The memory of Her Royal Highness will ever be revered by the people of this country for the conspicuous virtues of Her Royal Highness' life and especially for her admirable nurture of their future sovereign. The Executive Committee humbly request your Majesty to be graciously pleased to unveil the memorial in the sight of the present assemblage.

In reply the queen said:

> I receive with pleasure your loyal address. I am well aware of the feeling in Scotland which prompted the raising of this national memorial and assure you that I heartily appreciate the affection and admiration

manifested in this country for my dear husband, as well as the loyalty and attachment to me which has ever been the character of my Scottish subjects. I thank you heartily for the kind allusion you have made to my beloved mother on this day the anniversary of her birth. Her frequent residence in this your city and its neighbourhood proved how much she loved the Scottish nation.

And Victoria's part in the unveiling ceremony? At the conclusion of the queen's reply the Rt Hon. R.A. Cross, the Secretary of State, after exchanging a few words with the queen said, 'I have much pleasure in saying, by Her Majesty's command, that it is her desire the statue be now unveiled.'

Within seconds, the canvas which covered the statue and the wrappings of the pedestal were removed to reveal the statue to the gaze of the general public. Thereafter the four sculptors were introduced to the queen. Only then did Victoria leave the dais and, accompanied by the principal sculptor, members of the royal family and officials, spent some time admiring the statue.

Throughout the ceremony Queen Victoria appeared to be completely relaxed, but what were her thoughts? She surely recalled Albert's last visit to Edinburgh on 23 September 1861, to lay the foundation stones, possibly the last public engagements he carried out. It was an overcast day with an unusually cold and biting wind blowing. Victoria had remained at Holyrood, but Albert had been subjected to two very long ceremonies, which included prayers and therefore a need to remain bareheaded. Less than three months later Victoria's beloved Albert was dead.

After the Charlotte Square unveiling, Victoria returned to Holyrood. John Steell and Professor Herbert Oakeley, who had organised the music for the event, arrived at the palace and the Queen honoured both men with knighthoods.

And there was one final piece of good news for the city during that memorable royal visit, for it was announced that Queen Victoria was to bestow a knighthood on Lord Provost James Falshaw.

Sir James Falshaw has a unique distinction: he is believed to be the only Englishman to have been elected Lord Provost of the City of Edinburgh. His family hailed originally from the Yorkshire Dales, but he was born and educated in Leeds.

Falshaw qualified as a civil engineer, a fortunate choice of career, for this was a period when engineers were in great demand for railway construction. He came to Scotland in 1845, initially to Nairn, where he served on the Council, and in 1858 he moved to Edinburgh. The Yorkshireman retained his keen interest in local government, and two years later he stood for election in the city but was defeated. In 1861, however, he succeeded in being elected and served for sixteen years.

With his engineering qualification, Falshaw was an invaluable servant to the city and freely gave of his knowledge for many schemes, particularly those involving water and roads. He was keenly interested in improving housing for the poorer people of Edinburgh.

In 1872 Falshaw was defeated by James Cowan in the election for Lord Provost, but two years later, when Cowan was elected to the House of Commons, Falshaw became Edinburgh's first citizen. A number of schemes were promoted during his term of office, including the Moorfoot Hills Water Development, the Arboretum, opening West Princes Street Gardens to the public, roofing the Waverley Market, and widening both Princes Street and the North Bridge. The Falshaw Bridge over the Water of Leith at the west end of Glenogle Road is named after him.

Sir James declined to stand for parliament but continued with his interest in railway development, being chairman of the North British Railway. He died in 1889 at the age of seventy-nine.

Sir John Steell

Although born in Aberdeen in 1804, John Steell spent most of his life in Edinburgh. A childhood friend recalled an incident when the future sculptor was about eight years old and the two families lived 'on the steep road ascending to Calton Hill', where they played on the plainstanes (pavements). One day Steell took a piece of chalk and in two or three strokes 'dashed off without the least apparent trouble, a figure of a galloping horse, of large size, so entirely different and to exceed in point of character and excellence anything that children ever did'.

Steell studied at Edinburgh and then went to Rome. On his return he quickly attracted attention with his magnificent Alexander and Bucephalus, which was sited on the west side of St Andrew Square. In 1917 it was removed to its present site in the quadrangle at the City Chambers, to make way for the Gladstone Memorial.

Alexander and Bucephalus in the City Chambers quadrangle

The Wellington statue, east end of Princes Street

Gladstone was in turn repositioned in Coates Crescent during the mid-1950s, as he was causing traffic congestion in St Andrew Square.

Attempts were made to entice Steell to London because no commission for an important public statue in bronze or marble had been given to a sculptor in Scotland. He elected to remain in Scotland with considerable success and was appointed Queen Victoria's sculptor in Scotland in 1838. He is also credited with having introduced artistic bronze casting into Scotland.

Many examples of Steell's work can be seen in the vicinity of Princes Street, including: the Duke of Wellington (at Register House); Sir Walter Scott and Professor John Wilson (in East Princes Street Gardens); Queen Victoria (on the roof of the RSA building); Allan Ramsay (at the Mound entrance to West Princes Street Gardens); Thomas Chalmers (junction of George Street/Castle

Allan Ramsay, at the Mound entrance to
West Princes Street Gardens

Thomas Chalmers, at the junction of
George Street and Castle Street

Street); Prince Albert (Charlotte Square) and Viscount Melville
(Melville Street/Crescent).

In addition, Steell completed statues of the Marquis of Dalhousie
and the Rt Hon. James Wilson, who started life as an apprentice hat
manufacturer in Hawick, became a politician and established the
Economist newspaper, was financial member of the Council of India
and introduced paper money into India. Both of these statues were
for Calcutta. Steell was also commissioned to complete a copy of the
sitting Scott and a Burns, both for New York. He died in 1891.

The National Trust for Scotland and the square

Charlotte Square was initially residential, but by the beginning of the
twentieth century there was a significant change to office use. The
4th Marquess of Bute was very conscious of the importance of

retaining Adam's influence and in the early 1900s he was responsible for the restoration of nos. 5, 6 and 7 Charlotte Square, which included returning the roof line to the architect's original elevation. Other proprietors on the north side followed suit. In 1949, at the invitation of the 5th Marquess of Bute, the National Trust for Scotland established offices at no. 5 Charlotte Square.

During the late 1980s there was evidence of a move away from the square, no doubt influenced by the attraction of modern open-plan offices with adequate facilities for new technology, which were not available in older buildings and could only be achieved at the expense of severely damaging the fabric of these Georgian houses.

Following the death of the 5th Marquess of Bute nos. 5, 6 and 7 Charlotte Square passed, through The National Land Fund procedures, into the ownership of the National Trust for Scotland in 1966, in part settlement of death duties. The 6th Marquess, a former President of the Trust, expressed the hope that Charlotte Square would become the Trust's permanent home. no. 5 became the Trust's headquarters and no. 6 is leased as the official residence of Scotland's First Minister. no. 7, the Georgian House, is open to the public, and visitors can view a fine interpretation of an original Charlotte Square house. Also at no. 7, the Trust provided a flat as the official residence

The First Minister's official residence, Bute House

for the Moderator of the General Assembly of the Church of Scotland (the Moderator's residence is now in Rothesay Terrace).

The Trust announced in April 1996 that they had purchased six adjoining properties, Nos. 26–31 Charlotte Square, with the express intention of carrying out major restoration. They intended to occupy these premises, which are on the south side, as their headquarters with exhibition and gallery facilities.

The National Trust for Scotland also expressed their hope that Charlotte Square Garden would be restored to its original layout, including a more appropriate design of railings, pavement and road surfaces.

Hopefully, one day, visitors to Charlotte Square will see it as envisaged by its designer Robert Adam.

The restored south side of the Square

3

'CABIN, DECK AND STEERAGE'

The poor who lived in the once desirable houses of Edinburgh's Old Town must have cast an eye enviously beyond the valley of the former Nor' Loch to the elegant residences of the affluent and influential.

Geographically only a short distance separated the two classes but the social gulf was enormous. To the north of the North Bridge were the households where several full-time servants were employed while in the vicinity of the High Street families lived in abject poverty.

Investigative journalism is a much hackneyed phrase in modern newspaper writing but it is not new. In 1866 the *Edinburgh Evening Courant*, prompted by the deplorable standard of housing in the town, published a series of articles between 20 October that year and 19 January 1867.

This exposé shocked and shamed the wealthier classes into action and within a month £100 had been sent to the newspaper for the benefit of the needy families. By modern standards this may not seem a great deal of money but 130-odd years ago it was enough to provide four hundred families with two bags of coal each and 'the remainder of the money has been bestowed in gifts equally beyond the risk of misapplication.' A large selection of warm clothing was also donated.

There were two schools of thought on the improvement of living conditions – one idea was to open new streets through the denser parts of the town, while others believed that the problem could be solved by 'thinning' the more closely-packed and ruinous buildings in the old closes. While the experts argued the poor suffered.

The *Courant* was hard-hitting in its criticism of the ignorance of Edinburgh's rich about the conditions in which the poor suffered. 'Much less is known . . . of the closes of Edinburgh than of many parts of the interior of Africa; and the internal arrangements of the

Red Indian's wigwam are much more familiar to the Christian public than is the condition of the hovels in which many of our towns-people live,' the paper declared.

Practically every house visited in the investigation consisted of a single room, and in some it was impossible for a man of average height, wearing a hat, to stand upright. In several instances, families were discovered living in attics measuring 4 ft wide, 12 ft long and the height varying between 3 and 6 ft. Rents for such facilities were between one and two shillings (fivepence and tenpence) per week, paid in advance. Overcrowding was common with families of eight living in one apartment. Facilities regarded as standard in the present day house were non-existent, and there was no provision for the disposal of rubbish, which was kept on landings, behind doors and even under beds until the dustcarts came round.

The *Courant* conceded that it was unreasonable to expect that water and a WC could be provided for each house as many of the flats were not suitable for further conversion, but surely it would be possible to have one well at least for each court and also receptacles for filth outside the houses. But what must be provided, the newspaper insisted, were houses at rents within the reach of classes who were paying between £3 and £5 a year. 'Is it not possible to erect houses – perhaps of brick – of even a room and closet, with plenty of water, that would give a sufficient return on such rents?' asked the paper.

Among the worst accommodation visited in the course of the investigation was at Crombie's Land, in the middle of the West Port, the street which runs from the west end of the Grassmarket. It was here, just a short time before, that there had been an outbreak of cholera, and the doctors firmly argued the buildings should be demolished.

Dr Thomas Chalmers, the prominent theologian, was one who had long worked for the improvement of housing in this area and he shared the views of the medical men that this deathtrap should be removed. Crombie's Land had been the cause of great concern to the authorities because of the deplorable state of the tenement 'land'. It was entered through a narrow dirty passage, leading to a small, confined, filthy court. The rooms on the first and second storeys were reached by way of rickety stairs and gangways 'remarkable for their dirty condition'.

At the time of the reporter's visit three rooms had been closed off because it was here that eight residents – four from one family – had died from cholera; the disease had simply moved from door to door.

It was estimated that seventy people lived in Crombie's Land, described by Dr Henry Littlejohn, Edinburgh's Medical Officer of Health, in his report on the sanitary conditions of Edinburgh, as being one of the most overcrowded tenements in the town, having been 'built specially for the poor with an eye to a large rental, with small, ill-ventilated rooms, and a great deficiency in sanitary conditions'.

Another medical man who inspected the building said that he had seen enough 'to convince me that such a place must not only be a hot-bed of disease, but a great and continual nuisance to the locality, both morally and physically'.

One flat, measuring 10 ft by 6 ft, was 'home' for four people. When the visitors remarked there was no window, the tenant sarcastically pointed out that there was, drawing their attention to the small opening above the door where glass had been inserted. Rent for this room was 1s.6d. a week. Despite the dilapidated condition of the building, it was only twenty years old! The proprietor had purchased the ruin for £38. He had added two storeys and was obviously a nineteenth-century DIY man, having carried out the work 'with my own hand'.

The landlord, a former seaman, described his tenants in the following manner: first floor 'cabin'; second 'deck' and to the rear 'steerage'.

Roofs were built of thin wood covered with layers of metal, believed to have been made from old pots and pans which had been beaten down. This hovel, which contained twenty-seven rooms, yielded rents of between 1s.6d. and 2s. (7½ and 10p) a week.

In contrast there was, close by, a block of buildings which illustrated what could be achieved by a caring landlord and co-operative tenants. It had been purchased twelve years previously, repaired and let to thirty tenants at weekly rents of less than 2s. The common passageways and stairs were clean, there were cellars and drying greens to the rear, a water supply to each level and a soil pipe. Accommodation consisted of a room, measuring 18 ft by 13 ft, and a closet, 11 ft by 8 ft.

Tenants were required to keep their dwellings and stairs clean and in return the proprietor agreed to ensure that all repairs were carried out. The stairs were washed twice a week, Wednesday and Saturday, and the owner confirmed that the occupants were well behaved; they took a pride in their homes and when a flat became vacant there were between twenty and thirty applicants.

How, asked the *Courant*, with rents lower than in the worst hovels in the Grassmarket and West Port, was it possible to provide such superior accommodation at lower rents? The proprietor was content with a net return of ten per cent.

Many of the dwellings were beyond saving, and, with walls between three and four feet thick, would be difficult to demolish. Surprisingly, the point was made that building costs had risen appreciably. Among the reasons given were rises in wages and reduction in working hours in the building industry. It was believed that, where possible, restoration would be more economical than demolition.

But were wages a major factor in costs? For those residents in work, labouring was the main occupation, and a man could expect to be paid between 12s. and 16s. a week (60p and 80p). Shoemaking and repairing was a popular occupation, although the rewards were small – 9s. to 14s. (45p to 70p) for between eighty and ninety hours a week. Many earned a little money by selling firewood, and this was frequently a family concern. A quantity of wood was purchased for sixpence, broken up, bundled, and sold round the doors. On a good day there would be a profit of fourpence. Some women found work as seamstresses, making mutches (caps) at a penny each or as washerwomen.

Lack of education was prevalent. A ragged school had been established by the minister of Greyfriars, and while this had met with some success in the densely populated area around the Grassmarket, this was a task far beyond one man. The *Courant* asked:

> Could not George Heriot's Foundation, which has already done so much good in providing education for the children of the better class of working people in the city, be brought to bear to some extent on a class below that which it has already reached, and of whose necessitous state there can be no doubt? Without detriment to the work it is doing, might not a little also be done for a Heriot ragged school?

The area bounded by the High Street, Cowgate, St Mary's Wynd and Niddry Street was the most densely populated district of the town. The closes were narrow, confined, dirty and very high; it was also the

centre for crime and vice. The most common addresses to appear in
the police records were Hyndford's Close, Blackfriars Wynd and
South Foulis Close. Here the worst of Edinburgh's criminal frater-
nity lived next to many respectable people, who, because of
circumstances, had sunk to the lowest level.

Extreme filth was evident and the overhanging wooden house
fronts in some instances filled these narrow passageways, preventing
light or even fresh air from penetrating the darkness. These appen-
dices were not part of the original design, and their removal would
go some way towards improving the situation.

The Council were, to a certain degree, criticised for allowing the
filth to accumulate, the problem being that there were only two scavengers in the area, where it would require a dozen men to do the job
satisfactorily. Regulations did exist requiring the tenants to sweep
and wash the stair on a regular basis, but this could not be done –
none of the residents had a brush!

Cant's Close had one of the narrowest passageways in the town,
only 3 ft 6 inches wide, but its buildings stood six and seven storeys
high. The houses were substantial, the stairs were in good condition,
but very dark. Despite living on the top floor, a widow who was a
shirtmaker told the *Courant* reporter that she required artificial light
when she was working. This woman explained that she was paid
4½d. for each shirt and, after deducting her overheads for thread,
light and heating, her reward was 2d. for an eight-hour day.

In nearby Dickson's Close lived a basketmaker and a sweep who
each paid an annual rent of £4. The former earned between 1s. and
2s. (5p and 10p) a day, but complained that he had received an
account for 6s. (30p) for poors' rates.

Blackfriars Wynd had at one time been a centre for the Roman
Catholic ecclesiastics, with residences, chapels and other church
buildings. But these uses had been abandoned. Some buildings had
been removed, while others were subdivided into dwellings. Among
those which had survived was Cardinal Beaton's Palace at the corner
of Blackfriars Wynd and the Cowgate. Sadly this structure had deteriorated significantly.

The first floor of this once distinguished building was occupied by
a shoemaker at a rent of £12 a year. Evidence of its former use as a
church was revealed by the presence on the wall of a framed photograph of the late Bishop Gillis. What had once been the wine cellar

The plaque at the corner of
Blackfriars Street and the Cowgate
which marks the site of Cardinal's Beaton's Place

had been converted into houses. Halfway up the wynd, a former chapel had been very badly subdivided and one of the passages had been partitioned into rooms which were let at 1s. a week. In one of these apartments lived a gardener, his wife and five children; their accommodation measured only 12 ft by 5. There had been an outbreak of cholera in the area, resulting in the death of a mother and two children.

In an open space between Blackfriars Wynd and Todrick's Wynd was dumped the filth from the surrounding area. It was alleged that the rubbish was removed daily but this was questionable.

The main occupation for those who could find work was hawking fish, fruit and firewood. Eating houses abounded in the area and they were renowned for their tripe suppers, 'as muckle as a man can eat' for a penny. Also on the menu was a plate of potatoes for the same price, and they could be washed down with a champagne bottle of skeechan (treacle beer) for another halfpenny.

Crime was prevalent and gangs were on the streets looking for drunks, who would be dragged into the nearest close and robbed – if they had anything worth stealing. The police believed that these criminals could obtain enough money this way between a Saturday night and Sunday morning to live for the remainder of the week. Several houses had been identified as the haunts of known thieves.

One Sunday evening an intrepid newspaper reporter (accompanied by two detectives and a policeman) inspected two of the criminal dens. In one he saw a number of youngsters, well-known to the police as thieves, seated in corner of a room, and silence descended as the visitors entered. The furniture consisted of two tables, a few chairs and beds of sorts. Sitting beside a fire was a young woman, aged about twenty, who was in charge of the premises. She had convictions, had spent time in jail and was installed in the house to carry the rap for any detected crimes associated with the house. Her duties included selling drink, for which she received a small percentage of the takings.

In the second house visited, the only occupant was a young woman, who was reading a book. But as the visitors left the premises and walked to the end of the close in Blackfriars Wynd, the police identified the gang who used the house as their meeting place.

Similar circumstances prevailed in Todrick's Wynd, Hyndford's Close and South Foulis Close. These closes and the stairs leading from them to the upper storeys were in complete darkness and entry would have been impossible (and dangerous) without the light from the policeman's bull's-eye lamp. What had been windows on the stairs were now nothing more than openings, and several deaths (accidental or suspicious) had been reported to the police.

Despite the sordid reputation of this area, children were 'oot playin'' at two o'clock on a Sunday morning. They were aged between seven and twelve and no one seemed to know, or care, who their parents were.

A great deal of effort had been made by the parish minister, the Rev. Maxwell Nicholson, who had set up the Tron Church Industrial School. This establishment, in existence for several years, was very successful in training and finding work for girls who might otherwise have finished up on the streets. The older girls were taught kitchen and laundry work and in the relatively short time the school had been in existence, a hundred girls had been found jobs. At the time of the report there had been very few adverse comments from employers, and a further 120 were attending the school.

The south side of the Canongate beyond St Mary's Wynd, although relatively free from vice, suffered greatly from poverty.

Many families relied on soup kitchens for their food. Unfortunately this was a system which was open to abuse. Most families were grateful, but a few sacrificed their meal by selling the tickets and using the money (usually a halfpenny) to buy drink. Rents in this area ranged between 6d. (2½p) and 1s.6d (7½p) a week.

Some of the problems were, however, self-inflicted. One man earning £1. 5s. a week rented a house for £9 per annum. This he considered to be beyond his means and persuaded the landlord to rent him an inferior property for £5. When, some time later, a cellar became available for a rent set at between £2 and £3 a year he approached the owner with a view to using it as a house for his wife and family. The proprietor refused the request.

In another instance a house-decorator, earning good wages, was living in a room measuring 9 ft by 3½ ft.

Food for the poor was frequently tea and garvies (sprats). A mother and daughter explained that their income was derived from three sources. Part of their time was spent binding carpet shoes (slippers); for this they were paid 8d. a dozen and might complete two dozen in a week. The couple also collected 'sweepings' of paper, twine and rags from warehouse floors. The coarse paper was taken to a shop in the New Town, and in an average week the women were likely to be paid 9d. Envelopes and notepaper were sold for ½d. a pound weight. Twine was purchased by the 'stick' boys at a rate of 1d. a handful. Cinders were also collected and anything combustible was salvaged; the rest was thrown into the street.

Whitehorse Close, Robertson's Close, Campbell's Close, Malloch's Close, Brown's Close and Tolbooth Wynd, located on the north, lower end of the Canongate, were described as a disgrace to the city. All were open and airy, yet because of the filth that had been allowed to accumulate the smell was intolerable. There were facilities to dispose of the rubbish but many of the residents were quite content to throw the waste immediately in front of their doors. If a hole was closer than the depository, it was used, thereby adding to the health problem.

Rat's Close, located to the rear of Campbell's Close, was nothing more than an open sewer, created by tenants disposing of their waste by throwing it from the windows. The only difference from times gone by was the absence of the warning cry of 'gardez-loo' – as the scavengers frequently found to their cost. Window sills were inches thick with rubbish which had gathered over a period of years.

The investigators reported: 'We have seen something of the worst parts of London and of the large provincial towns of England, as well as the back slums of Dublin and Belfast, but we do not remember ever seeing anything so horribly dirty as these closes.'

Lack of sufficient cleaning staff was frequently mentioned as a cause of the accumulation of so much filth, and one scavenger explained that he was expected to keep nine long closes free from rubbish – an impossible task.

It was revealed that only £8.10s. had been paid the previous year to wash the closes. Surely it was possible to wash these passageways once a month and not annually, as was the case at the time of the investigations. Householders were not blameless: they disposed of their refuse outwith the regulation time of morning and evening. But was it reasonable to expect these people to keep smelly rubbish in their houses, the newspaper asked.

A great deal of criticism was levelled at proprietors for their greed. The subdivision of property could be achieved at very little cost, but this could result in rental increases of a hundred per cent. It was imperative, insisted the newspaper, that the Town Council take action in terms of the Provisional Order to have many of these sub-divisions removed.

The quality of the work came in for criticism and was demonstrated adequately when one of the 'walls' was moved by the touch of a finger. Profiteering was rife; a room with closet was rented for £5.10s. but by installing a partition the owner was able to demand £4.5s. for the bigger room and £3 for the dark, sloping closet.

The poorest families in this area were living in High School Wynd off the Cowgate and the breadwinner was usually employed in labouring jobs. Incomes varied between half-a-crown (12½p) and 15s. (75p) a week, depending on the availability of work.

At the foot of High School Wynd lived a widow with seven children, one born five months after the death of her husband. Her home was a sunken cellar, but she was an independent woman who managed to live without public support 'except during a few weeks when the children had fever and measles'. This courageous woman travelled regularly to Leith, where she purchased casks for 1s. each. These she broke up and made into bundles of sticks which she sold to the shopkeepers as firewood. The proud woman did not approve of sending her children round the doors to sell the wood, although by so doing her income would have been greater. The oldest of the family was a boy aged twelve who had a regular income of 2s.6d. (12½p) earned by 'going messages' and helping his mother with the firewood. Life was hard for the family; the children were sparsely clothed and went barefoot.

Bull's Close in the Cowgate had seen better days but in the mid-nineteenth century it was notorious for its filth. The once fine wooden-fronted dwellings were in reality beyond habitation. Yet in the midst of the squalor there was a gem. Not far distant lived Mary Pyper, over seventy years of age, slightly-built and blind. But Mary had achieved something in life, for she was a successful poetess. Her father had enlisted in the army, was believed to have been posted abroad, and from that time all contact was lost.

Mary Pyper obtained a limited education, thanks to the efforts of the church elder, and she had a particular interest in poetry. She had a knowledge of Shakespeare, Milton and Thomson. Burns she described as being 'often rather coarse'. This remarkable woman was a lady of principle and, after the death of her mother, she worked hard to achieve a reasonable standard of life and to pay off a debt for which she was not legally responsible.

On being advised this was not necessary, Mary replied: 'There's a law within us that tells us what's richt an' what's wrong; I got a share o' the benefit, an' I'm entitled to pay it.'

Mary's mother had been confined to bed for six years and the daughter had to look after her and earn enough to provide for two. During the time of her mother's illness, Mary turned to writing poetry. Attempts to obtain subscribers were usually met with polite refusals which, in a moment of frustration, prompted her to write:

> I asked a lady to subscribe;
> She answered – she would see.
> But oh! I find she still is blind
> Alas! for her and me.

In time, however, Mary's persistence brought success, with Elliot of Princes Street accepting responsibility for publishing while Constable undertook the printing. Both gentlemen gave all profits to the poetess. Dean Ramsay, in an introduction to the volume, wrote that the poems are 'of no common order of excellence, both in diction and sentiments'.

Mary's writing was recognised far beyond Edinburgh and a number of her poems appeared in an English hymn book entitled *Lays of
the Pious Minstrels*.

> An Epitaph – A Life
> I came at morn – 'twas Spring, I smiled;
> The fields with green were clad;
> I walked abroad at Noon – and, lo!
> 'Twas Summer – I was glad.
> I sate me down – 'twas Autumn eve,
> And I with sadness wept;
> I laid me down at Night, and then
> Twas Winter – and I slept!

Mary Pyper's volume of poems ran to at least three editions.

Nearby lived another woman who occupied a 'room', which in
fact consisted of a small part of a partitioned lobby. Her accommodation measured eight feet by four-and-a-half. Her bed consisted of
the straw and rags which lay in a corner and the floor was cluttered
with jars and pieces of crockery. This woman's only companion was a
cat, which entered and left through a hole in the roof.

Yet, despite her frugal way of life, this woman must have had a
reasonable education, for she enjoyed a small income working as an
'amanuensis'; in other words she wrote letters on behalf of others
who were incapable of performing such a simple task. As evidence of
her occupation, pens and ink bottles stood on a shelf. This woman's
background was a mystery, but there was a suspicion that at one time
she had enjoyed a much higher standard of living.

More evidence of the creative ability, which existed in the
appalling conditions of the Old Town is exemplified by James
Annan, a shoemaker who lived in the vicinity of Blair Street. When
business was slack, and that was frequently, Annan also resorted to
writing poetry. He described himself as one of 'nature's poets' and
humorously complained that poets before him had used up the
primroses and daisies in their works, but he was not dismayed for
there were nettles and dockens! A verse from one of the shoemaker's
poems reads:

> The mountain steep where wild flowers blaw,
> And purple heather bloom;

A singing linn does gently fa'
'Mang banks o' yellow broom.

Annan spent several years on the stage before deserting the boards. Did he regret that decision? He was philosophical in his response. Those he had known in that profession had been dead for twenty years!

A Stevenlaw's Close had existed for centuries, and at one time had been the abode of Edinburgh's wealthy merchants, but by the mid-1800s things had changed considerably. Here could be found some of the worst living conditions in the town, and the rents were high. Poverty abounded, work was unobtainable, and consequently food was scarce.

When the investigators called at one flat, they found a family of mother, father and five children; they were having breakfast – at two in the afternoon. The family had to wait until the mother returned with a little money earned by selling sprats. None of the family had attended school. There was only one bed, with a single covering, in the house. Clothing was sparse and furniture non-existent.

Public assistance was difficult to obtain because of bureaucracy. Relief could be refused by the Parochial Board if a wife refused to go to the area where her husband was born or declined to be admitted to the poorhouse.

Moving away from the town centre, the area of Greenside, just below Leith Street, was recognised as being undesirable. Many of the houses were described as being 'dark, damp and uncomfortable, particularly those which are sunk three or four storeys below the level of the main thoroughfare'. The drainage was in a very poor state and back lanes and courts were 'abominably dirty'. Yet many of those homes were occupied by residents who, by the standards of the time, were relatively well-off, earning £2 a week. They were, however, living in atrocious conditions, paying rent of only between £2 and £3 a year – in many cases to satisfy their craving for drink.

Many meaningful efforts were launched to help the poor and destitute, mainly through churches, small organisations and individuals, but these well-intended projects were uncoordinated and incapable of dealing with the vast problem.

The poor and homeless were not ignored by the authorities and the House of Refuge in the Canongate and the Night Asylum in the

High Street catered for many less fortunate members of society.

The refuge was maintained in a clean and tidy condition although the sleeping apartments were overcrowded. Many of the residents were elderly. Any man seeking night accommodation was required to arrive no later that 8 p.m., given a roll for supper, and taken to a room which had a wooden sleeping bench round the walls. No covering or blankets were provided, and a stove was the only heating. The residents were expected to leave without breakfast. Women and children were provided with porridge and milk before being turned out at 7 a.m.

In theory only strangers were admitted to the Night Asylum, which had facilities for forty men and forty women. The password for men was 'in search of work'; women were 'in search of a husband'! Supper and breakfast were provided and each resident received a blanket. Every effort was made by the superintendent to obtain work for these unfortunate people, and many successes were achieved.

One disadvantage of closing the doors of these centres at an early hour was that someone arriving in the town destitute could be in the position of having no shelter for the night, although places were available, and such an individual would be forced to sleep 'rough'. Frequently space was available in a police station, but regulations prohibited the use of these premises for anyone other than a prisoner.

A law-abiding citizen who spent the night at the refuge would be given a bread roll on arrival, and no other food. A prisoner held at the police station was provided with a roll and a pint of milk for both supper and breakfast.

Dr Littlejohn was appointed as the city's first Medical Officer in 1862, and three years later he published his important report on the sanitary conditions of Edinburgh.

Littlejohn's findings contained four fundamental conclusions:

(1) Paving and drainage of the closes must be brought up to a satisfactory level.

(2) Housing for the poor must be improved by the introduction of water and gas, the cleaning of common stairs and repairs being carried out.

(3) There should be a reduction of overcrowding by limiting the

number of residents in each apartment, reducing the height of tenements and removing accommodation that was beyond repair.

(4) Areas such as the Cowgate and St Mary's Wynd should be widened, and streets formed to pass at right angles to the long closes to make cleansing easier.

William Chambers, the well-known publisher, was elected Lord Provost on 10 November 1865. He was acutely aware of the conditions in the poor areas of the town and within a month he spoke at a Council meeting on the need for sanitary improvements. There had been outbreaks of fever, and Littlejohn had, as a matter of urgency, recommended that all the closes should be flushed with water purified with chloride of lime. The Lord Provost told the meeting that such action could only be considered to be a temporary expedient and that more stringent measures were required.

He said that in order to tackle this major problem it would be necessary to obtain a provisional order in respect of drainage and general sanitary improvements, and an Act to carry out extensive structural alterations throughout the town.

Lord Provost Chambers told his fellow Councillors:

> Almost every day since I was elected Lord Provost I have perambulated the closes in the old town. I have scrutinised every one of them on the north side of the High Street from the North Bridge to New Street; and on the south side from the Old Fishmarket Close to St John Street. Besides going up and down these closes, looking into every accessible hole and corner and sometimes ascending stairs to see the conditions of dwellings, I have gone to the tops of the taller buildings in order to get a good bird's-eye view of the whole concern. In these vastly interesting excursions I have been accompanied by the City Architect with his maps, and in various cases have had the satisfaction to go in company with the Dean of Guild and other members of the sub-committee charged with the duty of making these investigations. So far as I have gone I can fully bear out the published opinions of Dr Littlejohn as to the absolute necessity for opening up the closes. The great question is, how are the closes to be opened up? For that lies at the basis of all sanitary reform.

Chambers put forward radical proposals, which included the removal of large sections of old closes to make way for more functional roadways. The Edinburgh City Improvement Act received royal assent on 31 May 1867 and covered many areas in the Old

Town. Considerably more than £500,000 was spent on the scheme and this was reflected in the rates bills, something the Lord Provost appreciated. 'I fear that many of the inhabitants consider that they are taxed enough already, but be that as it may, there is here a great, I should almost say a blessed object to be gained and we shall render the whole city more healthy, improve its appearance and doubtless extend its trade and resources,' he said.

Among the streets affected were Market Street, Cranston Street, Jeffrey Street, Blackfriars Street, St Mary's Street, Guthrie Street, Lady Lawson Street, Marshall Street and Howden Street. Chambers, one of Edinburgh's more enterprising Lord Provosts, is remembered by Chambers Street, which also formed part of the improvement scheme, and on 5 March 1891 a statue was unveiled there in acknowledgement of his work. Further evidence of Old Town improvements of more recent times can be seen on that stretch of streets between the castle and Holyrood.

As already mentioned, the series of articles which appeared in the *Courant* during the 1866–67 period resulted in contributions in the region of £100 being sent to the paper spontaneously for distribution among needy families. It had never been intended to establish an official fund and in time all contributions were allocated.

Then, in 1883, a Mr Harris contacted the *Courant* about the plight of children in the Old Town. He ran the West Port Refreshment Room and was well aware of the suffering of many of the children round about. On 13 March the paper carried a story exposing the situation. Next day two letters appeared in the *Courant* urging that immediate action be taken to alleviate the problem, and two days later a letter was received from 'A Friend' in Glasgow, enclosing twelve postage stamps as a contribution to a fund 'for the poor in the West Port'. And so, like the phoenix of mythology, The Courant Fund for Poor Children rose from the ashes.

In under three months a sum of £142.7s.11½d. had been subscribed to provide food for children. As the newspaper pointed out, one of the characteristics of the fund was the interest that had been shown by youngsters themselves. Donations had come from schools, among them The Grange Academy and Institution, and the Liberton Niddrie Public School. The Children's Church connected with the Free Church at Stockbridge had also made a donation. One small girl had been responsible for two collections totalling £3.5s., the money having

THIS IS THE FIRST BUILDING
ERECTED UNDER THE
IMPROVEMENT ACT OF 1867

THE RIGHT HONOURABLE
WILLIAM CHAMBERS
OF GLENORMISTON
LORD PROVOST

The *Courant* campaign for better housing was successful,
as this plaque at the top of St Mary's Street shows

been raised from about fifty of her friends who saved for several weeks
and gave sums varying from 3d. to 1s. One father wrote to the *Courant*:

> I am deputed by my little boys to send the enclosed 12s.6d. which has
> been collected for the Destitute Children's Fund. The subscription
> began by the younger child (five years old) bringing a shilling from
> his box, and saying he wanted to give it for the poor children.

Another feature of the fund was that donations did not come entirely
from wealthy families, and in several cases money was sent by members
of the staff in the 'big houses'. Within three months more than
500 donations had been received. As an example of what was
achieved, in one week ninety children were provided with breakfast
or dinner daily, in one of eight refreshment establishments which
had agreed to participate in the scheme.

Although the *Courant* itself no longer exists, the Courant Fund for
Needy Children still goes on.

4
BUILDING THE BRIDGES . . .
AND A ROYAL SNUB

With a valley to the north and to the south, the ridge of the Old Town was somewhat isolated from the green fields eyed by developers in the second half of the eighteenth century. Two bridges were proposed and their construction proved vital to the expansion of Edinburgh. The North and South Bridges, popularly known as 'the Bridges', remain an integral part of the city's communications.

For many years there had been talk of a bridge over the site now occupied by the Waverley Station. One of several proposals was that put forward by John, 11th earl of Mar, who, in 1728, visualised a link stretching from Libberton's Wynd, adjacent to what is now George IV Bridge, across the northern valley to the site of Register House. The bridge would consist of three arches; no houses would be permitted on the structure and the cost would be met by selling sites at each end of the development, while the vaults and arches would be used for warehousing. But this was nothing more than the dream of a homesick Scot in exile after the turmoils of the Jacobite rebellion of 1715.

Expansion of the town was vital, and the Town Council looked covetously to the land on the north side of the Nor' Loch, which lay beneath the castle and the Old Town ridge. In 1759 the Council applied for a Bill to incorporate this land within the town's boundaries, but landowners opposed the scheme and long delays followed.

For four years the town's efforts were frustrated, but, thanks to the efforts of Lord Provost George Drummond and the Parliamentary Trustees, who made over to the Council a sum of £3,000, the local authority pursued their objective. A little progress was made when part of the Nor' Loch was drained in 1762. The foundation-stone for the North Bridge was laid on 21 October the following year.

On 1 August 1765, the contract for the bridge was signed. The work was to be completed by Martinmas 1769 at a cost of £10,140. The contract required a structure of five arches and an overall length of 1,134 feet. Good progress was made, and by midsummer 1769 the arches were complete. Then disaster struck.

The area of the Nor' Loch had long been used as a dump, and spoil from the closes and alleys in the vicinity had been tipped round the bridge site. Consequently the site was, to a certain extent, made-up land. Furthermore, the piers had not been constructed to the required height, and, to overcome the problem, about eight feet of soil had been added to raise the level at the south end.

As a result, on 3 August, when the work was nearing completion, and following heavy rain, the side walls and abutments burst. The vaults at the south end also gave way and five people were killed. Eleven others were seriously injured.

Major reconstruction took place and an action was raised in the Court of Session, followed by an appeal to the House of Lords. The eventual cost of the project was £17,354 – considerably more than the original contract figure.

The bridge was passable in 1772 but there were minor problems about the balustrades. Complaints were made that because the balustrades were open, pedestrians were being blown from the pavement into the mud in the middle of the road. A year earlier, the balustrades at the south end had been enclosed to screen the view of pedestrians from the sight of the 'blood and slaughter' in the market below! And the vaults were put into use, when, in 1774, the Council directed that all beggars found on the streets were to be imprisoned therein and fed on bread and water.

Despite its shaky start, the old North Bridge provided good and uninterrupted service until 1873–74 when, having considered various reports, the decision was taken to widen it.

Its original width was 40 feet, splaying to 50 feet at both ends, but, as a consequence of the laying of tram lines, the middle section was widened to 54 feet by throwing out massive iron brackets and box girders. Although the bridge remained sound structurally, the North British Railway were in 1891 promoting a Bill for the reconstruction of the Waverley Station, and it was suggested that perhaps this was an ideal opportunity to replace the bridge. The bridge was considered to be in a stable condition, but it was recognised that the piers would hinder the railway station proposals. The Council also accepted that with the ever-increasing volume of traffic, serious consideration would have to be given to the future of the North Bridge.

Two years later the railway company, who were ready to start work on the redesigned Waverley, again consulted the Council. After much consideration, and having taken into account the strong possibility of cabling the tramway system, together with the problem of increased general traffic, the Town Council resolved to rebuild the North Bridge. This decision was no doubt influenced by a contribution of £30,000 from the railway company.

Details of the new structure were fully documented on the invitation sent to the selected few invited to witness the laying of the foundation-stone:

> The New Bridge is to be constructed of iron girders resting on stone piers and abutments. It will consist of three spans of 175 feet each, the north abutment being in line with the south face of the General Post Office and the south abutment being at the south end of Market Street, the clear available space below the Bridge being 525 feet, in place of 360 feet in the Old Bridge. The width between the parapets of the New Bridge will be 75 feet, while that of the Bridge as altered more than 20 years ago was 54 feet. Each span will be formed of six steel-arched ribs, over which there will be a system of steel bracing supporting the roadway. The parapets and outer facing of the arches will be of ornamental cast-iron work. The contract price of the Bridge (apart from the properties at the south end) is about £90,000. The engineers are Messrs Cunningham, Blyth & Westland, C.E., Edinburgh: the architect is Mr R. Morham, City Superintendent; and the contractors are Sir William Arrol & Co., Ltd, Glasgow, with Messrs William Beattie & Sons, Edinburgh, sub-contractors for the mason work.

The foundation stone was laid by Lord Provost Andrew McDonald on 25 May 1896. Such was the interest of the citizens that barriers had to be placed between the east end of Register House and the Post Office, at the foot of East Register Street, and across Princes Street from the Waverley Steps. In addition, the street was closed at the High Street approach. Vast crowds assembled in Jeffrey Street, on Calton Hill and on the platforms of Waverley Station. The windows of the General Post Office were also used as vantage points.

Whereas the building of the first bridge had taken nine years, the replacement structure was erected in two-and-a-half years. The contractors took possession of the site on 12 April 1895, and the first half was open to traffic on 12 October 1896. The second half of the project was completed in a period of only eleven months.

The demolition was particularly difficult and was carried out without interfering with the railway traffic or the tramway system. All south-bound road traffic continued to use the bridge, while north-travelling vehicles were routed by way of Cockburn Street and Princes Street.

First the east side was demolished and replaced; then the west side was similarly treated. There were three fatal accidents during the work. Little of interest was found during the demolition – a pewter jug and several moulded gravestones; but no trace of the foundation stone laid in 1763.

Meanwhile, Edinburgh's Town Councillors were as proud as peacocks. They had negotiated the construction of the much-needed North Bridge with almost one-third off the actual cost of £100,000, the balance being met by the railway company. The ratepayers had benefited greatly, so why not put the icing on the cake and have a royal opening of the bridge?

And so on 3 November 1896, ten months before the proposed official opening, Town Clerk Thomas Hunter was instructed to write to Queen Victoria formally requesting her presence in the Scottish capital to carry out this important task.

With almost three weeks having passed and no official response from the Palace, it was assumed that she had graciously consented to attend the opening.

There was, however, a shock in store for the Council when a letter dated 24 November arrived at the City Chambers from Windsor Castle. It read:

Dear Mr Hunter,
I have had the honour to lay before the Queen your letter of the 3rd. inst., in which you submit a request on behalf of the Lord Provost and Corporation that Her Majesty may be pleased to visit Edinburgh at any time after the beginning of next August for the purpose of opening the New Bridge.

After careful thought the Queen, with much regret, feels obliged to abandon any hope of being able to comply with this request.

But Her Majesty has to fulfil one long-standing engagement, which, added to those consequent upon next year's celebrations, compel the Queen to recognise the impossibility of undertaking any further fatigue.

Her Majesty is, however, very anxious to visit Edinburgh again, and trusts to be able to do so before very long.

The Queen has heard with great interest of the construction of the New Bridge, and of other important improvements which are to be effected in that part of the city.

Yours very faithfully,
Arthur Bigge.

The Council were philosophical at the rebuff. After all, Her Majesty was seventy-seven years old, and the following year would celebrate her Diamond Jubilee. That no doubt would be a great strain. Disappointed but undaunted, the Council met and agreed that the Prince of Wales (the future Edward VII) would be an acceptable substitute.

This time, however, the Council adopted a different approach. Lord Provost McDonald, who had been elected two years previously, contacted Lord Rosebery as a go-between, in the hope that the prince would honour the town with his presence. His Royal Highness wouldn't.

It was now well into 1897. The situation was becoming desperate and the list of 'royals' was diminishing.

'Write and ask the Duke of York' (later George V), the Town Clerk was next told, with a suggestion that might be useful to use the good offices of the Earl of Rosebery who had a home at Dalmeny, near the city.

In due course a reply was received by the Town Clerk. It was dated 5 August 1897, from Cowes, and read:

Dear Sir
I am desired by the Duke of York to write to you in answer to your invitation, through the Earl of Rosebery and say that their Royal Highnesses much regret that it is quite impossible for them to accept it, and to open the North Bridge. The Duke and Duchess will only remain two days at Dalmeny, and it is unfortunately impossible to undertake any further engagements. Had the circumstances permitted of this, it would have been a great pleasure to their Royal Highnesses to perform the ceremony.

Believe me to be,
very faithfully,
Derek Keppel, Equerry-in-Waiting.

There was consternation in the City Chambers – three requests and three refusals. What next?

'Town Clerk, write again to the Duke and ask him to reconsider his decision!'

Mr Hunter, in his letter, agreed that perhaps it was inconvenient to visit Edinburgh while at Dalmeny, but pointed out that the duke was going to the Highlands. Perhaps . . . on his way back . . . it might be possible to honour the city . . . ?

The reply was swift and to the point. By this time the prince was at Osborne, and the letter was dated 12 August (only a week after his first refusal). This communication informed the citizens of Edinburgh that:

> I have to acknowledge receipt of your letter of 10th inst., and in answer I am to say that the Duke gave the most careful consideration to the invitation of the City of Edinburgh to open the North Bridge, and that His Royal Highness regrets very much that he is not able to alter his decision, which I was instructed to convey to you in my let-ter of the 5th inst. Their Royal Highnesses' visit to the Earl of Rosebery is of an entirely private nature, and is to last only one day besides the Sunday; and it is almost certain that they will not pass through Edinburgh on their journey south.
>
> I am,
>
> Yours faithfully,
>
> Derek Keppel, Equerry-in-Waiting.

At this point the Council conceded defeat and agreed that the Lord Provost be granted the honour.

It was an overcast morning on 15 September 1897 as the now Sir Andrew McDonald (one of the queen's Diamond Jubilee knights) prepared to perform the official opening of the North Bridge. The town decided to make it a memorable occasion. Flags were flying from every window in the vicinity; bunting stretched across the street, and flags floated from the lamp-posts on the bridge. Large crowds had assembled in the High Street and the access to the bridge, and the police were hard pressed to keep the way open for the official party.

At 12.30 p.m. the bridge was closed to vehicles. At the City

Chambers, the Lord Provost, Councillors bedecked in cocked hats and scarlet robes, and other dignitaries had assembled. But there was one final hitch. Lord Rosebery's train from Dalmeny did not arrive until 1 p.m., and the official party left twenty minutes late!

All had gone well in the end but a certain degree of disappointment remained. After all, it was Queen Victoria's Diamond Jubilee and there had been a hope that this major thoroughfare might have become known as the Royal North Bridge.

Commenting on the opening of the North Bridge, the *Edinburgh Evening News* said:

> The old North Bridge served well enough for the requirements of the city, and might have served, but circumstances forced the construction of the new highway. It will perhaps meet the requirements of a century, and even in the future days of progress, it will also impress the modern Athenian by the nobleness of its proportions, its admirable breadth, and its excellent design. It will remain, at least, the greatest engineering work of the latter end of the century in Edinburgh, and it will perhaps serve to dispose of the idea that beauty cannot be evolved from rigid lines of steel.

The *News* continued: 'Edinburgh can well afford to be proud of its New Bridge, which is not greatly surpassed even in many of our river cities or in London itself.'

Major repairs were carried out in 1933, when the brick vaulted decks were replaced with reinforced concrete. This was, of course, in those days when the carriageway was built from granite setts and the bridge carried two tracks of tramlines.

Then, in 1989, Blyth & Blyth were appointed by the former Lothian Regional Council to carry out a structural assessment of the bridge. Simultaneously they were appointed by the Scottish Development Agency as lead consultants for painting, flood-lighting, and maintenance repair work. Their investigations revealed a degree of deterioration. Work was carried out during 1990, and on 22 November 1990, Councillor Eric Milligan, then Convener of Lothian Regional Council, and later Lord Provost of Edinburgh, switched on the flood-lighting. Today the North Bridge is capable of carrying 40-tonne vehicles.

With the North Bridge in existence it was only a matter of time before the route was extended to give a major access to the south. In

1775 a scheme, estimated to cost £8,600, was considered. But these proposals included a tollhouse at the southern end of the development – not a popular idea – and for nine years the venture lay gathering dust in the Council offices.

In 1784, however, Lord Provost James Hunter Blair called for further reports. A design was approved, the necessary Act of Parliament obtained, and on 1 August 1785 the foundation stone of the archway which spans the Cowgate was laid. The work was completed and the road opened to traffic less than three years later.

But how many arches are contained within the South Bridge? The figure of between 19 and 22 has been quoted, but only one – that over the Cowgate – can be seen. The others are 'lost' among the lower levels of the South Bridge buildings.

Many of Edinburgh's old buildings disappeared as a result of the bridge construction, including Niddry's Wynd, Marlin's Wynd, and Peebles Wynd. Niddry's Wynd was replaced by Niddry Street, although the present thoroughfare is located some distance to the east of the old wynd. Part of the old Marlin's Wynd has survived the ravages of redevelopment, but this came about by good fortune rather than design.

Marlin's Wynd, according to tradition, took its name from Jean Merlion, a Frenchman, who was employed to pave the High Street. He lived in the passageway and asked that he be buried there. It is said that his grave was marked by six flat stones.

The last sermon was preached in the High Street's Tron Kirk in 1952. In the early 1970s excavations in the building revealed the remains of Marlin's Wynd, which ran from the High Street to the Cowgate. During excavation work for the South Bridge many coins from the reigns of Edward I and Edward II were found.

Peebles Wynd was located roughly on the line of the present Blair Street. It had been a favourite quarter for the bakers of Edinburgh, with their bakehouses and living quarters crowded closely together.

The old properties were purchased for modest sums, but the sites were sold at a handsome profit. The first lots (located on the east side of the street) were sold by auction on Wednesday 8 November 1786. The first site, with a frontage of 49 feet to the bridge and 37 feet to the High Street was offered at £1,400 and realised £2,860.

Early in 1788 it was reported that fifty-two properties were ready for occupation or nearing completion. Demand for construction

The only visible arch of the South Bridge which crosses the Cowgate

South Bridge with the frontage of Edinburgh University (minus its dome)

sites on the South Bridge was brisk, and one major attraction was the opportunity to use stone from the demolished closes.

The construction of this much-needed thoroughfare was undoubtedly the ultimate achievement during Lord Provost Blair's term of office. Sadly, he did not live to see the project completed, but his efforts did not go unrewarded, and today his name is perpetuated in Blair Street and Hunter Square.

There is a curious story told regarding the design of the South Bridge. From the Tron the street slopes downwards until it reaches what is now known as Chambers Street, when it rises sharply past the University. But why not a conventional design with a gradual slope throughout its length?

At the time plans were being prepared, College Street North (which ran roughly on the line of the present Chambers Street) was still in existence, and at the eastern extremity was Adam Square. This square was immediately adjacent to the proposed road, and contained the residences of some of the wealthiest and most influential of Edinburgh's citizens.

When, to their consternation, these property owners discovered that the proposed design would have resulted in the square being overlooked so that the common people could peer into their homes, pressure was brought to bear and the design altered.

Apparently it was all too much for those wealthy residents. What with the shock of what might have been and the introduction of commercial properties close by, it is said that they all departed, having acquired houses in more exclusive areas of the town.

5

THE THEATRE ROYAL . . . AND
AN ILL-FATED SITE

Shakespeare Square stood at the junction of North Bridge with Princes Street, pretty much where the General Post Office building came to be raised. It was certainly not one of the most attractive of Edinburgh's squares, and, completed in 1778, contained shops, lodging houses and a theatre – the Theatre Royal.

Architecturally this building had little to recommend it. One nineteenth-century writer described it as 'one of the plainest and most commonplace buildings in the city and were it not for its colonnade front, erected by Mr Murray in 1830, it might have been mistaken for a granary or barn'. Internally, however, the theatre was described as being elegantly fitted. Above the entrance was a statue of Shakespeare, with figures depicting the tragic and comic muses. The hall had cost £5,000 to construct and was opened in December 1769.

While its outward appearance may not have been particularly appealing, it gave Edinburgh audiences the opportunity to see the best of the London performers. When it opened the admission charges were: boxes and pits, 3s.; lower gallery, 2s.; second and upper galleries, 1 s. Takings amounted to approximately £140 a night.

On 21 September 1854 came the news that the theatre and adjoining properties had been acquired for the GPO building. Demolition followed, and on 23 September 1861 Prince Albert laid the foundation-stone for the new work, which was completed five years later.

Destroyed by fire

Not far away, at the foot of Leith Street, which slips off the east end of Princes Street opposite Shakespeare Square, lies another site long associated with public entertainment. But the ground at the corner of Broughton Street and Little King Street was destined to be plagued by misfortune, and all five theatres which were built here were destroyed by fire. Four of them were named the Theatre Royal.

As far back as 1789 a lease was entered into between Walter Ferguson, writer, and Robert Inglis, mason, for the site. After several transactions it was acquired by Natali Corri, a dealer in music and musical instruments, who converted the existing amphitheatre into concert rooms and then a theatre. It was known as the Pantheon, later the Caledonian, and finally the Adelphi. This theatre was managed by Robert Henry Wyndham, who was well-known in the theatrical business and had made appearances at the Shakespeare Square Theatre Royal.

On 24 May 1853 the Adelphi was destroyed in a fire, which also damaged St Mary's Roman Catholic Chapel (it had not yet attained cathedral status). The outbreak was discovered at approximately 4.45 p.m., and the flames spread so rapidly that within an hour only the four walls remained. It reopened on 19 December 1855 as the Queen's Theatre and Opera House, under Wyndham's management.

When the Theatre Royal Shakespeare Square closed, the Queen's adopted the title. Thereafter followed a bizarre sequence of disasters in which, over a period of eighty-one years, four theatres on this location, all named the Theatre Royal, were destroyed by fire.

By far the worst conflagration struck on Friday 13 January 1865,

The Theatre Royal in Shakespeare Square

resulting in the deaths of six people, the only occasion on which there were fatalities.

It was approaching 4 p.m. on that fateful day and the staff were completing their preparations for the evening performance of the pantomime *Little Tom Tucker*. Cassey, the theatre gasman, was lighting the rows of gas jets which were attached to the 'borders' (strips of painted canvas which stretched across the tops of the scenery to hide backstage from the audience). These lights were required to illuminate the stage, and it was a routine which Cassey had carried out frequently.

With quick efficiency he lit the back row and was in the process of attending to the jets in front when the border caught fire. It was not the first time this had happened, and Cassey was not particularly worried, as the problem had been solved by removing the canvas to prevent the flames spreading. This time, however, the outbreak was more severe and the gasman rushed along the 'flies' (wooden platforms which were used by the staff when moving scenery) yelling for the assistance of Syme (fireman), Stewart (head carpenter) and Glen (general assistant); but his pleas for help went unanswered.

Why? Because members of the staff had on a number of occasions raised false alarms, and the fireman may have assumed that it was another practical joke. Perhaps, of course, the call was never heard. Had Syme responded immediately to the call for assistance, the lives of six men and the theatre itself might have been saved.

Cassey found Syme in the carpenters' workshop and explained what was happening, but already precious minutes had been lost. The staff immediately rushed to where the fire was now raging, intending to cut the scenery support ropes, dropping the canvas backing and stamping out the fire. But luck was not on Syme's side on that Friday the thirteenth. Apparently, in his rush to investigate, he had dropped his knife and none of the others had one. A hose was turned on the fire but by now the situation was beyond their control and the men had no option but to abandon the building and raise the alarm.

Wyndham, who was lessee, was in London. His wife had left the theatre to visit her daughter in Ainslie Place and learned of the outbreak as she made her way back. Her brothers, Edward and Richard Sacker, were walking in Princes Street when a pedestrian gave them the news. They rushed back to discover that the back entrance was already inaccessible. But by using a ladder they reached the wardrobe room, located at the front, overlooking Broughton Street and immediately above a spirit dealer's shop. As a result of their efforts a large quantity of valuable silk, velvet and satin dresses and other props were saved. As these items were thrown through broken windows, members of the public bundled them into cabs which took them to a temporary store.

The interior of the theatre was soon consumed but none of the local residents was aware of the disaster until the flames had burst through the roof. As the fire continued unabated, people in various parts of the town noticed a glow lighting up the late afternoon winter sky and spectators gathered round the theatre.

Not until 4.30 p.m. was the first hose playing on the Theatre Royal building, but it was already obvious that there was no chance of preventing total destruction. The decision was then taken to ensure the safety of the adjoining residential property.

Fifteen minutes after the arrival of the firefighters the theatre roof collapsed and the flames continued relentlessly. The noise was described as 'like that of a mighty furnace'.

Worse was to follow when it was discovered that the attics of the line of houses immediately adjacent to the Little King Street side of the theatre were alight. There was no delay as the residents set about salvaging their possessions. Soon the flats on the opposite side of the street were similarly affected and rafters and joists could be seen burning furiously. Spectators willingly joined in the rescue operations, carrying some of the bigger household items downstairs. Soft furnishings were thrown from windows, often to the surprise of those below. As more engines arrived, all efforts were concentrated on protecting living accommodation. This was eventually achieved but not without sacrifice. Fire damaged the upper structures and lower properties suffered badly from the effects of water.

By 5 p.m. the number of spectators had grown to such an extent that three officers and 250 soldiers were brought from the castle to control the crowds.

As the afternoon turned into early evening two engines and eighty men arrived from Leith to help. There was a problem, however, for the water pressure could not meet the demand. A decision was taken to withdraw the Leith Dock Commission engine, leaving the artillerymen from Leith Fort to carry on. Fifty Leith policemen were also on the scene, providing valuable assistance.

The situation became critical at about 6 p.m. when the authorities became concerned about the state of the north wall of the theatre leaning outwards. St Mary's Chapel was the adjacent property and it had been evident for an hour that the wall was in danger of collapse.

When the severity of the fire was evident, Bishop Strain, assisted by four priests, removed all paintings and other valuables from the church and house. These included the large painting showing the entombment of the Saviour which hung above the altar. Shortly after 5 p.m. a chimney stack fell from the theatre onto the cupola of the cloister and into the vestry. There were two men in the vestry and rescuers immediately rushed to their assistance. One was dead; the second was alive but jammed against a wall and crying piteously for help.

Among those on the scene was the Lord Dean of Guild, George Lorimer, a much respected businessman in the town. He had been present for most of the duration of the fire and immediately became actively involved in the efforts to rescue the injured man. While they worked frantically in dangerous conditions, Lorimer and his colleagues were warned that the theatre's north wall was in danger of collapsing onto the church. However, they persisted in their efforts to free the trapped man.

Some heeded what they were told, left the building and lived; others died in the desperate effort to save a life, as the wall finally caved outwards onto the group of men below. When it was considered safe, a team of rescuers went into the debris in a forlorn hope of finding someone alive.

After ninety minutes they found the first body. He was in a sitting position and was later identified as George Sweeney, aged 67, a butler who lived at 15 Leopold Place. He left a widow and a grown-up family of four. One hour later the remains of John Clark. aged sixty-six, 4 Middle Arthur Place, were located in the rubble. A widow and adult family of seven were left to grieve. Ironically, Clark had spent forty years in the fire service in Edinburgh and for much of that time he had been captain of the Fountainbridge detachment. He had been retired for only a few months.

A 26-year-old clerk, Thomas Henry Leeke, was found a few minutes later. He had gone to the church to help in saving the pictures and was trapped when the chimney stalk collapsed. He was the subject of the ill-fated rescue attempt. His wife and seven-year-old daughter lived at 51 Broughton Street.

By 3 a.m. on Saturday only those three bodies had been recovered. The only good news was that the fire was out – there was nothing left that was combustible. After another couple of hours searching through the rubble the bodies of two victims were discovered lying side-by-side, but a considerable distance from where the other bodies had been found, suggesting that the two heroes had made a last unsuccessful attempt to run for safety as the wall gave way.

It was quickly established that they were the remains of John Taylor, believed to have been fifty-five years of age, who worked as a stonemason and had lived at 4 St James Square with his wife, a 16-year-old daughter and sons, fourteen and seven respectively; and Lord Dean of Guild Lorimer of Mayfield Terrace. He was survived by his widow and a family of four. John Taylor was no stranger to danger. On 24 November 1861 he had been involved in rescue work during the 'Heave Awa' tenement collapse in the High Street when thirty-five people died.

At 7 a.m. the body of the last victim was removed from the building. It was that of 54-year-old Bernard McVie of Baxter's Close, Lawnmarket, married, with six children whose ages ranged from five to seventeen.

Damage to the theatre was complete; that to St Mary's and the priests' house was considerable, one-third of the chapel being destroyed. The pulpit, which was adjacent to the wall of the theatre, was relatively undamaged although heaps of masonry had fallen all around it. Also destroyed were railings in front of the altar and the altar steps.

Examination of the remains of the theatre walls confirmed that they were in danger of further collapse, and the site was barricaded while demolition work was carried out. The church could not be used for services, and arrangements were made for the congregation to attend St Patrick's Church in the Cowgate until St Mary's could be reopened for worship.

Three of the victims were buried on the Tuesday following the fire. George Sweeney was laid to rest at the Grange cemetery, following a service at his home at 2 p.m. Half an hour later Thomas Leeke's coffin was taken to Warriston Cemetery. The mourners included uniformed members of no. 8 Battery of the City of Edinburgh

Artillery Volunteers. Mr Leeke had been a serving sergeant.

Then at 3 p.m. the body of John Clark was carried from his son's house in Middle Arthur Place to the Grange Cemetery, where there was a big turnout of Fire Brigade men.

The following day John Taylor was buried in Warriston Cemetery. The whereabouts of the resting place of Bernard McVie are, to me, unknown.

The funeral of Lord Dean of Guild Lorimer also took place on Wednesday. This was an impressive occasion and in many respects resembled a miniature military funeral. George Lorimer's family home was in Mayfield Terrace, and prior to his burial in St Cuthbert's graveyard at the West End, a service was held in his Newington house.

It was conducted jointly by the Rev. J.E. Cumming, minister at Newington Church (where Mr Lorimer was an elder) and the Rev. Dr Paul of St Cuthbert's. Simultaneously, the Rev. Maxwell Nicholson held a service at Newington Church in Clerk Street for representatives of the public organisations who were later to join the funeral procession. At 1 p.m. the bells of Newington and St Cuthbert's began to peal and they continued until the committal had been completed.

The cortège went along Blacket Place and at this stage the procession was led by the High Constables with the insignia of office draped in crape, followed by a line of carriages. Immediately behind the Lord Provost's coach, which carried Bailies Cassels and Alexander, came the hearse drawn by four horses. To the rear of the hearse were twenty carriages occupied by relatives and friends, then forty private vehicles.

The procession from Newington church was led by eight police constables, who marched four abreast. They were followed by the representatives of many public organisations; masonic lodge journeymen No. 8; directors of the western cemetery; Provost and magistrates of Leith; High School Club; rector and masters of the High School; chamber of commerce; Merchant Company; incorporation of guildry; City Road Trust; Lord Advocate; Dean of Guild Court; society of High Constables; city officers with halberds craped; sword and mace bearers with the insignia draped with crape; Council Officer; Town Council and officials; City Clerk; Treasurer; Convener; and Magistrates. As they moved off, the mourners who had attended the service at the Lord Dean's home took up positions to the rear. The procession stretched for three-quarters of a mile.

It was a typically dismal Edinburgh January day and heavy rain fell for most of the afternoon. Nevertheless, citizens turned out in large numbers to line the streets and pay their homage, and the shops closed. As the cortège approached the corner of the North Bridge and Princes Street the construction men working on the GPO building stood cap in hand and eyes to the ground in silent tribute, not a surprising gesture, for George Lorimer was respected by all in the building industry. He was recognised by the men as one of the best of employers, and to those men 'he extended both his hand and his purse while they were in distress or difficulty.'

Among those at the graveside were Bishop Strain and other members of the clergy from St Mary's, and also Mr Wyndham and most of the male members of the theatre cast. An hour had elapsed since the remains of Lorimer had left his home. The coffin was carried by the Master and five Past-Masters of the Masonic Lodge Journeymen No. 8. The walk was lined by the High Constables, and members of the Town Council and magistrates joined the family at the graveside.

But there is one mystery – where was George Lorimer buried?

A contemporary account of the committal ceremony is quite specific: 'The lamented Dean was buried in the family ground adjoining the wall next to Castle Terrace (in fact King's Stables Road) beside his father and mother, two brothers and two sisters, the dates of whose deaths are recorded on a handsome tablet at the head of the grave.' There is one George Lorimer named on this stone, and he died, aged fifty-two, on 1 September 1833 – thirty-two years before the Theatre Royal fire; this obviously refers to the father.

Close to the church door which faces Princes Street, however, there is another Lorimer stone, which includes the inscription: 'In memory of George Lorimer born 17 January 1812, died 13 January 1865', which is the date of the Theatre Royal fire. Reports at the time gave his age as fifty-three, and the details on this stone indicate that George Lorimer was in his fifty-third year at the time of his death. Perhaps George Lorimer was buried beside his parents, and for some inexplicable reason his name was never recorded. There is certainly enough space on the gravestone for his details to be inscribed.

The tablet near the church does give full details of this branch of the family; was the name of George Lorimer, Lord Dean of Guild, included as a memorial, rather than to mark his resting place?

Once More (1875)

A new Theatre Royal rose from the ashes and was completed in 1866 at a cost of £17,000. In 1874 the theatre was sold for £11,000 but within a year disaster struck once more and this time destruction was swift. Only half an hour after the fire had been discovered at 2 p.m. on Saturday 6 February 1875 the building was a blazing inferno, and by 4 p.m. only the four walls remained.

At the time of the outbreak there were few people on the premises. Mrs Fraser and two assistants were busy in the wardrobe room working on dresses for the current show, the pantomime *Jack in the Beanstalk*, and a cashier was in the foyer box office.

Shortly before the fire, the cast had gathered in a room, known as the treasury, to be paid their wages. Others were wandering about the stage. Smoking was banned, and this rule was strictly observed by staff and cast. At this time there was no indication of the disaster that was about to strike.

Mrs Fraser became aware of a rush of air through the room just after two o'clock. At the same time there was a loud noise from the area of the gas room at the opposite side of the stage.

The box-office assistant was startled when the inner glass doors swung outwards, caused apparently by a gust of wind so strong that pictures were blown from the walls onto the floor.

Those on duty immediately left the theatre, but already black smoke was pouring through the roof over the stage. Within minutes, part of the roof had been destroyed and there was great concern for the safety of nearby flats in tenements six and seven storeys high. In Little King Street blistering was noticed on the wooden window frames, which were in danger of catching fire. Instructions were given that these flats were to be evacuated and this duty was carried out by Sergeant Crawford (who had been on duty at the previous fire) and a team of constables.

The first firefighters on the scene were from the Central Fire Station and Rose Street. They immediately concentrated on the south and west walls of the theatre, but shortly afterwards the firemen were redeployed to protect the residents in Little King Street, where windows on both sides were alight. Bit by bit the theatre building gave way, and when the steam engine arrived at 2.45 p.m. the fire was at its height.

The engine added another three hoses to the firefighters' efforts. For a time, water was poured onto the roof of St Mary's in an effort to hold back the flames, and, when it was believed that the church building was secure, attention was turned to the north wall of the theatre which was sloping outwards. The wall was monitored with fearful anxiety for it was the corresponding wall in the former theatre, which had collapsed in 1865 resulting in the loss of life. When the theatre had been rebuilt iron rods were inserted to strengthen the structure. It was now under test.

The front of the theatre in Broughton Street remained intact and this was attributed to the design, which included a brick wall between the auditorium and the entrance. Meanwhile, on the south side, in Little King Street, flames continued to shoot through windows in the theatre and from the large door used for moving scenery. It now looked likely this wall was in danger of collapse, and a hose was taken up Little King Street and fed in through the scenery door, while a small engine at the top of the street continued to play an important part in the operation. A six-storey tenement to the south of the burning theatre was now under threat, but prompt action soon had this outbreak under control. As a precaution, however, firemen continued to play water on the roof.

The scene was graphically recorded:

> By and by a fireman appeared, hose in hand, on the very top of the chimney-stack overlooking a burning area and very picturesque he looked. The glare of the flames below was reflected from the brass helmet and he stood out in statuesque relief against the grey lowering sky. The object which secured such an excellent picture was, however, not so obvious, for the jet of water which the man threw towards the fire-lake below must have been as ineffectual as a streamlet turned on Vesuvius in eruption. Long before the water could have reached the flames it must have been converted into steam and carried away heavenwards.

Just when it seemed that the situation was under control a new crisis arose. In a shop near the entrance to the stalls, there was a large stock of whisky which was valued by the owner at £1,000, although insured for only £400. Flames were now moving eastwards, and if they reached the shop, an explosion was inevitable. The fire authorities were aware of the problem and when flames broke through the partition wall, a hose was diverted from another area to head off the danger.

Shortly before 4 p.m. the conflagration had reached the semicircular partition which separated the entrance corridors and passageways from the interior. Soon all was devoured and, with nothing between the street and the interior, the devastation was all too evident. From time to time the flames would rise, but there were a dozen hoses at the ready to douse any further threats.

At the express demand of the Lord Provost further assistance was requested from Leith, and within a short time a further engine was in action. Not surprisingly, and considering the history of this site, the fire attracted a large number of spectators, and the 1st Battalion, The Royal Scots were summoned from the castle to restore some order; this was achieved, but only with difficulty.

As the time approached 5.30 p.m. the Leith Docks fire-fighting equipment had also arrived, but by now it was too late – the Theatre Royal had been gutted, and all that could be done was to concentrate water on glowing embers, the walls of the church, and nearby residential properties. In the meantime, work had started on barricading the devastated area and that was completed by 10 p.m.

It was a particularly sad occasion for R.H. Wyndham, who had managed three theatres on this location, all of which had been destroyed by fire. The popular and successful pantomime *Jack in the Beanstalk* had only two weeks to run. The expenditure on this show was £2,000 and Wyndham had planned to stage an opera, followed by a new production of *Rob Roy* (on which a considerable amount had been spent on 'props'), to mark the end of his career at the Theatre Royal.

Among the many items destroyed were manuscripts and marked editions of plays which had been given to Wyndham by the widow of the famous Eton-educated actor, Charles Kean, who died in 1868. The leader of the orchestra, Mr Daly, had left a violin valued at £50 in the theatre. Unfortunately, he did not even own the instrument but had it on loan. The fire also meant that a considerable number of actors and theatre employees were out of work.

An investigation of the ruins on the Monday following the fire failed to establish the cause of the outbreak, but it was believed that it had started in the lighting above the stage.

Yet Again (1884)

Little time was wasted in replacing the Theatre Royal and the site was sold for £5,000 following the fire. A new building was designed and construction work completed in three months, at a cost of £12,500. The hall had a capacity of 2,300 and opened on 27 January 1876 with a performance of Boncicault's *Shaughraun*.

There were advantages in living in Little King Street. It was in the centre of the town, with access to a plentiful supply of shops; rents were relatively cheap, as reflected in the large number of poorer families who occupied these tenements. But this was also a street where tenancies were accepted with a certain amount of trepidation. The Theatre Royal was constantly in the minds of the locals because of its reputation for being fire-prone, and the year 1884 was no exception.

Only nine years had elapsed since the building had been gutted, when disaster struck again. Such was the intensity of the heat that attic flats in Little King Street caught fire and flames spread to the roof of the (now) cathedral and the archbishop's residence. Fortunately, there was no loss of life.

Experience had shown that previous outbreaks had started in the vicinity of the stage, but on this occasion the seat of the blaze was immediately above the entrance. In less than two hours the Theatre Royal had been consumed.

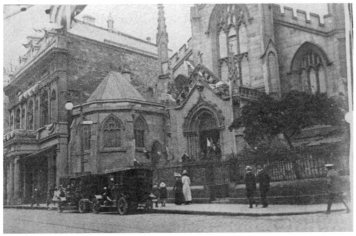

The Theatre Royal and St Mary's Cathedral. On the right is the first traffic signal in the city, at the junction of Broughton Street and York Place. It went into operation on 21 March 1928.

The alarm was raised about noon on 30 June 1884 by Mr Paterson, a bookseller at 15 Broughton Street, who was walking nearby. He noticed black smoke and a smell of burning around the theatre. He immediately alerted the St James Police Station before returning to the theatre, where he warned Peter Crabb, a member of the staff, who was about to leave the building. Crabb ran to the area identified by Paterson which was a 'props' room, measuring 20 feet by 12 feet. By this time the flames were spreading to a corridor behind the gallery.

Unbelievably, a company were on stage rehearsing a drama entitled *The Nightingale,* which would have had its first performance that night. While Crabb turned off the gas, an actor played a hose onto the now burning woodwork, but to no avail. The fire spread quickly, covering the refreshment bar, the workshops and the entrance to the gallery. In no time it spread along the roof and finally reached a sunlight window.

Fortunately many of the company's effects were saved, including live rabbits and birds which were required in the production.

The fire brigade soon arrived with a force of between twenty-five and thirty men. It was found that the fire had got into the roof above the entrance and the theatre was now beyond being saved. A decision was taken to move the equipment to St James Place, behind the theatre, and hoses were taken into the building from there. But such was the relentless progress of the blaze that the firemen were forced to withdraw.

As might be expected, spectators were now arriving in large numbers; for a while it was thought troops might have to be called out to control them, but a joint effort by the police, High Constables and Councillors soon restored order.

With the blaze now out of control, assistance was required from Leith but in reality it was too late. For a time the flames were prevented from spreading from the entrance hall to the dress circle, which enabled staff to rescue the pictures which had decorated this once fine theatre. The adjoining tobacconist's shop was, however, destroyed, with the loss of stock valued at £200.

Within an hour of the alarm being raised, there was concern for the safety of all the surrounding buildings. The theatre roof was burning furiously and at the stage end a seven-storey tenement was threatened. The windows were open and at all of them the faces of anxious tenants could be seen, trying to calculate when it would be necessary to start throwing furnishings to the street below.

On the theatre side of the street, the tenements, six storeys high, were in even greater danger. Here, in subdivided flats, lived some of the poorest people. These families (forty of them) made every effort to save their precious belongings by throwing water onto the wooden window frames, and the flats at the lower levels were secured. The heat eventually became so overpowering that the attic properties had to be abandoned to their fate. On several roofs the lead melted and ran down the outer walls.

By this time the firemen were being hampered by the loss of pressure and water could not reach premises above the second level; but the problem was soon overcome and efforts continued to save the flats.

There was sadness for many of the residents. What the flames had failed to destroy was considerably damaged by water. The Miles family, husband, wife and three children occupied a single attic room. Mr Miles had been unemployed for seven months but had recently found a job. Now he had lost everything.

Many of the families were not covered by insurance. For a time a large tenement in St James Place was also in danger and many of the families, no doubt aware of previous outbreaks, took the precaution of removing household items to the opposite side of the street. A change in wind direction saved the situation.

Fire again . . . this time 1884

Meanwhile, a great deal of attention was being paid to St Mary's Cathedral, where the roof of the servants' quarters at the archbishop's residence caught fire. Quick action by the residents themselves soon extinguished the flames.

In the year prior to this fire a great deal of money had been spent on the theatre, the interior having been painted throughout and expensive decorations provided for the dress circle, private boxes and corridors.

In the week preceding the latest catastrophe, the famous French actress, Sarah Bernhardt, who died in 1923, had appeared on the Monday and Tuesday. The remainder of the week had been taken up by the Majilton company in *Round the Clock*, prior to the opening of *The Nightingale*.

And Finally (1946)

The end for the Theatre Royal came on the night of Saturday 30 March 1946, when it was gutted in one of the fiercest blazes in Edinburgh for a long time. It was not an old theatre, having been completely refurbished only ten years previously and the cost of damage was estimated at £75,000.

Minutes before the outbreak was discovered, Scots comedian Tommy Morgan and his cast had played to a packed audience in the very popular *Hail Caledonia* show. By 10.40 p.m. the last of the public had been ushered from the hall and only a handful of staff remained, the assistant manager, night watchman, usherettes and cleaners.

About 11.15 p.m. assistant theatre manager Peter Robertson was still in the office when a cleaner reported seeing smoke in the gallery. The watchman, 56-year-old William Fraser, investigated, called the Fire Brigade, and then calmly played a hose on the flames. The first engine arrived within two minutes, but despite the efforts of units from London Road, Leith, Victoria Dock, Musselburgh and Dalkeith, they were unable to save the theatre.

Two turntable ladders were used and searchlights were played on the building to help the firefighters. At one stage the flames were shooting 40 feet into the air and the blaze spread rapidly. Around midnight the roof collapsed. As a precaution, families nearby were evacuated and taken to temporary accommodation in church halls.

Fortunately, the fire safety screen had been dropped immediately after the performance and although part of the stage and scenery were damaged, the dressing-rooms, workshops and 'props' were relatively unaffected.

Around midnight the flames burst through the roof and it was not long before large sections of timbers crashed into the pits, causing the fire to spread rapidly on the lower level. An hour later the fire was all but out, although firemen remained on duty throughout Sunday as a precaution. All day the site was visited by countless sightseers, many of whom were regular theatregoers who each week had paid a few shillings to see the current show and had been entertained by such household names in Scottish music hall as Harry Gordon, Dave Willis, Jack Anthony, Tommy Lorne and Will Fyffe.

The property owners were confident that the Theatre Royal would be rebuilt and a figure of £100,000 was quoted. It was hoped that work would start quickly and the theatre would be open by the end of the year. These optimistic views were not, unfortunately, shared by the authorities.

It was the immediate post-war period, building materials were in short supply, and there were many projects, such as housing, which carried a greater degree of priority.

At a meeting of the Town Council's Streets and Building Committee in the City Chambers on 5 June 1947, the Town Clerk reminded the Councillors that a special sub-committee had met in December 1946, when the question of obtaining an alternative theatre site had been discussed. The owners had subsequently informed the Council that they preferred the existing site, as they were more hopeful of obtaining a Ministry of Works licence to rebuild the ruined structure than for new work. After much discussion the Committee signified their approval, but it was close and went in favour of the applicants, Edinburgh Varieties Ltd, only on the casting vote of the chairman, and was subject to confirmation by the Town Council.

One week later the full Council decided by 40 votes to 13 to continue consideration. A new Theatre Royal was now becoming a controversial subject and George Willis, MP for Edinburgh North, expressed his concern in the House of Commons that a licence had been granted when houses were so desperately needed.

In July the Town Council indicated that they were not opposed to the replacement of the theatre, but believed that it must form part of a major redevelopment involving an area bounded by St James' Square, York Place, Calton Hill and the top of Leith Walk. That work would have to be carried out in stages.

The matter dragged on and the owners appealed to the Secretary of State for Scotland against the refusal of the Council to grant consent to replace the theatre. On 17 September 1948 this appeal was dismissed. The Secretary of State took the view that reconstruction on the same site would prejudice the redevelopment of the area as a whole.

In announcing his decision, however, he said he regarded the provision of a new theatre in this area as desirable in the public interest and indicated to the Council that he would be glad if they took steps to make a new site available as soon as possible. On 3 November 1950 the Council, by a majority of 36 to 13, resolved to grant consent for a theatre for a limited period of thirty years.

Two years later it was reported that work would commence 'in a few months time'. But that was subject to obtaining a Ministry of Works licence and the Ministry made it clear that the restoration of the Theatre Royal was automatically ruled out by the ban on building work costing more than £5,000 which applied to any place of entertainment. No promise had been given regarding the issue of a licence but they indicated that the Ministry would keep the matter in mind. Nevertheless, the work would have to wait until steel was more readily available and the building materials supply improved.

The Ministry indicated that they were sympathetic and aware of the special circumstances relating to the Theatre Royal and the pressure on theatre accommodation caused by the Edinburgh Festival, and they accepted there was a genuine need for more theatre space in the city.

In 1953 there were reports that the theatre would reopen the following year. This was immediately denied by the Ministry of Works, who said that no licence had been granted nor had any work been approved in principle.

The saga of the Theatre Royal site dragged on, and in 1954, eight years after the fire, the owners put it on the market. Two years later the Town Council considered a proposal to erect a garage and filling station on the land which only ten years previously had 'housed' the Theatre Royal, one of the best-known halls in the country. Fortunately, the local authority deferred making a decision on the application pending further details.

Was it the thought of a filling station alongside the cathedral that prompted the Roman Catholic authorities to act? At a service in St Mary's on 16 December 1956 the congregation were told by Father Patrick Quille that the church had bought the site of the former theatre 'with a view to further development'. Father Quille added that it was hoped to make the cathedral worthy of the capital of Scotland.

'We felt we must buy the site of the theatre to make sure the amenity of the cathedral would be preserved,' he said.

The Theatre Royal/St Mary's Cathedral site has changed beyond all recognition during the post-war era. Major redevelopment has been carried out in the vicinity. After a long battle the remains of the Theatre Royal were demolished, releasing the cathedral from its previously cramped location, and it now enjoys a broad promenade to the front. Here also are three major sculptures by Leith-born and locally educated Sir Eduardo Paolozzi.

Around the corner, Little King Street remains in name but, thankfully, gone are the high tenements where successive generations of residents nightly heard the reactions of the theatre audiences . . . and lived in constant fear of yet another fire.

St Mary's Cathedral has expanded over the site of the old Theatres Royal

6

THE GREAT FIRE OF EDINBURGH
AND THE AFTERMATH

Throughout many centuries, the danger of fire was a constant concern for the citizens of Edinburgh. Timber or thatch roofs, wooden-fronted houses, open hearths in the homes, all led to blazes which destroyed properties over the years in the tall, narrow and congested closes round the High Street.

But none was more horrendous than what became known as the Great Fire of 1824, which devastated a large part of the Old Town. The disaster had one major beneficial outcome, however; it cemented the formation of the world's first municipal fire service.

That fire reached proportions unknown in the town; none before had caused such widespread havoc. The outbreak burned over a three-day period, destroying buildings on the south side of the street

The scene of devastation after the great fire

between Parliament Square and the Tron Kirk.

On 24 June 1824, a serious outbreak occurred in the same area and the ruins had not been cleared away when, on 15 November, a fire was discovered in a seven-storey tenement at the head of Old Assembly Close. It was first noticed about 10 p.m. when flames burst from the premises of a copper-plate printing firm and spread rapidly upwards through the roof.

By 11 p.m. the three adjoining premises were alight and, with smoke belching from every window, it was soon apparent that nothing could be done to save them.

The firemen then turned their attention to the surrounding houses, but their attempts to prevent the outbreak from spreading were hampered because of the difficulty of gaining access through the maze of closes. After several hours the blaze was isolated in the east, but little could be done to prevent it spreading westwards. By 3 a.m. the *Courant* newspaper office was alight and was soon totally consumed. Two hours later the gable end of the building collapsed.

Meanwhile, the fire was also spreading downwards towards the Cowgate, where the mass of old timber buildings were quickly consumed. Soon the whole area was a blazing inferno.

The fight to save the town took a turn for the better after the flames penetrated to the west side of the *Courant* office. Here the adjoining property was one storey higher and consequently the flames could not reach the timber roof.

By 9 a.m. on Tuesday the fire appeared to be smothered. Fortunately, there had been little wind during the night, but danger remained, for a stiff breeze was now blowing, and sparks were flying. Consequently, the firemen continued to play water on the smouldering embers.

Suddenly, however, the cry went up – the Tron Kirk was alight! This was a major surprise, for the church was a considerable distance from where the fire had been checked. Nevertheless the firefighters had to act quickly, for the flames were shooting from the south-west corner of the church tower. The wooden balustrade had already fallen and the flames were being fanned by the south-westerly wind. A window had given way and, through the space, sparks had set the old church alight.

Several fire engines hurried to the scene; using long ladders the firemen scrambled onto the roof. For a time they managed to contain the outbreak, but the seat of the fire could not be reached. Soon the old Dutch spire, made of wood and lined in lead, was alight.

The men had to retreat as molten lead ran down the roof and walls. Only forty-five minutes after the fire had been discovered, the spire collapsed. This enabled the firefighters to get back onto the roof but the fire was still rampant. Fortunately, a more powerful engine owned by the Board of Ordnance arrived and the fire was brought under control.

But still more trouble was to follow. At 10 p.m., exactly twenty-four hours after the first outbreak, fire was discovered on the east side of Parliament Square. It began on the top floor of an 11-storey high tenement, overlooking the Cowgate.

The firemen, who had been on duty all that time, were severely handicapped, as their equipment was unsuitable for outbreaks at such a height.

The danger spread in all directions, until, by early morning, a vast area was alight. Flames were shooting to unbelievable heights, illuminating the pavements and silhouetting the spire of St Giles, which was undamaged. For a while, however, the nearby Commercial Bank building was in considerable danger.

By 8 a.m. the fire had burned itself out and the devastation could be surveyed. Walls had collapsed, bringing debris into the square; along the High Street four lands (tenements), each of four storeys were destroyed. Looking towards the Cowgate, two wooden lands in Conn's Close had disappeared and in the Old Assembly Close four lands of seven storeys were gutted, as were six tenements in Borthwick's Close. Four lands standing six to nine storeys high suffered a similar fate in Old Fishmarket Close.

Little was to be seen apart from heaps of rubble and many insecure walls. Along the front of Parliament Square four double lands of between seven and eleven storeys were destroyed. So dangerous were the walls left standing that they were quickly demolished. Some were blown up and others were pulled down using chains; these jobs were carried out by soldiers and sailors called in to help with the emergency.

In all, twenty-two fire engines had been in use, coming from as far away as Dalkeith Palace and Musselburgh. The insurance companies had a number of appliances at work, while the military made a major contribution.

Several deaths resulted from the fire – reports varying between eight and thirteen – and more than four hundred families were made homeless.

A fund launched to assist those who had suffered realised £11,596. The damage caused during these three disastrous days was estimated at more than £200,000. Should such a calamity occur today the cost would be multi-millions.

James Braidwood appointed

The 1824 fire was to convince the authorities that a municipal fire brigade was not only desirable but necessary. Firefighting had principally been the responsibility of the insurance companies, who had a vested interest in protecting their clients' properties, and, of course, the company money. But it was not an efficient service.

The year 1824 had been a bad one for fires. In February there had been a serious outbreak in Niddry Street, followed by another in June opposite the Royal Exchange (City Chambers). These incidents had resulted in meetings to discuss the unsatisfactory arrangements for firefighting in the town.

Finally, a committee came to the conclusion that Edinburgh could have a reliable fire service for an initial outlay of £1,400. It was estimated that the annual expenditure thereafter would not exceed £500. The Town Council also agreed to make an annual grant of £50 towards the maintenance of the service and additional payments from the insurance companies brought the total to £335. On the understanding that the yearly charge to their funds did not exceed £200, the police authority agreed to administer the scheme.

And so, with the Council and six insurance companies each contributing £200, the world's first municipal fire service was established. But they were still in the process of organisation when called on to answer the biggest possible challenge in what was literally a baptism of fire.

James Braidwood, the son of Francis Braidwood, a well-known Edinburgh cabinetmaker, was appointed to command the brigade, with the glorious title of Master of Fire Engines. He was only twenty-four years old, and had been educated at the High School.

The apparatus consisted of three engines costing £530 and four smaller appliances which were purchased for £210. The larger units were operated by twenty men, with an additional four to pull them

James Braidwood, Edinburgh's first fire-master

through the streets. Ten water carts were also provided to be used in conjunction with the engines. Uniforms too, were supplied, consisting of leather helmets, blue tunics and white trousers. Total cost for the eighty men? Only £181.19s.1d.! But by 1826 it was apparent that the running costs had been grossly underestimated – to the tune of one-third. Constant repairs to apparatus was the principal reason, although wages were a contributory factor.

During the early years of the service the firemen did their training on one day a week – at 4 a.m., 'an hour which did not interfere with their ordinary occupations'. The firemen were mainly tradesmen, and it was known for spectators to be called upon to assist, for which they were compensated.

Braidwood resigned his Edinburgh appointment to take up a similar post in London in 1832. There his task was a mammoth one, and included responsibility for the royal residences and numerous prominent buildings.

He had held the London post for twenty-eight years when he was killed, leading his men in a major outbreak. It was Saturday 22 June 1861, and the flames were raging through Tooley Street, London Bridge. The fire was described as the worst in London for 100 years and possibly since the great fire of 1666. Wharfs and warehouses were mainly affected, but to a lesser degree houses and shops were lost. Damage was estimated at £2,000,000.

Suddenly, about 7 p.m., a bulging wall caved in, burying Superintendent Braidwood. Such was Braidwood's reputation that on the Sunday Queen Victoria twice sent messengers to the scene for news of the fire brigade chief. His body was not recovered until Monday; he left a widow and six children. In an obituary, the *Illustrated London News* said that Braidwood had raised the Edinburgh Fire Engine Establishment to such a state of efficiency 'as to become the model for all similar institutions in the country'.

James Braidwood was buried at Abbey Park Cemetery, London, in the same grave as his stepson, killed in a fire six years previously.

A newspaper reported: 'The route of the procession was nearly as crowded as the occasion of the funeral of the Duke of Wellington. There was a great muster of volunteers, policemen and firemen with twenty mourning carriages. The Duke of Sutherland and Earl of Caithness attended as mourners.'

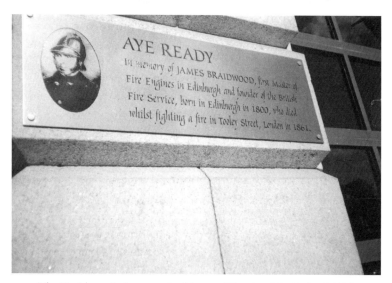

The Braidwood plaque at Lothian and Borders Fire Brigade HQ

London was quick to recognise its debt to Braidwood, and when Cotton's Wharf was rebuilt a memorial was erected to the man from Edinburgh, and one of the streets leading from Tooley Street to the river was appropriately named Braidwood Street.

Yet, in his home city Braidwood was barely recognised outside firefighters' circles. It is only recently that a plaque commemorating him has been placed on the Fire Brigade HQ building in Lauriston Place.

7

HIGH STREET TENEMENT COLLAPSE
AND HOW A LEGEND GREW

Above the entrance to Paisley Close in the High Street, more or less opposite Blackfriars Street, is the effigy of a boy and the unlikely quotation of the words of an Edinburgh laddie: 'Heave awa' chaps, I'm no' dead yet.' Controversy has always surrounded the actual words used, variously quoted as 'Heave awa', lads', 'Heave awa', boys', and 'Heave awa', men'.

These words were allegedly spoken by Joseph McIver at the height of a major disaster when, on 24 November 1861, the properties at 99 to 107 High Street, between Bailie Fyfe's Close and Paisley Close collapsed. Thirty-five people were killed and it is unlikely that the rescuers paid a great deal of attention to the rambling of one boy who was almost certainly in a state of shock.

The property where the catastrophe occurred was a tenement which consisted of shops on the ground level with five storeys of flats and attics towering 85 feet high. The ground area of the tragedy site measured no more than 60 feet by 60 feet. It was flanked on both sides by wooden-fronted buildings which were substantially lower, and of a type built about the beginning of the seventeenth century.

At one time this address was the abode of wealthy families. Here, William Fettes, a future Lord Provost and founder of the famous college, lived above his mother's shop. At the time of the building collapse, eighty-three poorer families were resident.

It is not difficult to visualise the scene immediately before disaster struck on the Sunday morning. Most of the families were asleep, but luckily others were not at home, being either at work or wending their way towards the High Street after a night out.

The hands of the Tron Kirk clock were approaching 1.30 a.m., and a cold wind blew as two policemen walked their beat up the High Street. Suddenly the relative quietness was shattered by a distant rumbling, and clouds of dust blew out, throwing a complete screen over the area. It was some time before the policemen were able to establish the exact cause and, to their utter horror, they discovered that the front of the building between 99 and 107 High Street had caved in, crashing to the ground and taking with it all floors of the building.

The policemen ran to their police station, where Lieutenant Milligan was on duty, to raise the alarm. It was obvious that this was a major incident. The fire brigade were soon on the scene, and the town's magistrates were informed of a possible disaster.

From the wreckage pitiful cries for help could be heard, but because of the vast amount of rubble which had fallen into such a confined space – outwardly masonry had gone no further than the pavement – rescue was difficult.

Nevertheless, the work of releasing the victims went ahead, despite the cold and danger, for it was not known when any of the adjoining buildings might collapse. To illuminate the area, the tops were removed from street lights so that the full blaze of gas was available for torches.

Very quickly twenty-two bodies were recovered and a further thirteen people taken out alive and rushed to the Infirmary. But many more – the exact number was unknown – were still missing. By now large crowds had gathered in the High Street; to keep them back barricades were thrown across the street. As the bodies were brought out, the rescuers were surprised to find how few showed any evidence of physical injury, and, in almost every case, death was due to suffocation. A vast number of the victims were found prostrate in bed.

And so to the story of hero Joseph McIver, so graphically told in the *Weekly Scotsman* of 30 November 1861:

> At an early hour, while the work of clearing away the rubbish was proceeding, one of the detachments of firemen discovered a foot protruding from the debris. The men set vigorously to work around the spot and soon ascertained that a boy was buried there. But the unfortunate lad was so closely wedged between the rubbish and the joisting that he could not be got out until the beam was cut in two.
>
> During the process of sawing through the beam, the boy was heard repeatedly to say, 'Heave awa' men: I'm no dead yet.' And on his ultimately being extracted, happily not much injured, he immediately called for a drink of water. Considering his extremely critical position, the patience and firmness of this lad was truly wonderful.

And so young Joseph McIver became immortalised with his effigy above a close in Edinburgh's most famous street.

There were a number of lucky escapes, among them Police Sergeant Rennie. He had been patrolling on the side of the street where the collapse took place, but crossed to investigate a disturbance. Seconds later the building disappeared.

A family of eleven, the Baxters, were also fortunate to escape with their lives. All had retired for the night except the father, William. He had just placed his trousers on the back of a chair when he heard a noise like the 'rumble of chuckie stones'. His wife, a superstitious woman, remarked excitedly, 'That is a warning.' The family were quickly roused by the parents and escaped by the back passage.

Three policemen who lived in the building were fortunately on night shift, but, alas, the wife of Constable Mackenzie was killed. Another lost forty sovereigns in the rubble. The money had been drawn from the bank the previous day as the constable had intended emigrating to Australia.

Many days passed before the debris was cleared and the cause of the disaster investigated. According to contemporary reports, the building had been erected about the end of the seventeenth century from timber which came from the Burgh Muir. The wood was later faced in stone, and investigations revealed that the beams were full of dry rot.

It has been suggested that the building fell without warning, but only two days before the collapse, Mr Cairns, who occupied one of the ground floor shops, had discovered some fallen plaster. He called in a master mason, who failed to detect any danger. Even those who got out before the building gave way spoke of a ten minute interval from the signs that something was seriously wrong to the collapse itself.

But the disaster achieved one thing above all else; it drew the attention of the authorities to the deplorable state of the buildings in the poorer parts of the town. Meetings took place and the Council agreed to hear a deputation. As a result, Dr Henry Littlejohn was appointed to be the town's first Medical Officer of Health on 30 September 1862.

In 1865 Littlejohn prepared 'A Report on the Sanitary Conditions of the City of Edinburgh', which had far-reaching consequences and resulted in the demolition of many slums, improvement to other

Heave awa' . . . A tribute to Joseph McIver

properties and the rebuilding of tenements. Numbers 99 to 107 High Street rose from the rubble, and the names Paisley Close and Bailie Fyfe's Close are once more displayed on that familiar tourist route.

Curiously, if you ask any of the older residents for directions to Paisley Close the response is likely to be raised eyebrows and a shake of the head. But mention 'Heave Awa' Close' and recognition is instant!

8

A REAL BOY'S OWN HERO

During the second half of the nineteenth and well into the twentieth century, successive generations of boys were reared on a literary diet of adventure stories such as *The Young Fur Traders*, *The Coral Island* and *Martin Rattler*, which flowed from the fertile mind of the Edinburgh writer, R.M. Ballantyne, who was born at 25 Ann Street.

Pure fiction, of course, and no doubt his early writings were influenced by the five years he spent as a young man in Canada, working as a clerk for the Hudson Bay Company and trading with the Indians. But did Robert Michael Ballantyne, on Wednesday 9 October 1867, take part in a real-life, brave, but alas unsuccessful bid to rescue a young girl trapped in a blazing smoke-filled tenement in Edinburgh's Royal Mile?

The premises were the solidly built Chessel's Court, 240 Canongate, dating from the 1720–30 period. It was about 12.30 p.m. on that fateful day. The pavement was, as usual, crowded, and the street congested to the extent of 'almost total obstruction'.

Meanwhile, in a workshop to the back of the court and adjacent to Pirrie's Close on the west, Thomas Hammond, a 34-year-old fireworks maker and tobacconist, was completing a London order for rockets.

As Hammond was filling one of the fireworks, the powder ignited and sparks flew about the shop, which was littered with inflammable material. Fire broke out, and the paper used in the manufacture of the rockets caused dense smoke, initially concealing the flames. The smoke spread quickly through the back entrance of the shop, which opened onto the tenement stairway; it was drawn up the stairwell and into the houses. The residents automatically made their way on to the stair, only to find their exit blocked by the smoke. There was only one way of escape – through the windows; but some of the trapped people were 60 feet up. Worse was to follow.

In the shop were two kegs of powder, one of which was open. There was an almighty explosion which was heard all over the town, as powder, rockets, and fireworks ignited. The two windows in Hammond's shop, three in the basement workshop occupied by Duffy the basket-maker, and three large windows in the flat above were blown out with such force that the glass was embedded in buildings across the street. An iron bar weighing 4½ lbs and part of a window frame were found inside the bakery shop opposite, while flames were soon leaping from the windows and stretching halfway over the roadway.

Firemen were quickly on the scene, but twenty minutes passed before their engine appeared. Hoses were connected at the head of St Mary's Wynd and Riddle's Close, which let the firemen attack flames from both front and rear.

As desperate cries for help came from the upper windows rescue operations began. From a third floor window Mrs Henderson bravely dropped her four children, one by one, into the arms of Police Sergeant Auld. Auld was knocked unconscious by a blow on the chest as he caught the fourth youngster. He quickly recovered, however, and was able to assist George Riddle, a chimney sweep, to rescue the mother and another woman by using a ladder.

Meanwhile, two women were spotted leaning out of a fourth-floor window from which smoke was belching. A rope was passed to the women, who were now out on the ledge. One was persuaded to tie the rope round her waist, and, as she swung, she was caught by the policeman; the second woman was similarly saved. And Charles Stewart heroically brought out four other women by ladder.

But there was sorrow too. Mrs Jessie Ferguson jumped from the fourth floor, and as she lay dying on the pavement her last words were, 'My poor bairn's in the garret.'

The Scotsman reported:

Mr R.M. Ballantyne, who arrived on the ground shortly after one o'clock, hearing that Mrs Ferguson had said this, proposed to Mr Slater, a slater, and Mr McPherson, Inspector of Streets and Buildings, that they should try to go up the staircase and search for the child.

Mr McPherson was compelled by the smoke to return in a few minutes but Mr Slater and Mr Ballantyne, keeping their heads as low as possible, succeeded in making their way to the fourth storey.

Some idea of the difficulty and danger of this search may be formed from the fact that Mr Ballantyne had to go four times to the windows to get a little air while engaged in the search. In one of the houses Mr Slater and Mr Ballantyne found a young girl lying on the floor not far from the door. Mr Slater took the poor girl in his arms and carried her swiftly downstairs to the court and through the pend into the front street.

Unfortunately the girl was dead.

Was the R.M. Ballantyne referred to in the newspaper account the famous author? Interestingly, the occupations of those involved in rescue work are identified, with the exception of Ballantyne, who is referred to by name only.

Five people (including 12-year-old Mary Ann Emslie, Hammond's message-girl) died, and three of the Hammond family were among people injured in the blaze. The death toll would have been much higher, but for the bravery of the firemen and some outstanding rescues performed by members of the public.

The town were quick to recognise the heroic efforts of the rescuers, and on the afternoon of Saturday 25 November Lord Provost William Chambers, magistrates, and Councillors assembled in their robes together with the Trustees of the Surplus Fire Fund at the City Chambers to honour some of those citizens who had 'distinguished themselves in saving life'.

Lord Provost Chambers told those present that the cause of the calamity was well known. It was the improper manufacture of fireworks on the street floor of a high dwelling-house. The sudden fire had filled the staircase with smoke, resulting in escape being impossible. Realising that escape by way of the stair was cut off, some mothers had thrown their children from the windows before jumping themselves.

'It was mainly in attempts to save them by ladders, ropes and blankets that the heroism I speak of was displayed', continued the Lord Provost. 'These attempts were, I am glad to say, successful in several instances; but whether so or not, invited the approbation of the authorities, along with such marks of favour as were in their power to bestow.'

He went on to explain that the awards were funded from the Surplus Fire Fund, the balance from money raised by public subscription and otherwise for the relief of the persons who suffered from the great fire of 1824.

Many claims had been submitted to the Surplus Fire Fund for assistance over lost property, but this was specifically excluded from their remit. One man had claimed £163 and there was no reason to believe that it was not genuine, but the Lord Provost believed that anyone who owned property of this sort of value should insure it adequately. Also in existence was the Accident Fund, which had been established some years previously to compensate householders who had suffered following the collapse of buildings in the High Street. (Was this 'Heave Awa' Close', which collapsed with the death of 35 persons?)

From the Accident Fund many poor people had been compensated with small sums of money. Claims had been submitted amounting to £544. 13s. 3d. for losses both at Chessel's Court and in a second fire in North Gray's Close a few days later. This fund had paid out £204.

Within six weeks of the fire a number of people had been given monetary awards totalling £23, and the meeting at the City Chambers was to present a further £20 and silver medals. The Lord Provost said that, apart from the awards, he had written to several people thanking them for their help. Among them was a young army corporal on leave, who had given considerable help to the police. In addition to rewarding the soldier, a letter had been sent to his commanding officer, and that letter had been read out before the regiment.

Lord Provost Chambers told the guests that he had witnessed some of the dangerous rescue work which had taken place, and that it was with this in mind that he was pleased to announce that the city was to purchase a fire escape.

With regard to the awards, the Lord Provost explained, it might have been possible to obtain medals for at least two individuals from the London Society for rewarding outstanding efforts in fire rescue. The Council had decided, however, that an Edinburgh award was more appropriate. The inscription read: 'Presented to – in recognition of his meritorious services in saving life at the disastrous fire in the Canongate, 9th October 1867.' On the reverse side was the town's coat-of-arms.

Lord Provost William Chambers thanked each recipient individually as he presented the awards, and to R.M. Ballantyne he said:

I am delighted to admit you into this Legion of Honour. You have distinguished yourself on many occasions previously, both here and elsewhere, by your services in the cause of humanity and it is gratifying to me, as Chief Magistrate of Edinburgh, to be able to present you on this occasion with one of our medals of honour.

Those citizens of Edinburgh honoured that day were:

William Craig Auld, Sergeant, Edinburgh Police – medal and £5
George Riddle, chimney sweeper, Bell's Close, Canongate – medal and £5
Andrew Slater, slater, Canongate – medal
Peter Wight, clerk, South St Andrew Street – medal
John Watson, baker, 18 Bristo Street – medal and £2
John Burke, slater, 6 Greenside Court – medal and £2
Gilbert Simpson, colliery sub-manager, 17 Keir Street – medal
William McKenzie, builder, Hope Park – medal
Peter Watson, slater, 2 Big Jack's Close – medal and £2
Constable James McIntee, Edinburgh Police – medal and £2
Constable John Taylor, Edinburgh Police – medal and £2
R.M. Ballantyne, 6 Millerfield Place – medal

R.M. Ballantyne, 6 Millerfield Place. At last a lead to establishing the identity of the elusive hero. A check of the Edinburgh Street directories for the years following 1867 showed only one R.M. Ballantyne. This clue, however, only partly solved the mystery. But all was revealed in the census returned for 1871, where, under the address '6 Millerfield Place' appeared the names 'R.M. Ballantyne, his wife Jane and son Francis'. The solution appeared under the heading 'occupation', where the following entry had been made: 'Literature. Books for the young. Art (painting).'

9

MOB RULE IN THE WEST BOW

Historic Greyfriars churchyard contains a fine collection of centuries-old, ornate gravestones, which serve as reminders of some of Edinburgh's famous, wealthy, and distinguished citizens. Almost certainly, however, the stone most likely to be missed by the casual visitor is a long, plain and simple memorial, now partly covered in a green deposit which makes the inscription difficult to decipher.

Close inspection will reveal the name John Porteous and, more sinisterly, a word rarely seen on a gravestone – 'Murdered'. The full wording on the memorial reads: 'John Porteous a Captain of the Edinburgh City Guard Murdered 7 September, 1736. All Passion Spent 1973.'

For more than 250 years, this has been the Porteous resting place, and for most of that time the grave has been marked by nothing more than a wooden post. This is not surprising, for his death, despised as the man was, is remembered as one of the most shameful incidents in Edinburgh's history and resulted in the government taking reprisals against the Scottish capital.

The year 1736 had opened relatively quietly in Edinburgh with no hint of the drama that was to follow. Petty smuggling was an 'occupation' followed by more than a few men, and from time to time the law-breakers were apprehended by the Customs officers.

Such was the fate of Andrew Wilson from Pathhead, near Kirkcaldy, who, aggrieved by the seizure of his contraband, resolved to recover at least the equivalent value of the appropriated property. Consequently, on 9 January 1736, Wilson, accompanied by George Robertson of Bristo Port, Edinburgh, and a number of associates, robbed the collector at Pittenweem of a sum of money. Curiously, the robbery had been carried out so openly that Wilson and Robertson were arrested the same evening and the money recovered. In due course the pair stood trial in Edinburgh and were condemned to death – a sentence which the citizens of Edinburgh considered to be severe.

The pair were incarcerated in the Tolbooth, and in accordance with the custom of that period, on the Sunday prior to the date set for their execution, the condemned men were taken to St Giles' Cathedral for the church service, accompanied by four guards.

Suddenly, Wilson seized two of the soldiers, at the same time yelling at Robertson to escape. Robertson vaulted the pews and, almost as if by a prepared plan, the congregation stood aside and allowed the prisoner to go clear. At this Wilson calmly sat down.

There was no doubt where the sympathy of the Edinburgh citizens lay, and there was considerable anxiety among the town officials as 14 April – the date fixed for the execution – approached. Concerned that an attempt might be mounted to rescue the second man, the magistrates ordered that the guard be doubled and that the officers and men of the Trained Bands attend the execution. In addition, members of the City Guard were each issued with three shots and, by special order, the weapons were loaded before marching off on duty.

As 2 p.m. (the time set for the death penalty to be carried out) approached, a battalion of regular troops then billeted in the Canongate were drawn up on each side of the Lawnmarket at the top of the High Street. In addition, reserve soldiers under arms were on call in the city guard room.

A vast crowd had assembled in the Grassmarket to witness the execution. The sentence was carried out, and confusing stories have been told about what followed. It was alleged that as the hangman mounted a ladder to release the body he was stoned by a number of boys. This was not an unusual occurrence on such occasions, but it is said that several of the Guard were struck and nerves were already on a knife-edge.

The Guard was under the command of Captain John Porteous, the son of a respectable Canongate tailor, who had followed his father's profession for a time before choosing to join the army as a career. In 1718, having left the army, he was appointed adjutant of the City Guard and eight years later he reached the rank of captain.

This promotion was surprising, for Porteous was an unpopular man with a violent temper and sadistic character. In July the previous year he allegedly quarrelled with a fellow officer, John Fergusson, and the pair came to blows while appearing before the Town Council. They were dismissed from their posts but later reinstated.

It was rumoured that Porteous was extremely angry at Robertson's escape and that he had been particularly brutal to Wilson on the days before the execution. The stone-throwing was the opportunity that Porteous had been seeking and he grabbed a weapon from one of the men and began firing wildly.

By the time the shooting was over four spectators were dead, two injured persons subsequently died, and eleven more were injured but survived. Some of the victims were not even in the crowd but were looking on from nearby windows, which illustrates how indiscriminate the firing had been. Porteous retreated his men up the West Bow and to the guard room in the High Street. At the outset he could have read the Riot Act but he had chosen not to do so. His duties completed, the captain made his way to the Spread Eagle Tavern, where the magistrates were already assembled.

The commanding officer was taken to the Council Chamber, questioned at length and formally charged with murder – he was not above the law. He emphatically denied the charge claiming that he had not given an order to shoot into the crowd, nor had he fired his weapon. The three shots authorised by the magistrates were still in his possession, two in his cartridge-box and the other in his firearm.

Porteous was brought to trial on 19 July and, despite his protestations, he was sentenced to death with the execution date fixed for 8 September. The trial had been a lengthy one, and had continued non-stop. It did not conclude until 9 a.m. the following morning, and Porteous had to wait a further seven hours before he learned his fate.

An appeal was immediately dispatched to London where, in the absence of George II, Queen Caroline ordered a stay of execution. The news reached Edinburgh on 2 September.

Once more the wrath of Edinburgh was roused, and very quickly it was being whispered in the coffee houses that Porteous would die on the date decreed by the court.

On 7 September a message was delivered to Lord Provost Alexander Wilson, warning him of the serious situation; but no action was taken. At approximately nine o'clock that night the rioters assembled at Portsburgh, and, preceded by a drummer, marched through the Grassmarket, increasing in number at every step. They quickly overpowered the City Guard and then turned their attention to the Tolbooth Jail, where, with some difficulty, they gained entry.

With the crowd in this mood it was impossible to find anyone who was prepared to carry a message, but finally the Lord Provost persuaded Patrick Lindsay, the town's Member of Parliament, to make contact with General Moyes, who was in command of the military garrison in the town. This officer refused to act on the basis of a verbal message.

It was now 11.30 and the mob were in the prison, where they took the keys from a terrified warder. The luckless Porteous was soon identified by the lynch mob and dragged by way of the West Bow to the Grassmarket. They stopped briefly at the foot of the Bow, where a shop was entered and a rope seized for the hanging; very considerately, a guinea was left to pay for the noose.

In the darkness, the rioters, carrying torches, manhandled their prisoner to the south side of the Grassmarket, directly opposite the West Bow. There they found a dyer's pole, over which they threw the rope. In a flash it was round the condemned man's neck and mob justice was carried out. Quickly and quietly the rioters dispersed, leaving on the ground the weapons they had stolen from the Guard armoury.

The 'sentence' on John Porteous had been carried out in a most barbaric manner and death followed after several abortive attempts. The victim fought ferociously to the end. It was not until several hours later that the authorities were prepared to venture into the Grassmarket and recover the body, which was later laid to rest in Greyfriars.

Not surprisingly, there was panic among the town authorities, for they knew that on this occasion they were answerable to London. When the full facts of what had taken place reached the south they were received with anger, tempered by a degree of horror. King George, who was in Hanover, was kept informed through a series of express messages.

A hurried meeting of the Edinburgh magistrates was convened, at which it was decided to put on a show of power. As a message to London the Council ordered the arrest of anyone remotely suspect. More than two hundred people were taken into custody, quizzed, and then released because of lack of evidence.

But a question much discussed among the law-abiding citizens concerned the unusually large number of strangers who had appeared in the town hours before the riots began. The Council were well aware that a disturbance was a strong possibility, so why had the City Guard not been instructed to monitor their movements? Perhaps they had been, but then their commanding officer was not exactly the most popular of superiors. And where were these visitors now? Had they left the town as quietly and quickly as they had appeared? Perhaps they were nothing more that morbid spectators.

London, too, was most anxious to bring the perpetrators to justice, and a number of officials (including General Wade) were sent to Edinburgh to assist the Lord Advocate with his inquiries.

A proclamation was issued offering a reward of £200 (a vast amount of money) for information leading to the conviction of anyone involved, but no one was tempted. The message was to be read on the first Sunday of each month in the churches for a year; but all was in vain.

A Bill was introduced in the House of Lords 'to disable Alexander Wilson, Esq., Lord Provost of the City of Edinburgh, from taking, holding or enjoying any office or place of magistracy in the City of Edinburgh or anywhere in Great Britain and also for imprisoning him; for abolishing the town guard and removing the gates at the Netherbow Port'.

The Lord Provost was arrested on 1 April and spent three weeks in prison before being granted bail. In due course he and four bailies, together with the Lords of Justiciary, were ordered to appear before the House of Lords. Immediately there was a problem – protocol. On their arrival at the Lords there was a debate as to whether the Scottish Justiciary Lords should attend in their robes and whether at the table or the Bar! It was claimed that, as this point had not been settled by the articles of the Treaty of Union (which united the Scottish and English Parliaments), it was their right to be seated beside the English judges. After a lengthy discussion, it was determined that the Scottish legal representatives should appear in their robes at the Bar; but they insisted that it was their right to appear within the Bar.

The Bill to punish Edinburgh for its misdemeanours was fought vigorously by the Scottish Members of Parliament, but after numerous amendments it passed through both the Lords and the Commons.

The clauses to imprison the Lord Provost, abolish the City Guard and remove the Netherbow Port which stood at the foot of the High Street and gave entry to the Canongate, were omitted and replaced with a fine of £2,000, this sum to benefit the widow of the luckless Captain Porteous. But the action also cost the town's taxpayers

89 West Bow as it is today. Legend has it that
the 1736 rioters took the rope from these
shop premises to hang Captain John Porteous

£1,446. 2s. 7½d., exclusive of lawyers' fees. Considering what the consequences might have been, the Edinburgh officials returned
well-satisfied with the outcome.

Citizens turned out in great numbers and travelled miles to the
east of the town to meet the party. Lord Provost Wilson, by nature a
quiet man, got word of what was going on and returned to
Edinburgh by a different route. Wilson ceased to be Lord Provost on
13 July 1737, by virtue of Act of Parliament, and he was succeeded by
Archibald Macauley six days later.

Little remains of the old West Bow, although no. 89, traditionally
the shop where the rioters obtained the rope from Mrs Jeffrey's
premises, has survived. It is still a retail shop. But until as recently as
the 1960s you could still buy all types of ropes and twines from 89
West Bow, then occupied by William Bell (Ropes) Ltd. Not long
before the shop closed I called to see the manager, Alexander
Livingston. As I looked around the premises there lay bundles of
ropes and twines which to the casual visitor may have looked untidy,
but Mr Livingston knew exactly where anything could be located.

The shop counter, a substantial piece of dark, solid wood, stood just inside the door. It looked very old and marked from years of service and as my eyes moved along the flat, scored surface my thoughts automatically turned to the story of the Porteous Riots. Suddenly, and to my amazement, there, embedded on the counter was an old coin . . . surely not? Mr Livingston anticipated what I was thinking and explained the mystery:

> When I came to the shop in the early 1950s an old battered farthing was screwed to the counter. It was rather unsightly, and when a friend gave me five old-looking but worthless coins, I decided to remove the farthing and replace it with one of the newly-acquired coins. Over the years four of these coins were stolen, but if the characters who removed them thought that they were inheriting the golden guinea the laugh was on them for, in fact, they were worthless counterfeit coins used by gamblers in years gone by!

At the time of my last visit the fifth and last coin lay fixed in place with little chance of its being removed.

'You see,' said Mr Livingston with a laugh, 'every day for a week after I had put it in place, I applied layers of jewellers' glue just to make quite sure!'

Number 89 West Bow was a popular tourist attraction and for nearly twenty years the shop manager had a constant flow of customers not so much concerned about purchasing a length of rope (for legitimate purposes, of course) as with the shop's traditional connection with the death of Porteous. Visitors would call in from all over the world, particularly from America and Australia, and there were always a fair number of children with an interest in local history.

When, on the last working day of 1967, Alexander Livingston closed the door at 89 West Bow, it brought to an end an important link in Edinburgh's history and tradition. After more than 230 continuous years, a shop which had sold ropes and twines to countless generations of Edinburgh citizens would no longer provide this service.

No doubt Mr Livingston's final act was to take a last nostalgic look round the now empty premises. But were they empty? Within these four walls there surely remained centuries of memories – not least the mystery surrounding the identity of those rioters who smashed open the door, took a length of rope, and, leaving payment on the counter, then dragged the terrified Captain John Porteous to face his death on that dyer's pole, just across the road in the Grassmarket.

10

AN ELECTION – AND THE RIOT ACT IS READ

Come election time, be it parliamentary or local, Edinburgh is not exactly ablaze with enthusiasm, electioneering or canvassing, and this apathy is usually reflected in the relatively low turnout. This, the politicians will explain through a press release from a PR person, is because trends have altered and massive TV, radio and newspaper coverage ensure that the once popular hustings, meetings and 'door-knocking' no longer play a part in modern politics. In truth, there is a general apathy on the part of the electors.

How different from a parliamentary election which was held more than a century and a half ago when, dissatisfied with the result and the method by which it had been achieved, Edinburgh citizens went on the rampage. There were ugly scenes, the Lord Provost was threatened with violence and indeed assaulted, and military detachments were called out to assist the police to maintain order.

Eventually, after many hours of disruption, order was restored, but only after the Riot Act had been read. At that time, of course, the citizens of Edinburgh had no say in the decision – authority was vested in the Town Council!

The date was 3 May 1831, and for the last time the Town Council assembled to carry out this important duty. They were selecting the man who would replace William Dundas, who had been the Scottish capital's representative in parliament for the previous twenty-four years. There were three candidates, Robert Adam Dundas, nephew of the retiring member; Lord Advocate Francis Jeffrey; and Lord Provost William Allan, considered by most to be an outsider.

Dundas was not popular, for it was believed that his uncle, then Member of Parliament, had voted against the Reform Bill; consequently Jeffrey was the popular candidate among Edinburgh's residents.

The Councillors took their duties very seriously and the full Council (thirty-three members) turned up at the City Chambers for that historic vote.

The day started with a service at St Giles' Cathedral. About 11 a.m. spectators began to assemble outside the Council offices and very quickly the area was packed to capacity. The hands of the Tron Kirk clock were approaching 11.30 a.m. and a roar went up from the crowd as the popular Lord Advocate was spotted. His arrival was the signal for those present to voice their opinion on the suitability of the two main contenders.

Dundas was believed to be in the Chambers and it was rumoured that he had enjoyed breakfast with some of the Councillors.

Shortly before noon there was a rush for the few public seats which were available, when the news went round that the Council were assembling. At noon, precisely, the Lord Provost opened the meeting by stating that before dealing with the main part of the business, he had to announce that a number of petitions had been received and he instructed the clerk to read them. They contained 17,000 signatures – all in favour of Jeffrey.

This formality completed, the Lord Provost called for nomination of candidates to represent the city of Edinburgh in the House of Commons.

The name R.A. Dundas was put forward and that was the signal for another outburst of hostility; Jeffrey's nomination, on the other hand, was warmly received. Lord Provost Allan's candidature was noted with indifference.

The vote was taken, and the result was: Dundas 17; Jeffrey 14; and Allan 2. In a flash the news was conveyed to the highly charged crowd in the quadrangle below and immediately all hell let loose.

'A rope, a rope for Dundas', 'Burke (smother) the Provost' and 'Burn the Bailies' were only a few of the threats which could be heard coming from the menacing throng, and an attempt was made by the mob to rush the Council Chamber. Fortunately for those within, the attack was thwarted.

A considerable time elapsed before it was considered safe for the Lord Provost to leave the building, and it was only with difficulty that a passage was cleared through the throng. Strangely, in view of the tension which still prevailed among the crowd, Lord Provost Allan decided to walk to his home in Hillside Crescent, something he was to regret for the rest of his life! Gravely, and accompanied by a number of his friends, no doubt for moral support, and with a strong police presence, he struggled down the High Street and into the North Bridge.

The crowd were still in an angry mood. As he crossed the bridge the police cordon was broken, the Lord Provost manhandled, and for a time it was feared that his life was in danger. Eventually, the police regained control of the situation, but the outraged citizens pursued their quarry, throwing stones. In Leith Street, Edinburgh's first citizen was struck several times and finally had to seek refuge in a shop.

In the meantime, the sheriff had been summoned and he arrived accompanied by Captain Stewart. By now the crowd had turned their wrath on the police, and Stewart was badly injured. Finally the Riot Act was read, but to no avail.

A company of Irish Dragoons was rushed from Piershill Barracks, and under the protection of these soldiers the Lord Provost arrived home. Meanwhile, troops from the 79th Highlanders were ordered to the Assembly Rooms and others took up positions opposite the City Chambers.

Despite the vast crowd which had pursued the Lord Provost, many thousands had remained near the City Chambers in the High Street awaiting the departure of Jeffrey, the defeated candidate. As he left the building the noise was deafening. He was followed by his supporters to the Mound where his coach was waiting. No sooner was he aboard than, to his utter astonishment, the horses were removed from the traces and a band of men set off pulling the vehicle to Jeffrey's home in Moray Place. He thanked those concerned for the gesture and went indoors, but the crowd would not disperse.

Eventually Jeffrey appeared on the balcony and addressed them:

My friends. I sincerely thank you for this demonstration of your approbation; but may I recommend you to be peaceful and quiet and to confine yourselves to the cheering with which you have now greeted me. In less than another year I trust we shall come home better pleased with the result than we have done today. As you value my favour – as you esteem your own character – and the great cause in which we are all engaged – go quietly home and let it not be said by your adversaries that, in your call for liberty, you only mean riot and discord. Again let me beseech you to refrain from violence; we have our opinions and our opponents have theirs. They have given an erroneous one in my estimation; but let there be no personal violence. Let them enjoy their momentary and solitary triumph; for ours is the prevailing opinion and I have no doubt we will succeed. I am much fatigued by the proceedings of this day and I hope you will excuse me not addressing you at farther length, but I again entreat, go all quietly to your homes.

Jeffrey's persuasive eloquence was successful and the throng quietly dispersed.

But all was quite different in other parts of the town, where an explosive atmosphere simmered. At 6 p.m. the Dragoons were called out once more and they were supported by a naval detachment from Leith. Another three hours were to pass before any sign of peace was to return to the streets.

As midnight approached, more than twelve hours since the incidents of one of Edinburgh's most explosive days had started, the demonstrators had tired, and gradually went home. By the early hours of the following morning only a handful remained on the streets.

Despite the vociferousness of the demonstration, relatively little damage had been caused. Several windows were smashed at the house of Dundas, the newly elected MP, and a number of street lights had been subjected to the attentions of a small number of citizens.

But one man was conspicuous by his absence: R.A. Dundas, MP. Where was the obligatory victorious candidate's speech thanking his supporters and assuring all of Edinburgh's citizens that he would do all in his power to safeguard the interests of the city? So far as could be established, Dundas was still in the City Chambers, where he had been since early morning, afraid to meet the citizens who had not elected him!

Surprisingly, only one rioter appeared in court, and was sentenced to nine months' imprisonment.

Shortly afterwards, Lord Provost Allan's term of office came to an end (he had served his two years) and he was succeeded by John Learmonth.

The following year was a momentous one, with the passing of the Reform Bill. It was reported that on one Sunday countless thousands assembled on Calton Hill, eagerly awaiting the arrival of the express coach with the latest news. Eventually, it was established that Edinburgh would have two representatives in parliament.

There were three candidates: Francis Jeffrey and James Abercromby nominated by the Whigs (similar to the present day Liberals) and Forbes Hunter Blair (Tory).

The result proved how much the Town Council had been out of touch with the wishes of the people when, in 1831, they had elected Dundas. When the result was announced on 21 December 1832 the figures were: Jeffrey 4,036; Abercromby 3,843; and Blair 1,519. Both Reform candidates had been successful.

Following the announcement, Jeffrey told the assembled audience:

> It is the triumph, not of one man, or any set of men, but the triumph of principles, held in common among all free men of the earth. It is not the triumph of any party, however numerous or respectable in Edinburgh, but the triumph of a cause which has been rapidly advancing in every corner of the universe – and on the progress of which alone can be confirmed, the cause of liberty, independence, justice, peace, tolerance and intellectual improvement.

Abercromby said that the contest in which they had been engaged was happily concluded, 'and I do most heartily congratulate you on the triumph which we have gained'. The two elected members were then taken in triumph by coach to Jeffrey's Moray Place home.

The result was received with considerable enthusiasm by one newspaper, which commented:

> Fellow Citizens – Let us congratulate one another! The day is our own. Toryism has made its last expiring struggle in the city, where its power has been so long pernicious and so long overwhelming! We rejoice that our opponents have come to the poll and exhausted their utmost effort on behalf of their candidate, because it has revealed to us their strength as well as our own, and has given us the fullest assurance of our entire emancipation.
>
> Twenty thousand independent citizens assembled at the Cross on the day of nomination; they saw their opponents were but a handful; but with the full consciousness of their strength, they did not commit a single outrage upon any individual, or any single act of violence or disorder!

11

EDINBURGH'S LAST PUBLIC HANGING

As you walk on the south side of the Royal Mile, close to the junction with George IV Bridge, glance at the edge of the pavement and there you will see three brass blocks in the shape of an 'H'.

At one time there was a plaque on the adjacent wall explaining their significance, but it was removed some years ago and never replaced. In fact this 'H' marks the spot, at the head of the former Libberton's (or Liberton's) Wynd, where, on 21 June 1864, George Bryce of Ratho was hanged for the murder of a young nursemaid. It was the last public hanging in Edinburgh.

The scene was graphically described in a contemporary newspaper: 'From St Giles' Church to near the Assembly Hall was one dense mass of human beings and almost every window, and many of the house tops, were likewise occupied. For a considerable distance along George IV Bridge and down Bank Street there was an immense attendance of spectators . . . '

In fact it was estimated that the crowd numbered between 20 and 25,000.

Bryce was described as a young man of rather unprepossessing appearance. Employed by his father, who kept a small farm and public-house in the village of Ratho to the west of Edinburgh, he had formed a relationship with a young woman employed as a cook by Mr and Mrs Robert Tod who lived in large villa overlooking the village.

Also on the staff was Jane Seaton, a children's nurse. She knew Bryce, who was a frequent visitor to the big house. But Jane Seaton was suspicious of him – an opinion which, unfortunately, she had expressed too freely among the staff. So forceful were her views that the cook broke off the relationship.

Bryce was well aware of the circumstances, and he took to visiting the house at unusual hours. He was known to have been in the garden late at night and on at least one occasion had attempted to enter

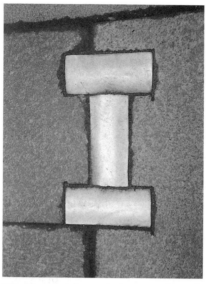

The brass bricks mark the spot where the
last public hanging took place in Edinburgh

the house by a window.

On the morning of Saturday 16 April 1864 Bryce finally snapped. Leaving home at 7 a.m. with a razor in his pocket he made his way to the Tod house. There he met his former sweetheart who, in response to his questioning, confirmed that Jane Seaton was in the house, but that under no circumstances was he to enter.

Brushing the cook aside, Bryce made his way to the nursery, where he confronted his victim. Swiftly he pinned the unfortunate woman to the floor and attempted to strangle her. Her screams brought Mrs Tod racing to the nursery; using an umbrella, she was able to distract Bryce sufficiently to allow Jane to escape.

The panic-stricken woman ran quickly down the path to the house of a neighbour, Mrs Binnie. Jane was just about to enter the house when she was overtaken by Bryce. He threw her to the ground, drew the razor, and slashed. She died instantly.

The trial took place in Edinburgh on 31 May, and although the verdict was a foregone conclusion, newspapers reported that it 'excited more interest than any since the time of Madeleine Smith'. (She had been accused of poisoning her lover in Glasgow, and the jury brought in a not proven verdict.)

At 8 a.m. on Monday 20 June, the day before his execution, Bryce was taken by cab from the Calton Jail to the lock-up in the High Street; the time had been chosen by the Governor to thwart demonstrations.

Slowly during the day spectators arrived in the High Street; as the evening progressed, vast crowds began to assemble near to where the scaffold would be placed. 'Every species of ruffianism, wretchedness and vagabondism was more than represented', a newspaper stated.

Their morbid curiosity? To watch the erection of the black-painted gibbet at the top of Libberton's Wynd, which descended steeply to the Cowgate. Work on the gallows began just after midnight and was completed by 2.30 a.m. The crossbeam was placed south to north so that the condemned man would be facing the castle. To give the occasion some form of decency, the scaffold was draped in black cloth.

One newspaper reported: 'The talk that prevailed amongst this wretched gathering was obscene and boisterous and the noisy mirth that occasionally broke out was made all the more dismal by the intervening sound of the hammer as the black-painted erection at the head of the wynd was rapidly bolted together.'

In the hope of making some extra money, the proprietors of cheap refreshment rooms opened their premises, 'and many were the stray customers that were tempted hurriedly to regale themselves on the stale commodities of these establishments'. Many of the spectators, tired after the long night, slept in the cold draughty stairs and closes nearby.

But the ghouls were up and about at an early hour, and by 6 a.m. the whole area outside the barricade was occupied. Others, thankfully, had different motives, and conspicuous in the crowd were preachers and groups singing psalms and holding aloft boards covered with extracts from the scriptures.

Excitement was running high when, at eight o'clock, the officials required to be in attendance on these occasions had assembled. The prison van was already in position outside the High Court building in Parliament Close, and Bryce was driven swiftly round St Giles' Cathedral, up the High Street, and across the square to the County Building.

Bryce was taken to a room to face the executioner, who immediately pinioned him. Edinburgh Council officers, dressed in uniform and carrying halberds, set out to lead the formal procession. They were followed by the condemned man, flanked by two ministers, bailies in their robes and other officials, to the place of execution.

Bryce mounted the scaffold, a prayer was said, and a white hood was placed over his head to conceal his face. Finally, as the body dropped, the previously noisy, boisterous crowd hushed – hit by the reality of the situation. Within seconds, hundreds of those present were in tears.

At 9 a.m. Bryce's body was removed to the Calton Jail for burial.

It was reported that this was the largest crowd at an execution in Edinburgh since a relative of Bryce had been hanged twenty years earlier!

12

THE CURIOUS STORY OF JAMES ROBB

Truth definitely is sometimes stranger than fiction. Consider the circumstances surrounding the murder of 17-year-old James Robb in 1862, and how the name of the alleged perpetrator was revealed in a letter to *The Scotsman* twenty-three years later.

And why should the informant wait so long before revealing his secret?

The story is a curious one, and the decision to reveal all was prompted by the discovery in 1885 of the body of a young girl in the Queen's (Holyrood) Park in Edinburgh. This sparked off an intriguing series of newspaper letters.

The penultimate day in the life of 'Jamie' Robb was 6 April 1862. It was just another Friday for the folk in the small community at Easter Howgate, Midlothian. They were mostly poor, but hard-working farm people; as they toiled in the fields, Mrs Thomson, who supervised the near-by tollhouse, busied herself about the premises.

It was between two and three in the afternoon when she became aware of a stranger standing in the doorway. He was between twenty and twenty-five years of age, about five feet eight inches tall and had long black hair, which tended to curl at the ends. He wore a dark cap, black jacket, moleskin trousers and hobnailed boots. Country folk can be suspicious of strangers, and the tollhouse keeper asked the stranger what business had brought him to her premises.

Fear gripped Mrs Thomson when the intruder demanded to know, in a voice which the observant woman noted bore a strong Irish brogue, at what intervals the toll money was collected and whether she had a watch in the house. With surprisingly little difficulty she was able to convince the man that neither money nor watch was in her possession.

By a twist of fate, as the stranger was about to leave, young James Robb – he was only seventeen – arrived at the house. He was a pack-laddie and well-liked in the district; he earned a living by visiting the farms and cottages, selling his cheap jewellery and watches. He was, unfortunately, unaware of the dark stranger's presence; before he could be warned, Robb had betrayed the purpose of his visit and explained what goods he was carrying. Nevertheless, the stranger left the tollhouse.

Not many minutes had passed when an agitated man and woman arrived at the tollhouse and explained that a short distance along the road they had seen a strange man carrying a pedlar's box. Although suspicious, they had continued with their journey; but not far away they had found the pack-boy lying on the road.

Robb was in an exhausted state, and blood poured from wounds on his head and face. He was barely conscious but was able to tell the couple that after leaving the tollhouse he had been joined by the stranger, who had struck him several times with a hammer before stealing the box.

A cart was brought from a nearby field and the lad was taken to Dr Stockwell at Penicuik. His injuries proved to be more serious than at first thought, and Robb was transferred to the Infirmary in Edinburgh. Robb's box was found intact, about 150 yards from where the assault had taken place. It was believed at the time that all that was missing was the boy's pocket watch. In hospital the young pedlar rallied, and his life appeared to be in no danger. Attempts were made the following day to obtain a written statement, but he was unable to hold a pen. At a later stage he was asked to write on a slate what he could tell of the attack, but he wrote only two words – 'hammer' and 'stone-breaker'. His condition deteriorated suddenly, and on the second day after the attack James Robb died.

A description of the alleged murderer was circulated throughout the county of Midlothian, but despite intensive investigation by the police no progress was made. Several suspects were detained, but as no evidence could be obtained connecting them with the crime, they were released.

There the matter rested, that is, until twenty-three years later, when, dramatically, on 1 October 1885, a letter was received by the editor of *The Scotsman* from Matthew Gray, 33 High Street, Portobello. It read:

Sir – Would you kindly find space for the following narrative? I think it will be interesting, more especially after the late mysterious affair which has happened in the Queen's Park.

Some twenty years ago or more, a young man by the name of Robb was found lying insensible in a ditch about two miles from Penicuik. He was conveyed to the Royal Infirmary, where he died two days after, of internal injuries. The police scoured the country round, detectives made all the investigations in their power to get a clue, but all to no purpose.

The only thing that came to light was simply that Robb had been waylaid and robbed of his money and watch and chain, but by whom and how, remains a mystery until this day. Like every other sensation it was a seven day wonder, and passed away to give place to the next.

Some time ago I was thrown upon the tide of circumstances which ultimately launched me in America, where I joined the United States Army. After a few weeks' stay on Governess Island I was drafted to fill up Co. A 13, U.S.A., then doing duty at Fort Shaw, in Montana Territory. Here the Company consolidated and was removed to Fort Steel, in Wyoming Territory.

When we arrived there we learned that three general prisoners had been transferred to our charge. Happening to be on duty one day over those prisoners, I got into conversation with one of them, who was a strong hardy Irishman. He soon gave me to understand that he was well acquainted with several districts of Scotland. I happened to ask him if he had ever been to Edinburgh.

'Oh yes', he replied, 'there was rather a curious circumstance happened to me the last time I was there.'

I asked him what it was, when to my utter astonishment he made the following statement:

'You see I had been in Glasgow working and I got on the drink and lost my job; so I bundled up and made for Edinburgh, where I tried to get something to do, but all in vain, so I determined to make for Newcastle.

'I got as far as a place called Penicuik, or rather, a bit the other side, when I came up to a young swell-like chap; he didn't look much of a man. So I just says to myself – What's to hinder me from tossing him over, and getting his tin?

'I passed the time of day with him, so I saw he had a splendid ticker. While he was putting it in his pocket I nailed him under the ear, and threw him into the ditch by the roadside, where I gave him a good benefit, so as he would not be able to make a noise until I got out of the way a bit.'

Sir, the whole thing flashed through my memory in a minute. I was convinced that I stood face to face with Robb's murderer. I preserved my feelings as much as possible and asked him how he came on then.

His reply was: 'Oh. I just about ship and made for Leith, where I got aboard a boat bound for Newcastle where I arrived the next day and had a good spree off the money and the watch, when I got the chance for a stoker on an American ship and came out here.'

Seeing his story was exhausted, I said, 'Are you aware you murdered that man?'

His face became livid white, he never spoke, nor did he ever lift his head from the pick he was working with, for the remainder of the day.

In the evening I related the story to the first sergeant, who was to report it to the commanding officer the next morning. But when morning came it was found that 'McCarty' had made his escape from the guardhouse nor was he ever seen or heard tell of from that night until I left.

On 3 October *The Scotsman* received a second letter from Mr Robert Blair, Hawthorn House, Greenfaulds, Cumbernauld, which read:

Sir, – I was painfully interested in the graphic account given by Matthew Gray in to-day's *Scotsman* of the murder of the young man Robb near Penicuik about twenty years ago. I remember the tragic affair and the mystery which has enshrouded it all this period. I am all the more interested as James Robb was a school companion of my own and we were, as boys, continually together.

He was a notable unselfish boy, and among all my school mates there was none I took to like 'Jamie' Robb. When the time came that school days were done, and we each had to take our separate ways in the busy world, I sadly missed my old friend 'Jamie'. When news reached me of his tragic murder, I mourned as for a very near and dear friend.

It is well that this hitherto mysterious affair is now so far cleared up and I feel obliged to Mr Matthew Gray for having sent his letter to *The Scotsman* for publication. James Robb was the son of Thomas Robb, travelling jeweller, who in my young days resided in the village of Kirknewton, a man than whom there was none better known and respected in most of the farms and villages of Midlothian.

The villain McCarty has accepted the guilt – the brand of Cain is upon him – and his tormenting conscience will not allow this foul deed to slumber. It is a matter for regret that prompter action was not taken and the murderer's flight frustrated.

The correspondence came to a close 5 October with two letters. The first, written from 30 Dundas Street, Edinburgh, was from the sister of the murdered man and read:

Sir, – As the sister of the late James Robb, murdered near Penicuik in April in 1862, I have to return thanks to Mr Matthew Gray in *The Scotsman* of October 2 containing the confession of McCarty, which at last has solved a great mystery and shown up the great apathy of the police at that period. I have also to thank Mr Robert Baird for his generous testimony to my poor brother.

– Jessie Robb Sinclair.

The final letter was again from Matthew Gray and read as follows:

Sir, – I am delighted to see through your columns that the memory of 'James Robb' is still fresh and green. I also could testify to James's excellent qualities, but, sir, enough, what I want to reply to is the last sentence of Mr R. Baird's letter, namely, that 'It was a matter for regret that prompter action was not taken and the murderer's flight frustrated.'

Let me remind Mr Baird that even in the 'American Army' there is a certain amount of 'red tapeism' that must be formulated before obtaining anything. Had I taken the law into my own hands I would in all likelihood have shared the same fate as the sergeant who attempted to chastise Charles J. Guiteau for his murderous attack on President Garfield. Only those who have passed that way have any idea of the utter helplessness of the law.

I also regret that I was not allowed to claim justice for 'Jamie'. But if Mr McGovan himself had been there I question if he would have taken prompter action under the circumstances.

However, I may say for the benefit of Mr Baird, although 'McCarty' was never heard tell of, it was generally surmised that he fell a victim to the Indians, who had but a short time previously received severe defeat from 'Uncle Sam's troops'.

Thus, with a letter to *The Scotsman*, the Easter Howgate murderer was revealed. But is there somewhere a file, heavily covered in dust, with the barely decipherable title: 'James Robb: Murdered April 6, 1862', and scrawled across it the word most hated by policemen: 'UNSOLVED'?

13

DR WILLIAM EDWARD PRITCHARD: A DOUBLE MURDERER

Edinburgh's many graveyards contain the remains of both victims and perpetrators of crimes. If you go into the elegant Grange Cemetery in what is now a very salubrious part of south Edinburgh you will find one particular grave without any difficulty. Enter by the east gate in Grange Road and walk straight ahead. It is only a short distance to where the tombstones are attached to the wall, ironically adjoining Lovers' Loan, and it is the fifth one along.

The stone is showing signs of wear but the inscription can still be deciphered. It reads:

> In memory of Michael Taylor who died 18th May 1867 aged 74 years, also of Jane his wife who died 25th Feby. 1865 aged 73 years, also of their beloved daughter Mary Jane who died 18th March 1865 aged 38 years.

But what the memorial does not reveal are the bizarre circumstances surrounding the deaths of the two women, mother-in-law and wife of Dr Edward William Pritchard, who was later to stand trial for poisoning them.

Michael Taylor was a successful Edinburgh silk and lace merchant and he and his wife lived in respectable middle-class Lauder Road. They no doubt believed that their daughter Mary Jane had made a good choice when she married the doctor and they gave him £500 towards establishing a medical practice in Glasgow.

Outwardly all was well and the marriage produced five children. But there was a seamier side to Pritchard. There were rumours of illicit affairs and debts. And there was a fire in which a young servant girl died.

The family moved house and 15-year-old Mary McLeod was employed as servant and children's nurse.

In late 1864 Mrs Pritchard began to suffer from bouts of sickness,

The grave at the Grange Cemetery where
Mary Jane Pritchard and her mother
Jane Taylor are buried. Both were
poisoned by Dr Edward Pritchard

which were treated by her doctor husband. As a way of convalescing,
Mary Jane travelled back to Edinburgh to her parents' home in
Lauder Road, where, by all accounts, her health improved remark-
ably.

She returned to Glasgow for Christmas and for a time she kept
well. By January, however, the symptoms had returned, and gradually her condition deteriorated. It was therefore agreed that the
elderly Mrs Taylor would come through from Edinburgh to look
after her daughter.

In the meantime the symptoms persisted, and Mrs Pritchard was
heard screaming with pain and demanding to see another doctor –
Dr Gairdner. Such was her agitated state that the doctor did not consider it appropriate to examine the patient at that time. He returned
next day and found Mrs Pritchard considerably improved – although
he had his suspicions. The following day Mrs Taylor arrived to nurse
her ailing daughter.

Mrs Pritchard continued to improve and on one occasion she
asked for tapioca, but then decided not to eat it. But her mother did

and was violently sick. The poor innocent woman recovered and expressed the opinion that she must have had the same illness as her daughter!

Then on 25 February 1865, following a meal of sausages, Mrs Taylor died. She was examined by Dr Paterson, who was suspicious. Nevertheless, Mrs Taylor's body was taken to Edinburgh for burial in the Grange Cemetery, just a short distance from her home in Lauder Road. The cause of death was given as 'apoplexy'.

Meanwhile, Mrs Pritchard's health yet again deteriorated. On the evening of 17 March she was found in a delirious state, demanding that attention be given to her mother, who was already dead. Dr Paterson was called. He prescribed a sedative, but by one o'clock in the morning she too was dead – exactly three weeks after her mother. Gastric fever was given as the cause of death, and her body was taken by train to be interred beside her mother at the Grange.

Suspicions were growing, however – two deaths in three weeks, mother and daughter, and this, 'coupled with certain hints that had been received', resulted in intensive police investigations. While he was in Edinburgh arranging his wife's funeral, the police were granted a warrant for Dr Pritchard's arrest. He was picked up at Queen Street Station, Glasgow, as he stepped from the late-night Edinburgh train.

The Edinburgh authorities were informed and a post-mortem examination was carried out by Professor Douglas Maclaggan and Dr Henry Littlejohn, Edinburgh's Medical Officer of Health. Their findings revealed particles of antimony in Mrs Pritchard's liver. Her mother's body was exhumed on 31 March and again traces of antimony were found.

Shortly after 8 a.m. on 3 July 1865, Pritchard was brought from the Calton Jail to the High Court building in the centre of Edinburgh to face trial.

Dr Edward William Pritchard, tall and stout with long thin hair and balding at the crown, stood accused of murdering his mother-in-law Jane Taylor and his wife Mary Jane Pritchard by poisoning.

The first witness was Catherine Lattimer who had worked as the family cook for ten years. She explained that she had gone to Carlisle for two weeks, and that Mrs Pritchard had been fine when she left.

Asked how her mistress was when she returned, she replied, 'Not very well.'

'What was wrong with her?'

'She said she had a cold.'

'How long was she confined to bed?'

'Four or five days.'

'Was she sick?'

'Yes, at times.'

'Did any medical man attend her?'

'Dr Gairdner was the first.'

'Did Mrs Pritchard tell you herself that she was sick?'

'Yes.'

'Do you remember her going to Edinburgh to see her mother?'

'Yes.'

'Did she appear to be quite well then?'

'No, not quite well.'

'She returned a few days before Christmas. How was she?'

'A good deal better.'

A week later her sickness returned. She was confined to bed three weeks later, suffering from sickness, pain and cramp. Eventually, Mrs Pritchard insisted on seeing another doctor and a servant was sent to ask Dr Gairdner to call.

Sixteen-year-old Mary McLeod, housemaid and children's nurse, was asked if Mrs Pritchard had been attended by any doctor, other than her husband, before she went to Edinburgh.

'No.'

'Did she get any medicine?'

'Yes, a bottle; the contents were white like milk.'

'Anything else?'

'Yes, red powders. Dr Pritchard gave the prescription.'

'Was Dr Pritchard beside her when she died?'

'Yes.'

'Was he weeping?'

'Yes. He said, "Come back to your dear Edward." '

But the trial took a sensational turn when the witness, with extreme reluctance, was forced to admit that there had been a sexual relationship with Pritchard; that she had been pregnant, and that the accused had administered a drug to procure an abortion. Damningly, the witness was forced to admit that the doctor had promised to marry her should his wife die.

Professor William T. Gairdner of Glasgow University told the court that he had made two professional visits to Mrs Pritchard. He had been called by Dr Pritchard at the request of his wife. He said that he found Mrs Pritchard considerably exhausted and at the same time suffering from excitement caused by stimulants, and that he was very much puzzled by the symptoms.

Professor Gairdner had written to Mrs Pritchard's brother, Dr Taylor of Penrith (a former college friend), drawing his attention to his sister's illness. He admitted under cross-examination, however, that he did not indicate to Dr Taylor that he had suspected poisoning.

Apothecary John Campbell told the court that in November, December and February he had supplied the accused with strychnine, tartar emetic, laudanum and tartarised antimony. The witness had been particularly struck by the large quantities of the latter drug bought by Pritchard, who had also bought a considerable amount of chloroform during the latter part of the previous year.

Professor Maclaggan, who held the chair of Medical Jurisprudence at Edinburgh University, said that the post-mortem examinations of both women had revealed large quantities of antimony – in his opinion that was the the cause of death. Dr Littlejohn confirmed the findings.

The court was told that Dr Pritchard's two bank accounts were overdrawn. Mr J.D. McBrair, trustee of Mrs Taylor's affairs, revealed that his client was in possession of trust funds of £3,000, of which £500 had gone to Dr Pritchard in June 1864, and by Mrs Taylor's will, Mrs Pritchard would have inherited £2,000.

In a declaration made before Sheriff Alison, Dr Pritchard said that he had been married for fifteen years and had attended his wife in his capacity as family doctor. He was satisfied that Mrs Pritchard had died as a result of gastric fever.

Pritchard claimed that he had administered no medicine, only champagne and brandy to support her strength. And six weeks before death, a little chloroform to induce sleep.

There were several uncomfortable minutes on the fourth day of the trial when the defence introduced two of the Pritchard children as witnesses. The first was Charles, aged eleven, who, because of his tender years, was not put on oath but was reminded by the judge that he must tell the truth.

'I am Dr Pritchard's eldest son. I lived with him in Glasgow. I was there when mamma died. My pappa and mamma lived happily together. Mamma and pappa were very fond of one another,' he told the charged court.

And 14-year-old Jane said: 'I lived a good deal with my grand-mother in Lauder Road. Pappa was often there with my grandmother. Grandmother and pappa were fond of each other. I have often heard her speaking very kindly of him and him of her.'

The trial took a curious turn on the fifth day when questions were asked about Battley's Solution, today a little-known concoction.

Thomas Fairgrieve, druggist, with a shop in Clerk Street, Edinburgh, confirmed that Mrs Taylor was one of his regular cus-tomers and that she habitually purchased Battley's Solution. Similar evidence was given by the representative of another Edinburgh firm. But what was the purpose of introducing questions on this medicine, which was not even mentioned in the charges?

Battley's Solution was a mixture of opium, alcohol and water and was probably used as a painkiller. Unfortunately, it could also be addictive, and Mrs Taylor used it in surprisingly large quantities. Was it possible that antimony or aconite could have contaminated the solution sold to Mrs Taylor, one of the expert witnesses was asked under cross-examination? This was not possible, the court heard. In other words, if traces of antimony had been found in Mrs Taylor's Battley's, it had not been introduced at the time of preparation.

It took the jury only fifty-five minutes to reach their verdict of guilty.

Pritchard was told by the judge that he would be taken to Glasgow and there, on 28 July, he would suffer death by hanging.

There was one final, curious twist to the Pritchard case. On the day of the hanging, *The Weekly Scotsman* reported:

> This morning Dr Edward William Pritchard, the Glasgow poisoner, suffered the extreme penalty of the law for the murder by poison of his wife and mother-in-law at the common place of execution . . . The crimes for which this wretched man suffered punishment have not been equalled in their horrible atrocity since the case of Palmer.

Palmer? The case would have been fresh in the memories of many people, but today he is unknown. Dr William Palmer is believed to have poisoned his wife in 1854, his brother in 1855, and a friend later in the same year, all for financial gain. He was, however, convicted only of the murder of his friend, and was hanged at Stafford on 14 June 1856.

14

DID THE KELLY GANG COME TO TOWN?

The Australian bushranger Ned Kelly is either a notorious hoodlum who got his just deserts on the gallows for murdering policemen, or a folk hero who fought bravely against the colonial rulers of Victoria and New South Wales. Arguments still rage in Australia and his story has been turned into a film and book.

He was finally captured in 1880 after evading police for two years and his gang scattered. But did two of the Ned Kelly mob make it to Scotland and carry out a series of armed robberies in the Edinburgh area?

On the evening of Friday 4 February 1881, Robert Veitch, a man in his twenties who worked as a commercial traveller for J. Marshall, fruit merchant, Market Street, Edinburgh, was making his way home to his father's house at Deanpark farm on the Queensferry Road. He was about 40 yards from his destination when he noticed two men acting suspiciously. They crossed to where Veitch was walking, produced revolvers, and demanded money.

At first the young man thought that it was a joke, but on realising the seriousness of the situation he lashed out with an umbrella and made a run for home. As he fled, Veitch was struck with what was described as a life-preserver cosh. Foolishly, Veitch, his father William and sister Emily set out to find the attackers, whom they soon spotted near John Watson's Hospital (now the Gallery of Modern Art).

As Robert Veitch approached, the men produced revolvers. Veitch lashed out with a stick and immediately five shots rang out, striking him on the left cheek and right ear. Emily sustained a fractured jaw and her father suffered injuries to his side. Nevertheless, the trio pursued the attackers; they eventually lost sight of them and only then did they seek medical attention.

Dr J.B. Carruthers was later to tell the High Court in Edinburgh that Robert and Emily were fortunate to escape with their lives.

About two hours later, James Stewart Dick, a druggist's assistant who lived in Caledonian Terrace, was walking in Ravelston Road with a young lady when they were approached by two men demanding money. Dick handed over four shillings (20p) and a hat, but managed to retain his watch. He later identified the hat at Leith police station. Before leaving the scene the robbers struck Dick several times on the head with a skull-cracker.

Meanwhile, news of the attacks had been passed to the Leith police. About 11.30 p.m. Sergeants William Arnott and Donald Reid were near the Customs House when they noticed two men acting suspiciously.

When questioned, the pair told the police that they were looking for their ship, the *Jem*, but the sergeants pointed out that the *Jem* was a tug and they could not be members of the crew. At this, the strangers became angry and the policemen decided to take them in for questioning. A struggle followed, a shot rang out, and Sergeant Arnott was hit on the head. Arnott drew his baton, and as firing continued, one shot struck Reid. The criminals made their escape, but Reid continued in pursuit, at the same time whistling for assistance.

Constables John Cameron and Thomas McConville were on duty at the Customs House, saw the struggle, and immediately joined in the chase. The suspects were eventually trapped in Commercial Street. One, later named as Fred Seymour, immediately put a gun to his head, fired, and died instantly. The second man, believed to be James Grant, also attempted suicide but the gun jammed. He then handed the weapon (described as being a 'British Bulldog' make) to Constable George Birse, who immediately arrested the culprit. Three policemen in all had been injured, and Arnott, Reid, and Constable Alexander Nicholson were taken to Leith Hospital. Dr George Johnstone, the resident surgeon, described Arnott's injuries as dangerous.

Meanwhile, the police investigations were proceeding. The arrested man had said little, but he let drop one piece of vital information, claiming that he had sailed from Australia on the *Melbourne*. It was quickly established that this vessel had docked recently in London.

Details of the two men were forwarded to the CID at Scotland Yard, and they in turn consulted the captain of the ship. He confirmed that the photograph of Seymour was in fact that of a man known to him as William Smith. He, together with J. Harnett and J. Harrison, had been taken on as able seamen on the *Melbourne* in Australia the previous November. Significantly, Harnett matched the description of Grant.

The captain also told the police that revolvers had been found in the men's bunks. They had been confiscated but returned to the men when they docked in London. Very importantly, he was also able to confirm that the revolvers were stamped 'English Bulldog'. Newspaper reports of the Edinburgh and Leith shootings referred to 'British Bulldog' revolvers being used. Could this have been an error?

Despite the important information provided by the sea captain on the identity of the accused (perhaps he had used a false name when leaving Australia), he stood in the dock at the High Court, Edinburgh, on 23 May as James Grant, indicted:

1. With having, in concert with a companion now deceased, attacked and assaulted with a life-preserver, Robert Veitch, traveller, on the Old Queensferry Road, leading from Edinburgh by Bellsmill to Queensferry.

2. With an attack upon Robert Veitch, his father William Veitch and his sister Emily Veitch, and having wilfully fired from a pistol a number of shots at them, several of which took effect upon the father and daughter, the latter having her upper jaw bone fractured, and whereby both were wounded to the effusion of blood and serious injury of their persons.

3. With having threatened to shoot James Stewart Dick, druggist's assistant, residing at Caledonian Terrace, Dalry Road, Edinburgh, striking him with a life-preserver and taking from his person by force, four shillings in silver money.

4. With having in Dock Place, Leith, attacked William Arnott and Donald Reid, Sergeants, and Alexander Nicholson and Thomas McConville, Constables, in the Leith Police force and shooting at them several times to the effusion of blood and serious injury to Reid and Nicholson and wounding Arnott to the danger of his life.

The accused pleaded not guilty, but the jury, after hearing the evidence, were out for only ten minutes before returning with their verdict of guilty.

Grant's crime was a very serious one, but the judge, Lord Young, resisted the temptation to send the convicted man to prison for life.

He nevertheless warned that he would have to spend a long time in prison, and in passing a sentence of fourteen years' penal servitude.

At this, the prisoner, who had attempted to interrupt the judge, folded his arms and said: 'I wish you would bring it in capital punishment as I intended to kill and I don't wish to lie.'

The judge proceeded to lecture Grant on his bravado, and concluded by telling him that, though the prisoner might not think so, there were wiser people in the world than he; also that he would do well to dismiss from his mind the idea that the wicked were better off when an end was put to their miserable existence.

At the time of the attack on the Veitch family, newspaper accounts gave their address as Deanpark farm: a contemporary map of the area shows Deanpark Nursery on land opposite what is now Stewarts-Melville College. On the Queensferry Road and present-day Orchard Brae corner of the nursery site, the map clearly shows buildings. Was this the Veitch residence?

The Veitch family were co-founders of the fruit and vegetable firm Veitch, Moir and Erskine. It survives to this day as Veitch Moir Ltd.

The heroism of the Leith policemen was rightly acknowledged by the Council and citizens of the burgh. On 2 June six members of the force, Sergeants D. Reid and W. Arnott, Constables J. Cameron, A. Nicholson, T. McConville, and G. Birse were each presented with thirty guineas and a silver medal.

But the mystery remains. Who were these criminals? Were their names really Grant and Seymour, as the police information suggests, or Smith and Harnett, the names under which they worked on the *Melbourne* on the trip from Australia? In all probability they left Australia under assumed names. If they were members of the Kelly gang, the police would surely be watching the ports and the hard men would undoubtedly conceal their true identity.

When Grant and Seymour arrived in Edinburgh is uncertain, but one curious piece of information was supplied by a retailer of boots and shoes, who ran a business in Union Place. On 1 February, three days before the attacks were carried out, several men visited his shop. The shopkeeper, 'who had experience of Australia', described the men as being of the bushranger type. One asked for a pair of 'guitars', which the shopkeeper immediately recognised as an Australian word for top boots.

15

A REAL DR JEKYLL AND MR HYDE

In the catalogue of Edinburgh's rogues the name of Deacon William Brodie stands out. Respectable businessman by day, one-time member of the Town Council, but by night a housebreaker and thief. The two sides of the man are generally regarded as the inspiration for Robert Louis Stevenson's story, *The Strange Case of Dr Jekyll and Mr Hyde*.

But what tends to be forgotten in the Brodie legend is that he was only one member of a gang of four, although undoubtedly the most prominent.

Brodie lived in Brodie's Close (named after his father Francis) in the Lawnmarket. His associates were George Smith, Andrew Ainslie, and Humphry Moore (alias John Brown). But their career of crime came to an end on 1 October 1788, when Brodie and Smith went to the gallows. Ainslie and Brown (by which name he was known at the trial), survived by turning King's evidence.

And the offence for which Brodie and Smith paid with their lives? In March of that year they robbed the General Excise Office of Scotland in Chessel's Buildings in the Canongate, and stole £16.

Smith and his wife were hawkers from Berkshire who usually toured England with a horse and cart. For some reason, however, they arrived in Edinburgh in 1787 with the recommendation that they would find suitable accommodation at Michael Henderson's inn in the Grassmarket.

The Englishman frequented Clark's, a gambling house in Fleshmarket Close. Among the regular visitors there were Ainslie and Brown. Smith had first met them at Henderson's inn, where Brodie was a frequent guest. Graham Campbell, Smith's servant, was later to tell the court that Brodie, Ainslie, and Smith were often to be seen in Smith's house, mainly to play cards and dice. But there can be little doubt that this house in the Cowgate was also the meeting place for criminals.

Brodie's Close in the Lawnmarket

Ainslie was described as a shoemaker, and at the time of the trial he was a prisoner in the Tolbooth, having been arrested shortly after the robbery. He was called by the prosecution, and the defence objected on the grounds that he had already been accused of the crime and therefore could not be considered to be a reliable witness. After legal debate Ainslie was allowed to give evidence. A similar objection was lodged against Brown, and further that he was under sentence of transportation imposed by an English court. But Brown had been pardoned and details were read to the court. His evidence, it was ruled, was admissible.

The full extent of the criminal activities of Brodie and the gang will never be known. It was evident, however, from what was revealed at the High Court that there was a ready market for the stolen property south of the border. There had been a number of serious robberies in the town but none more embarrassing than the break-in at the Excise Office.

The authorities received their first important lead when, late in the evening of 7 March, just two days after the theft, John Brown visited William Middleton, an employee at the sheriff's office, and told him he had detailed information about robberies which had taken place at the Excise Office and at a number of shops in the town.

Brown was on the run from a transportation sentence imposed in England, and he had seen an advertisement in the name of the Secretary of State promising a reward, and, if appropriate, a pardon for information leading to the arrest of the thieves who were involved in the robberies; hence his willingness to co-operate. He was taken to William Scott, Procurator Fiscal, and, having made a statement, Brown showed where a quantity of keys were hidden in Holyrood Park. On their return to the town, George Smith, his wife, Graham Campbell (Smith's servant) and Andrew Ainslie were arrested. It was now the early hours of Saturday morning.

Next day Brodie sent for his foreman, Robert Smith, who assumed that it was to do with the following week's work. In fact, Brodie was interested only in the arrest of George Smith and Ainslie. Brodie then told the foreman to purchase a waistcoat and breeches for him as he was 'going out of town'.

The hunt was now on for Brodie and that he was ever caught and brought to trial was thanks to the alertness of William Geddes, a Mid Calder tobacconist. He and his wife were returning from London to Leith on board the *Endeavour of Carron*. After the Geddes joined the vessel the owners and a stranger subsequently identified as

'Mr Brodie' (from Kay's *Portraits*)

'John Dixon' came on board. 'Dixon' appeared to be ill and was allocated a bed in the stateroom close to the fire.

When at sea 'Dixon' handed the captain a letter, which resulted in the vessel changing course and heading for Flushing in Holland. Before disembarking 'Dixon' handed a packet to Geddes with the request that he deliver the contents on his way through Edinburgh. This was an act that was to prove fatal for Brodie. The return journey to Leith was uneventful, and Geddes reached Mid Calder with the packet unopened.

But three weeks later, while on a visit to Dalkeith, Geddes read a description of Brodie in the newspapers and a report that he was wanted for robbery. Struck by the similarity between Brodie and 'Dixon', Geddes was suspicious, and opened the package. It contained three letters, two addressed to Michael Henderson and signed 'W.B.'. The third was addressed to Matthew Sheriff and indicated that the sender was 'John Dixon'.

In one of the letters to Henderson he made it clear that he had contacts in London and expressed concern that his description was being circulated in that city. He wrote: 'I saw my picture six hours before, exhibited to public view and my intelligence of what was doing at Bow Street was as good as ever I had in Edinburgh.' His letter to Sheriff indicated that he would not be returning to Edinburgh. He said:

> I have not yet received the trunk with my shirts and stockings, but will write Mr Walker to forward it to Ostend, where I will be under the necessity of buying some things. And I hope by the time I come to New York I will have some things waiting me there. Whether it is better to send them by the Clyde or Thames, you and Mr – will judge best.

And later: 'Direct [correspondence] to Mr John Dixon, to the care of Rev. Mr – at New York.' These documents were taken immediately to Procurator Fiscal Scott in Edinburgh. Brodie was traced to Holland and steps taken to have him extradited.

On 1 July a Messenger-at-Arms (Mr Groves) was dispatched from London to The Hague to negotiate Brodie's return to Edinburgh. Groves was advised that there would be no problem, and he was provided with a letter for Mr Rich, the consul in Amsterdam.

Brodie was already under arrest. Groves was told that should the authorities require an official application to the States General, he would be provided with the necessary documents; but it was emphasised that this would be unlikely.

Groves arrived in Amsterdam and went directly to the consul. Next day he was advised that, as most of the magistrates had gone to their country homes, nothing could be done before Monday. Groves was further advised that a formal application would be required. The consul immediately prepared the necessary documentation. The papers were checked by Groves, who had them amended by inserting after Brodie's name 'otherwise John Dixon'. In court, however, it was discovered that the paperwork was flawed and proceedings were delayed yet another day.

The hearing eventually got under way at 10 a.m. and Brodie was brought into court. Asked his name, he replied 'John Dixon.' He continued to give evasive answers to questions, but eventually he was released into the custody of the British officials.

William Brodie returned to Edinburgh to face one of the most sensational trials the Scottish capital had seen.

That Brodie was a showman there is no doubt. His trial and that of his co-accused George Smith opened on 27 August; at their request, they were conveyed to court in chairs, but with members of the City Guard on each side. Behind was a guard with fixed bayonets, while troops lined the street to control the large crowd. Brodie was well-dressed, but Smith was meanly attired.

Among those who formed the jury were three well-known Edinburgh men: William Fettes and James Donaldson, founders of the schools which bear their names, and William Creech, who published the Edinburgh editions of the works of Robert Burns.

The evidence against the accused was strong. Among the early witnesses called were John McLeish and James Laing, clerk and assistant clerk respectively in the Council offices, who were able to identify Brodie's handwriting. Asked by the defence how he was so certain, McLeish explained that in the course of his work he had seen many accounts and receipts bearing the accused's writing.

Even the co-accused, Smith, did much to bring about their conviction when, in the third of four statements dated 19 March, he identified certain keys and instruments which he said had been used in the Excise Office robbery. He also confirmed that among other false keys shown to him, one had been made by Brodie for the sole

'Smith at the Bar' (from Kay's *Portraits*)

purpose of gaining entry to the Town Chamberlain's room.

Smith added that Brodie had taken a number of impressions, but that Brodie had told him that it did 'not answer'. In addition, Brodie had made impressions for keys to get into the Chamberlain's cash-room!

Prosecution witness Middleton from the Sheriff's Office said that, accompanied by Smith and other witnesses, he had gone to Warriston's Close to the west of the Royal Exchange (now the City Chambers), where Smith removed a number of items, including a small key, from a hole in the wall. Smith confessed that the key had been used in a robbery at the Excise Office.

There was consternation, however, when James Murray (a sheriff officer) said that the items had been located in Allan's Close, to the east of the Exchange. Unable to resolve the conflict of evidence, the court adjourned to visit the site, entering by way of Mary King's Close. It was then established that Warriston's Close was correct.

The trial did not go well for the accused. Among the witnesses were Andrew Ainslie and John Brown, who were accomplices in the robbery but had turned King's Evidence.

Brodie's foreman, Robert Smith, admitted that on 9 March Brodie had sent for him and asked if he knew anything of the circumstances surrounding the arrest of Ainslie and Smith. He did not, but had told Brodie he hoped he had not been involved with them. Brodie did not answer. He later told the foreman that he was leaving town.

Smith admitted that Brodie kept picklocks, but claimed these were necessary tools in their work as cabinetmakers and carpenters and all employees had access to them.

Brodie's house had been searched and several curious keys, pistols and picklocks were found. Evidence was concluded shortly after 1 a.m. and at approximately 4.30 a.m. Lord Justice-Clerk Braxfield began summing up.

It was arranged that the court would reconvene at 1 p.m. for the jury's verdict. Their verdict was – guilty. The two criminals were sentenced to death by hanging, to be carried out on 1 October, a harsh sentence for housebreaking by today's standards.

Brodie and Smith were taken back to the Tolbooth, where, in accordance with the procedure for condemned men, they were chained by one leg to a bar in the cell. Their only exercise was by walking the length of the bar; even their beds were placed alongside.

At 11 a.m. on the day of the execution, Brodie wrote to Lord Provost Thomas Elder, requesting that his body be handed over to a named person so 'that he and my friends may have it decently dressed and interred'. His wish was granted, and it is believed that Brodie was buried in the graveyard at Buccleuch Parish Church.

Included in the letters which Brodie wrote while under sentence of death was one to the Duke of Buccleuch, asking him to use his influence to have the death sentence commuted to transportation. Brodie expressed an interest in Botany Bay!

16

THE CLERK WHO DUPED THE EXPERTS

Towards the end of the 1880s a frequent topic of conversation among collectors of literary and historical documents concerned the vast number of manuscripts which had apparently been unearthed in Edinburgh. As the years passed, more and more of these 'finds' continued to appear on the market, but suspicion was being raised about the authenticity of many of these papers.

Indeed, so strong did these stories become that, in November 1892, the *Edinburgh Evening Dispatch* decided to expose the whole affair by publishing a series of articles. For several weeks the paper waged its campaign, devoting an unbelievable number of column inches to the story.

But it had the desired effect, leading on 25 June 1893 to the appearance of Alexander Howland Smith at the High Court in Edinburgh, charged with creating forged documents. It was a trial which attracted worldwide attention and brought to light a forger who knew no bounds; there were few writers he had not copied, including Burns, Scott, Thackeray, Carlyle, and Ramsay.

On the historical side, 'Antique' Smith (a name he acquired because of his interest in old books) produced numerous documents, many relating to the '45. Others bore the signatures of Paul Jones, Mary Queen of Scots, Sir John Cope and Oliver Cromwell.

The first article appeared in the paper on 22 November 1892, and was based on a letter reputedly written by Robert Burns to 'Mr John Hill, weaver, Cumnock', which had appeared some time previously in the *Cumnock Express* and was described as being hitherto unpublished. Despite extensive inquiries no trace could be made of Hill or any of his descendants.

These disclosures had a great impact on the public and the response was fantastic; considerable correspondence followed in the columns of the *Dispatch* and the paper was inundated with suspect forgeries. In subsequent articles some forgeries were reproduced and

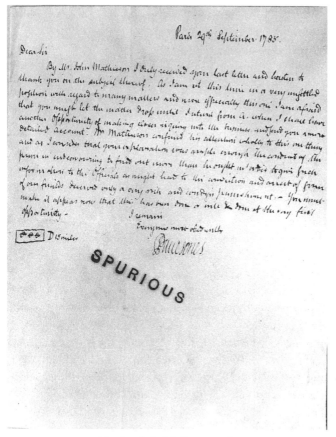

'Antique' Smith forgery of a
Paul Jones document (courtesy of the
Trustees of the National Library of Scotland)

a reader, unaware that Smith was a suspect, wrote to the paper indicating that the spurious documents bore a distinct resemblance in some ways to the writing of Smith, who had earlier been employed as a casual copying clerk by the correspondent.

Yet another letter told of the strange character who frequented bookshops in George IV Bridge, purchasing large quantities of old books which were of no interest to the usual collectors. No matter how large the parcel, the purchaser always declined the offer of delivery, preferring to struggle with his heavy load. He claimed that his interest in these apparently worthless publications stemmed from his occupation, which, he explained, was designing book covers. In fact there is little doubt that this mysterious figure was forger Smith and that his real interest went no further than the blank fly leaves, which he used for his spurious productions.

Gradually the pieces began to fall into place, and so confident was the *Dispatch* that it finally named the culprit as Alexander Howland Smith, who lived in lodgings at 87 Brunswick Street. He was described as being a man of just over thirty years of age (he was in fact thirty-three), with sallow complexion, dark moustache, and side whiskers; it was a perfect description of the wanted man.

By now letters were arriving from Canada, America, and New Zealand. It was reported that the president of the London-Ontario St Andrew's Society had purchased two doubtful Burns' manuscripts.

Police investigations were by this time complete, and on 5 December Smith was arrested. He appeared at the Burgh Court charged with uttering forged documents and was sent to the High Court for trial. Smith applied for bail, but this was refused. A few days later, however, he appealed and was released on a surety of £100. Shortly afterwards Smith successfully petitioned the court, restraining the *Dispatch* from publishing further articles.

The story did not escape the attention of the London newspapers. One reported that there was in Edinburgh 'a local industry devoted to the manufacture of famous documents', while another referred to 'Edinburgh's manuscript factory'. Needless to say, it was recognised in dour, douce Edinburgh as a public scandal.

The trial opened at the High Court, Edinburgh, on 25 June the following year, and involved four charges of fabricating documents. The number of charges is deceptive, however, for the prosecution had listed 162 documents to be produced in evidence, and it was expected that forty-seven witnesses would be called.

Andrew Brown, bookseller, 15 Bristo Place, Edinburgh, was the first to give evidence. He said that he had first become acquainted with the accused towards the end of 1886, when Smith had called at the shop and offered some autographs for sale. About two months later Smith had returned to the shop and produced, the witness thought, letters by the Earl of Mar and the Duke of Argyll. When asked how he had obtained them, Smith replied that they had come from the office of Mr Ferrier, W.S., who was in the process of moving and had instructed Smith to clear the vaults. This statement had

Smith's hut, or summer house, shown in the ground plan.
From a contemporary illustration.

been checked by the witness, who told the court that he had no reason to doubt Smith.

Under cross-examination, Brown admitted purchasing items from the accused on a number of occasions. He also admitted that he had paid Smith about £200 and, when pressed to answer as to whether or not he had lost or gained from the transactions, Brown claimed that he did not know.

Throughout the day a steady stream of witnesses gave evidence, including George Traquair Thin, bookseller, 54 South Bridge. He said that the Equitable Loan Company was in the habit of sending the firm catalogues of their two annual sales. Occasionally, interesting books appeared on the 'lists'. In the 1890 spring catalogue he noticed some manuscripts – Burns and Scott, the rebellion etc. – which were subsequently purchased. At the saleroom he had seen them only in subdued light, but he had no reason to question their authenticity, although closer examination in his own office raised serious doubts. He subsequently handed them over to the Procurator Fiscal.

Also giving evidence for the prosecution were James Dowell, auctioneer, and representatives of various city pawnbroking businesses; all had been defrauded by the wily Mr Smith.

But it was towards the end of the first day that the witness who was to play the greatest part in convicting Smith took the stand. George Frederick Warner was assistant keeper of manuscripts at the

British Museum and an acknowledged authority in his field.

Warner stated that in January he had been asked by the Procurator Fiscal of Edinburgh to examine a number of documents in connection with the case. This he had done and had come to the conclusion that all were spurious. Asked if he believed that they were the work of one hand, Warner replied that he did.

The British Museum expert said that he had studied ninety-eight items, including papers reputed to be in the writing of Robert Burns, Sir Walter Scott, and a number of other literary and historical pieces. Dealing with the Burns papers, Warner said that he had examined nineteen of them; eight were short letters and were clumsy, laboured imitations of the bard's handwriting. The remainder were mainly poems and were much better forgeries. Burns wrote freely and formed his letters; he made his final stokes freely and his writing had a natural slant from left to right. In the forged papers the slant was too exaggerated. The signatures, the witness stated, were all formed on one model.

Warner pointed out that the Burns letters concluded 'I remain', which, he said, was most unusual. Furthermore, one of the fakes had not been written by Burns, but was the work of Alexander Pope!

Even the paper used for the forgeries was not of the texture on which letters of that date would be written. It was coarse and had obviously been torn from books. Some poems had been written on

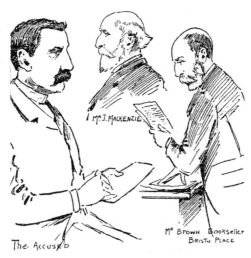

Contemporary sketches of the accused and two witnesses

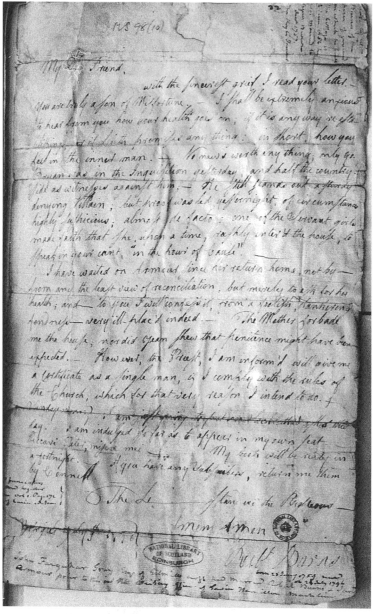

A genuine Robert Burns letter, dated 9 July 1786,
to John Richmond, clerk with William Wilson, WS,
about Jean Armour (courtesy of the Trustees of the
National Library of Scotland)

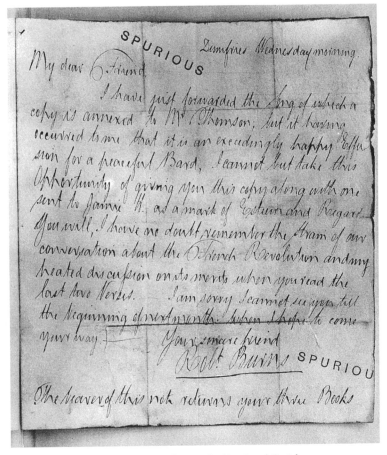

A Robert Burns forgery by 'Antique' Smith
(courtesy of the Trustees of the National Library of Scotland)

cartridge paper, while for others the forger had used a rough bluish paper similar to that available in legal offices for drafts. The paper had apparently been washed with a yellow substance and drawn over a wet, dirty surface to give the appearance of age.

The Scott letters had been written on rough paper which, in the opinion of Mr Warner, had been tinted. They showed a superficial resemblance to Scott's writing.

Letters by Lord Macaulay, James Hogg, and James Watt were examined and all were considered to have been forged. Only the Hogg letter bore any resemblance to a genuine document.

Warner also examined fifty-eight historical documents dated between 1638 and 1747, all of which, in his opinion, were forgeries. In certain instances dates were impossible, the handwriting was questionable, and the paper did not resemble that used for official documents.

After the devastating evidence given by the British Museum authority there could have been little doubt as to the outcome of the case.

When the court reconvened the following day, only one further witness, George Smith Inglis, a London handwriting expert, was called for the prosecution. He had acted for the Treasury on many occasions.

Inglis said that he had examined letters written by the accused, had compared them with the faked papers, and had come to the conclusion that all had been written by the same person. The Burns forgeries, he said, bore a general resemblance to the poet's handwriting, but there were certain Burns characteristics which were not evident in the spurious documents. Similarly, having studied the Scott forgeries, the witness was able to point out certain peculiarities common to Smith's writing and the forgeries.

Few witnesses were called for the defence, although on the first day of the trial James Gall Ferguson, curator of the Corporation Museum, Archibald Campbell, depute city clerk, Bailie Gulland, William Brown, bookseller, and David Lyell W.S. all expressed the opinion that the Burns, Scott and Macaulay papers produced in evidence were genuine.

And there was a brave, loyal, but fruitless attempt by Miss Agnes Smith to defend her brother. Miss Smith, 'a lady of prepossessing appearance', said that on one occasion she had gone to Mr Ferrier's office with a message from their mother for her brother. While she was there, her brother had shown her a room about the size of the well of the court; the floor was completely covered with documents and papers. There were also metal and wooden deed boxes.

Alexander had taken a lot of these papers to their home in Albany Street. She had never seen him bringing them but they were there. She was aware that for many years her brother had taken an interest in antiquarian matters and old documents.

The jury took only forty minutes to reach their unanimous verdict of guilty. The foreman, however, recommended the prisoner to mercy, on the ground that it was an unusual crime, and because of the easy facility of disposing of the spurious documents.

The defence asked the Lord Justice-Clerk to bear in mind that the charge had been hanging over the prisoner's head since January.

Alexander Howland Smith was sentenced to twelve calendar months' detention. The man who had fooled the collectors for more than six years served his time in the Calton Jail.

17

THE MEN WHO MADE A MINT

James Steele and Robert Ramsay were a pair of rogues; that was proved on 21 February 1930, when, at the High Court in Edinburgh, they pleaded guilty to charges of counterfeiting, in terms of the Coinage Act. Yet in one respect they had to be admired, for such was the quality of their work that the Royal Mint believed it to be the most remarkable of its kind to be brought to light in Great Britain.

Steele and Ramsay were both 45, and lived in the same flat at 13 Caledonian Road in the Dalry area of the city. Although time-served joiners, they occupied an old brick-built, two-storey building measuring 60 by 40 ft in Murieston Crescent Lane, ostensibly as a wireless repair and servicing business, although it is doubtful if they ever saw many customers. Not that they would have lost any sleep over that. The premises were isolated, and private lock-ups were the only other properties in the lane. It was a perfect location for concealing their illegal activities.

As in so many cases, it was a tip-off that brought the pair to the attention of the police. Miss Tennent, an assistant in the sub-post office at 3 Elm Row, noticed that a young boy called regularly to buy postal orders. He always tendered half-crown (12½ pence) coins, including some dated 1920. Nothing remarkable in that, except, as the observant assistant noticed, the coins were in remarkably good condition for their age.

Miss Tennent sought the advice of the local bank, where she was assured that the half-crowns were genuine. The lady was not convinced, however, and took the doubtful coins to the police. They in turn consulted the Mint, who confirmed Miss Tennent's suspicion about the genuineness of the money.

And so a trap was set. The post office was kept under surveillance, and on 16 January 1930, a boy entered the shop, laid four half-crowns (two dated 1920) and one shilling (5 pence), a total value of 55 pence, on the counter and asked for a ten shilling (50 pence) postal order.

In response to a pre-arranged signal the boy was followed to a stair in Union Place, where he was seen to hand over the postal order to a man. After a struggle the suspect was taken to Gayfield Police Station, where he refused to reveal his identity. In his possession, however, were coins similar to those identified by the Mint as counterfeit.

The arrested man was later named as James Steele, and a search of his bedroom at 13 Caledonian Road revealed the master dies in a securely locked box. Also in the flat was Robert Ramsay, and in his room police found a large number of counterfeit coins.

In the Murieston Crescent Lane building the police found a vast quantity of equipment, all identified as the tools of a counterfeiter. It took two days to dismantle and remove the machinery.

On 21 February the two men appeared at the High Court, where they pleaded guilty to three charges:

1. That between May 28, 1927, and January 17, 1930, in premises at Murieston Crescent Lane and in a house at 13 Caledonian Road, they had equipment used for counterfeiting.
2. That during the same period they falsely made and counterfeited 1,350 coins intended to resemble and pass for half-crowns.
3. That on various dates within that period, and in particular on January 16, 1930, in the sub-post office at 3 Elm Row, Edinburgh, and elsewhere in Edinburgh, Glasgow, and other parts of Scotland, they tendered counterfeit coins resembling half-crown pieces.

Mr Macgregor Mitchell, KC, appearing for the accused, told the court that the men, previously of good character and ability, had unfortunately allowed that ability to run into criminal channels. They had served their country in the Great War and had spent their spare time studying electricity, magnetism and engineering.

The Solicitor-General, Mr J.C. Watson, conceded that the Mint in all their records had no case of coining offences where such high skill and precision had been shown in the manufacture of counterfeit coins. The accused had all the facilities and machinery and it could only be used by capable men.

The Lord Justice-Clerk warned Steele and Ramsay that such was the gravity of the offences that they could have been sentenced to penal servitude for life in respect of either of the first two charges. Theirs was a deplorable case of misdirected ability. He sentenced them to three years' penal servitude.

The circulation value of the counterfeit money mentioned in the charges was just over £168, which would give each of the accused £84; not exactly a fortune by present-day standards.

But the matter has to be put into perspective. In 1930, five of their coins (equivalent to 62½ pence) would have purchased a bottle of whisky; a mere four shillings and sixpence (22½ pence) was the cost of a bottle of port, and cigarettes were one shilling (five pence) for twenty. Had one or other of the accused walked into the Fifty Shilling Tailors, 21 Princes Street, and laid twenty of his hand-made half-crowns (£2.50) on the counter he could have left wearing a spanking new ready-made Botany all-wool serge suit.

On completion of their sentences the two men apparently disappeared into obscurity, although it is known that Steele returned to 13 Caledonian Road, where he lived with his sister Lily. Then on 18 November 1964 James Steele, now eighty years old, had unexpected and unwelcome visitors – the police. Steele must have been considerably relieved when it was explained that they had called in connection with a complaint about noise from a joiner's workshop, but realised that they had come to the wrong address. Innocently, the old man let the guardians of the law into the flat.

What took place during that visit was not revealed, but by the time the police left, it was evident that Steele had ignored the warning issued by the Lord Justice-Clerk when he passed sentence thirty-four years previously. In the old man's bedroom, police found various pieces of machinery, dies, powder, and other equipment which would be required by a competent counterfeiter. In due course James Steele was charged that between 1 April 1958, and 18 November 1964, he manufactured more than 14,000 florins (10 pence pieces).

The accused appeared at the Sheriff Court on 8 December and pleaded guilty to the offence. Sheriff W. Ross McLean, QC, remitted Steele to the High Court for sentence and the sheriff was no doubt relieved at being spared the task of having to send a very old man to prison.

Two days later Steele stood on familiar territory as he heard Mr F. W.F. O'Brien, Senior Advocate Depute, tell the court that the coins were of a higher standard than any sent to the Mint for years.

Specimens were sent to the Royal Mint, and the Chief Assayer reported that the counterfeits are of excellent quality, produced by an expert craftsman, which would easily have deceived the public and banking institutions. No counterfeits of this standard had been submitted to the Mint in the course of years. It is perhaps a tribute to the excellence of the workmanship of the accused.

There was no evidence that Steele had used any other person to put the coins into circulation. The court was also told that the actual profit to Steele was something less than the apparent £1,400 value because of the cost to him of materials. His gain was in the region of £1,000.

Mr Nicholas Fairbairn, for the defence, said that Steele was a single man. He had worked at Miller's Foundry, Abbeyhill, until he retired in 1955, after an accident. Steele's only income was an old age pension, which he found insufficient to keep him. The accused, Mr Fairbairn went on to explain, bought metal for ten shillings (50 pence) a strip and from each strip he made forty-two florins.

Passing sentence, Lord Grant, the Lord Justice-Clerk, told Steele: 'This is a most remarkable case, and one of the serious features about it is the extremely good coins you were able to counterfeit.'

Lord Grant added that it was also an extremely serious offence, because Parliament indicated in the Act under which Steele had been charged that the minimum sentence ought to be three years' imprisonment.

'Nevertheless, I have power to mitigate that, and in view of your age I will limit the sentence to one of two years' imprisonment,' said Lord Grant.

An appeal was refused on 22 December. Lord President Clyde, sitting with Lords Carmont and Guthrie, said that, in their view, ample effect had been given by the court in sentencing Steele to two years. They could see no grounds for interfering with the sentence.

A bank official estimated that the coins which were the subject of the 1964 charge would have weighed approximately 3 cwt. 3lbs.

James Steele's sister Lily was later to tell the *Edinburgh Evening News* that she thought her brother was spending time in his room working with his model trains and photographic equipment, his two hobbies. Her brother had always been clever with his hands and had wanted to be an engineer. He went round every engineering shop in Edinburgh trying to get work but did not manage to. Instead he trained as a joiner.

Miss Steele said: 'When the police came they took away a lot of the coins he made which were hidden in the room. His work was admired by a Royal Mint man. Apart from the coins the police took away, I don't know what James did with the money.'

The 1964 conviction of James Steele surely ended the criminal career of a remarkable man. But it also left a number of unanswered questions.

Did the police really make a mistake when they called at Steele's flat on 18 November 1964, or were they 'acting on information received'? How many of the activities of Steele and Ramsay went undetected; were they 'going straight' between their release from prison in the 1930s and Steele's re-arrest in 1964? And what was their modus operandi to put the coins into circulation?

The purchase of postal orders appeared to work well initially, but this method eventually brought about the arrest of the counterfeiters. These postal orders were no doubt quickly converted into ten shilling and one pound notes, thus allowing the purchase of more expensive items without raising suspicion and at the same time reducing the number of counterfeit coins held 'in stock'. And was there another way of disposing of the relatively small value coins? Perhaps through someone who had a big turnover of small amounts? Or, most sinister of all, was there a 'Mr Big' behind the operation?

It is unlikely that any of these questions will ever be answered.

18

NUMBER ONE REGENT ROAD

On the face of it, Number One Regent Road, Edinburgh, sounds like a prestigious address. The property stood on an outstanding site in a desirable area of the city, with a commanding view of Holyrood Palace, Arthur's Seat, the Old Town and the castle.

The architecture too, was inspiring, having been compared with Windsor Castle, yet it was a property no self-respecting citizen would occupy out of choice. Why? Because Number One Regent Road was the official address of the notorious Calton Jail.

Like so many public buildings, the Calton Jail was constructed at different periods. First came the Bridewell, built between 1791 and 1796 with the help of a £5,000 grant from the government. The balance was met jointly by the town and county.

The Calton Jail, erected to the west of the Bridewell, was to follow. It was a long time in the planning, however, having been spoken of in 1786. Eventually an Act was passed in 1813 but it was not until September 1815 that work commenced, and it opened to receive its first prisoners exactly two years later. This building, which cost an estimated £20,000, had been intended for criminals only, with a separate unit for debtors. Lack of funds, however, meant that both classes shared the jail until 1847, when the development was completed with an extension to the east of the Bridewell. Subsequently, the three establishments were amalgamated to form the Calton Jail.

The Calton held prisoners from every part of Scotland prior to their appearance before the High Court and, if convicted, it was where they served their sentences – or were held pending transportation.

Following the end of public hanging in 1868, the death sentence was carried out within the precincts of the prison and, so far as I can establish, eight people (seven men and one woman) were hanged in the Calton Jail. Their stories are all different, sharing only the tragedy of death by murder, but some of them do reveal aspects of Victorian and Edwardian life, in particular a callous disregard for

The door from the condemned cell in the
Calton Jail is now in the Beehive Inn, Grassmarket

the welfare of children before strict laws for adoption were introduced.

Eugene Marie Chantrelle

It had all the ingredients of a cheap, sleazy novel. A 34-year-old teacher seduces his former teenage pupil, is forced into marriage, and finally murders her. This was no work of fiction, however, but a tragedy which took place in genteel, middle-class Victorian Edinburgh.

Eugene Marie Chantrelle was a Frenchman and teacher of languages at various schools, including the High School in Leith and an establishment in Buckingham Terrace. But Chantrelle met Elizabeth Cullen Dyer when she was a pupil at Newington Academy. A liaison developed, and in August 1868, with the 17-year-old girl seven months pregnant, the Frenchman married her. They set up home at 81 George Street, but the marriage was not a success.

Despite the respectable veneer, Chantrelle was a drunkard, a seducer, and a frequenter of brothels. He had assaulted his wife on numerous occasions. Ten years later, Elizabeth, now twenty-seven and the mother of three children (one only two months old) died, poisoned by her wayward husband.

Although Chantrelle had been arrested on 5 January 1878, it was not until 8 April that the Crown served the indictment on the accused. It was a 24-page document, of which three related to the charge that on the first or second day of January, 1878, he had administered in an orange or in lemonade or some other medium of food or drink, a quantity of opium or some other poison or poisons.

The trial opened at the High Court on 7 May that year, and lasted for four days. Such was the morbid curiosity of the Edinburgh public, that in the stampede for seats, several spectators narrowly escaped serious injury.

Mary Byrne, a servant in the Chantrelle household, told the court that on Hogmanay, Madame Chantrelle had been in good health and had taken the baby for a walk. She had been away for about four hours. On New Year's Day she had seen her mistress only briefly, having been given the day off. Normally Madame would have had a cooked breakfast, but on this occasion she asked for toast only, explaining that she had a headache. The servant returned about 9.30 p.m. and she was surprised when the accused answered the door. Madame was ill, he explained, adding that she had not eaten all day.

Mary Byrne visited Madame Chantrelle, who was in bed and looked ill. The gas was on (it always burned all night at a peep). There was a glass, containing a quantity of lemonade, which was most unusual, and some grapes on the bedside table. The patient asked for an orange to be peeled. It was quartered and only one piece eaten, the others being left by the bed.

Rising about about 6.45 a.m. Mary went downstairs to make a cup of tea. She heard a moan, like the sound of a cat, and she ignored it. But when it happened a second time she investigated and traced the noise to Madame Chantrelle's bedroom. On entering, she noticed that the gas light was out, contrary to usual practice. There was vomit on the pillow, and the patient was obviously very ill. She took her mistress's wrists and shook them violently but the only response was continued moaning.

Chantrelle was informed, but he was unable to communicate with his wife. He then told Mary he had heard the baby crying and asked her to investigate. The servant, who had heard nothing, found the three children sound asleep. In the meantime Chantrelle had opened the bedroom window and asked Mary if she could smell gas. Yes – a little – but there had been no evidence of it before she had left the room. The meter was then turned off.

Dr James Carmichael, who had a practice at 42 Northumberland Street, was called. The observant servant noticed that in the meantime the lemonade had disappeared, one quarter of the orange had gone, and the remaining two had been divided into four.

Carmichael suspected gas poisoning and the sick woman was removed to the nursery. A note was sent to Dr Henry Littlejohn, Edinburgh's first Medical Officer of Health, who lived at 24 Royal Circus, asking him to call. Littlejohn was also a police surgeon. He examined the light bracket and, being unable to trace a leak, ruled out gas.

Elizabeth Chantrelle was admitted to the Royal Infirmary, where she died a few hours later.

The court was told that the deceased had been seen by Professor Douglas Maclagan on admission. He also dismissed the gas theory and was convinced that opium or morphia was the cause of death. A post-mortem indicated no evidence of gas poisoning.

On 3 January (the day after Elizabeth died) the police removed a metal container and several bottles from the house together with soiled bedding. Chantrelle was known to have studied medicine and the police activities worried him. 'Did they want to make out that I have poisoned my wife?', he was alleged to have asked the servant.

Elizabeth Chantrelle was buried at the Grange Cemetery on 5 January and immediately afterwards her husband was arrested and taken to the Calton Jail.

In the meantime inquiries continued. A bolster slip from Madame Chantrelle's bed was examined, but the stain, measuring 15 by 10 inches, revealed no clue. However, an area 4 by 1 inch on a sheet produced a smell of opium. The body was exhumed on 10 January and, although the examination failed to confirm the cause of death, it proved to be inconsistent with gas poisoning.

George Todd Chienne, CA, manager of the Accident Assurance Company, George Street, identified policies taken out by Chantrelle on behalf of himself and his wife for £1,000 and a lesser sum in the name of Mary Byrne. The accused had been keen to purchase immediately, but the company had never issued a policy on the life of a woman, and approval was required.

The dead woman's mother Margaret Cullen or Dyer, who lived at 10 South Gray Street, told the court that the family did not approve of Chantrelle, who often ill-treated her daughter. Elizabeth on occasions sought refuge with her.

The jury took only seventy minutes to reach their unanimous verdict of guilty. Chantrelle was sentenced to be hanged on 31 May.

Immediately the condemned man asked for and was granted permission to speak. In a calm and distinct voice Chantrelle said:

> With regard to the stains that were found both on the sheet and the nightgown of Madame Chantrelle, I will make a few remarks on the chemical evidence of these stains. I have no desire to criticise the medical nor the chemical evidence that was given, nor shall I decide as to the correctness of Mr Falconer King's evidence, who was a witness for the defence . . . I am willing to admit that the dark stains on the sheet and nightgown – and I am speaking not so much in my own interest as in the interests of public morality I have forfeited my own life. I am quite willing to admit that these stains on the sheet contain sufficient evidence of opium . . . it neither proceeded from me nor Madame Chantrelle, but was rubbed in by some person I know not.

After several minutes the Lord Justice-Clerk interrupted, telling the accused he should not proceed further, and that his counsel would advise him where such representations should be made.

Shortly afterwards Chantrelle was taken to the Calton, pursued by some of the 1,000 spectators who had assembled in Parliament Square outside the High Court.

On the morning of the execution the condemned man was awake by 5 a.m. He dressed and had a light breakfast (coffee and an egg), followed by a smoke.

Had Chantrelle confessed? The Governor confirmed that a document had been prepared but it was believed to relate solely to the well-being of his children.

As the time for the execution approached, the condemned man was asked by the Rev. Wilson if he had anything further to say. In a low clear voice he replied, 'No, nothing, Mr Wilson.'

On the stroke of eight, Eugene Marie Chantrelle walked in procession the 50 yards to the storeroom, where the sentence was carried out.

Several hundred spectators had assembled on the Calton Hill, but their view was frustrated. A few who risked their lives by venturing onto the chimney stalks in Waterloo Place did witness the procession.

Chantrelle's was the first hanging in the Calton Jail.

Robert Flockhart Vickers and William Innes

When gamekeepers James Grosset and John Fortune and rabbit-catcher John McDiarmid set off armed only with walking sticks, on the lookout for poachers, they could never have thought that it would result in the deaths of two of them and the subsequent hanging of Robert Flockhart Vickers and William Innes.

The trial of Vickers and Innes took place at the High Court, Edinburgh, on 10 March 1884. The indictment alleged that on 15 December 1883, in a field at Redside Farm on the Rosebery Estate, in the Parish of Carrington, Midlothian, they had attacked and assaulted Fortune and McDiarmid by discharging loaded firearms at them, the effect of which was that both men subsequently died.

They were also charged with assaulting Grosset, gamekeeper to the Earl of Rosebery, by discharging firearms at him, causing injuries to his back and shoulder.

Grosset told the court that on the night of Friday 14 December he was out with Fortune and McDiarmid looking for poachers. It was a clear moonlit night, and windy – a favourable night for poachers. They carried no guns, only walking sticks. About 2.30 a.m. they decided to go home.

Back in his cottage, Grosset heard a shot. He immediately contacted Fortune and McDiarmid and they moved in the direction from which the shot had been heard. They saw two men walking towards them and they hid until the poachers were about 15 yards away. The gamekeepers then rose and challenged the accused.

Vickers and Innes then began to walk backwards up a slope and Grosset said that he called, 'There is no use going on like that. Stand still. I know you well enough.'

Innes told the three men to stand back and allegedly said to Vickers, 'You take that one and I'll go for this one.' The guns were then raised, and Vickers hit McDiarmid, who fell beside Grosset. Seconds later, Innes fired, and the shot grazed Grosset's back. Then Fortune fell from a shot fired by Vickers. With no delay Innes pointed the weapon at Grosset, but it misfired.

Grosset went on to tell the court that he had known Innes for seventeen years and Vickers for two to three. He immediately set off for Edgelaw Farm and asked farmer Robert Simpson to get medical help. Meanwhile, some farm workers went to help the injured men. Fortune had crawled 150 yards from the place where he had been shot.

Police Sergeant George Adamson of Gorebridge, having been told that Innes had injured himself, called at his house between 8 and 9 a.m. He was in bed and had a shot wound in the right jaw. Asked to explain the injury, Innes claimed that it had happened accidentally that morning when ramming the gun. He refused to produce the weapon but the sergeant found it in another room. Innes was taken to the Infirmary.

The police were unable to trace Vickers immediately, but located him on the Sunday. On examination, his gun was found to have been cleaned recently.

The local doctor, William Spalding, said that early on the Saturday morning he had gone to Grosset's house and found the three men who were suffering from gunshot wounds. Fortune was seriously injured, having been shot in the stomach. He had fifty-two pellets in his body, and this, the doctor believed, was fatal. McDiarmid had wounds on the shoulder, arm, and hand, but this was not thought to be life-threatening.

Professor Chiene told the court that McDiarmid's injuries were dangerous, but he did not think that they would prove fatal.

Fortune died on 18 December 1883 and McDiarmid on 8 January 1884.

Innes and Vickers were found guilty of murder by a majority of 9 to 6 at the High Court trial, the minority preferring a not proven verdict.

The accused men were told that they would be taken to the Calton Jail and be fed on bread and water; there they would be hanged on 31 March and thereafter buried within the prison.

From the time of their conviction the men met only once – on the scaffold. They exchanged not a word, but shook hands. At 8.12 a.m. a black flag was flown over the prison to signify that the sentences had been carried out.

Vickers, who was thirty-seven years of age, lived at Gorebridge.

He left a widow, and eight children aged between one and fifteen. Innes, aged thirty-seven, resided at Stobmill. His widow was left with children aged two, six, nine and ten.

Both men were described as being 'fond of a shot' – a common description for a poacher. The execution of Vickers and Innes was unique, for it was the only time that a double hanging took place in Calton Jail.

Jessie King or Kean

It was five past three precisely on the afternoon of 18 February 1889, and the muted chatter ceased suddenly at the High Court in Edinburgh. In the dock was Jessie King, the Stockbridge baby farmer and alleged murderess. The silence was broken only by the sound of shuffling feet as the jury returned. There was a short pause.

The Clerk: 'Have you agreed on your verdict?'

The Foreman: 'Unanimously.'

The Clerk: 'Will you return your verdict?'

The Foreman: 'A unanimous verdict of murder.'

The Lord Justice-Clerk: 'On the two charges I presume?'

The Foreman: 'Both charges.'

There was a brief delay while the jury's verdict was recorded, and then Lord Justice-Clerk Kingsburgh addressed the convicted woman: 'Jessie King, no one who has listened to the evidence in this trial will have failed to be satisfied that the jury could have come to any other conclusion than that they have come to in your case. Your days are numbered.'

Lord Kingsburgh then passed sentence that King would be taken to the prison and detained until 11 March and, on that date, between the hours of eight and ten (at this point the convicted woman began to wail) in the forenoon be hanged and thereafter buried in the prison grounds.

With the sentence completed, King was carried, semi-conscious, to the cells below. The trial had lasted four-and-a-half hours; six minutes was all the time the jury needed to reach their verdict.

In the cells King was handed over to Inspector Christie, and in an agitated state exclaimed, 'Oh to be hanged! What a death!' Later, when she had calmed down, she thanked Christie and the police for the kindness they had shown.

To avoid the assembled crowd, the prisoner was taken to

Parliament Hall and out through a private door to the adjoining Signet Library, from where she left unseen.

Jessie King had faced three charges:

1. In April or May 1888, in the house in Ann's Court, Canonmills, then occupied by Thomas Pearson, labourer, she strangled Alexander Gunn aged twelve months or thereby, son of Catherine Whyte, residing at 6 Huntly Street, Canonmills, and murdered him.

2. In September 1888, in the house at Cheyne Street, Stockbridge, then occupied by Pearson, she strangled Violet Duncan Tomlinson aged six months or thereby, daughter of Alice Maria Jane Stewart Tomlinson, domestic servant, 3 Coates Place, now in Edinburgh Royal Infirmary and did by putting her hand upon her mouth suffocate and murder her.

3. In October or November 1887, in the house at 24 Dalkeith Road, then occupied by Pearson, she did strangle, or in some other manner assault Walter Anderson Campbell, aged five months or thereby, son of Elizabeth Campbell, wireworker, Prestonpans, now deceased, and did murder him.

The third charge was subsequently withdrawn.

Catherine Whyte told the court that on 1 May 1887 she was unmarried and had twins. As she was working in service she was unable to keep the children and gave them to Mrs Henderson of Rose Street. When they were eleven months old, an advertisement was placed for someone to take them. 'Mrs Macpherson' (King) took Alexander, and was given £3.

A young boy, Alexander Brown, 18 Allan Street, Stockbridge, told of how he was playing in Cheyne Street and saw a parcel (he knew the house where the accused lived and it was near there). The lad was with some other boys, one of whom kicked the parcel, thinking it contained some old boots. Eventually they opened it, found the dead child, and called the police immediately.

Constable George Stewart explained that the parcel had been opened before he arrived but he was able to confirm that there was a presence of lime.

Jemima Tomlinson, 6 Wardrop's Court, mother of Alice Tomlinson (who at the time of the trial was a patient at Edinburgh Royal Infirmary) said that her daughter had given birth to an illegitimate girl at the Maternity Hospital. The grandmother explained that she had looked after the baby for three weeks before advertising for a suitable home. There had been many applicants and she had chosen 'Mrs Banks' (King), who said that she would take the child if she was healthy. King had mentioned a price of £2 to £3. The accused had told her the baby was for her sister, whose husband was piper to the Duke of Montrose.

The house at Cheyne Street where King shared a room with Thomas Pearson, who was absolved of any implications in the crimes, was occupied by Mr and Mrs James Banks.

Mrs Banks was suspicious of King and it was she who had alerted the police.

Detective James Clark searched the room and found a key to the locked closet. He told King that it was his intention to search the closet.

At this, the prisoner allegedly replied, 'Get a cab, it's there.' In the corner of the bottom shelf, the policeman found the body of a female baby. On the top shelf there was a mat, on which there was evidence to suggest that a small body might have lain there. Also in the closet was a tin containing chloride of lime and a piece of black cloth similar to that wrapped round the body of the child found in Cheyne Street by Alexander Brown.

When charged King admitted both offences.

Dr Henry Littlejohn and his son Dr Harvey Littlejohn gave medical evidence.

On 11 March 1889 Jessie King paid the penalty for her crimes. At 7.45 a.m. the bell began to toll with an eerie six-second gap between each strike, and it continued until the execution had been carried out at approximately 8 a.m. At 2.30 p.m. King was placed in a black-painted coffin, to which quicklime had been added. She was then buried alongside Vickers and Innes, the Gorebridge murderers.

Jessie King was thought to be the first woman to be hanged in Edinburgh for fifty-four years.

John Herdman

No trace remains of Milne Square, but it stood directly opposite the entrance to the Tron Kirk in the High Street. In the Edinburgh street directory of 1898 it is shown as 173 High Street. The entrance was through a close, and a contemporary street map suggests that there was also a passage leading to the North Bridge, roughly in line with the present arcade.

On 13 March 1898, the proprietors of *The Scotsman* purchased from the Town Council the cleared site on the west side of what was described as North Bridge Street, for £120,000. But part of Milne Square still existed, and at no. 7 there was residential accommodation of sorts.

Shortly after 7 p.m. on New Year's Day 1898 Constable Robert Combe was on duty at the junction of the High Street and North Bridge, when he was told by a resident at 7 Milne Square that a woman who lived in a room at the top of the tenement had been badly injured and was possibly dead.

Combe summoned assistance and with a colleague raced to the attic flat, where he found a woman's body lying in a pool of blood. She had head and face injuries.

The CID were immediately alerted. They quickly found that the victim lived with John Herdman and that they had argued violently during the day. When the police officers entered the stair they questioned a man, who was taken to the Central Police Office in the High Street. He was blood-stained and carried a knife.

Later, the flat, which measured 12 feet by 10 feet, was visited by a senior police officer and Sir Henry Littlejohn, the police surgeon. The room was lit by a small attic window; there was practically no furniture and the bed on which the body lay was made up on the floor.

It was soon established that the dead woman was Jessie Calder, aged about fifty, who had adopted her stepfather's name of Soutar. She worked as a laundress.

On 3 January John Herdman, a 52-year-old printer's machineman, appeared at the Edinburgh Police Court. The charge was that 'on Friday 31 December 1897 and Saturday 1 January 1898 in the house at 7 Milne Square occupied by him and in the passage leading thereto, he attacked and assaulted Jessie Soutar with a piece of wood or some other weapon, did strike her several blows on the head, face and breast and other parts of her person, stabbing her with a knife or other weapon on the body to the effusion of blood and did murder her'.

Herdman was about 5ft 7ins tall, slightly bald, hair turning grey, and had a thick military-like moustache.

His trial took place before Lord Young at the High Court on 21 February.

Anne Connor explained to the court that there were four houses, each of one room; these were entered off a common passage, where the murder had taken place. The deceased had lived with the accused but she had been away for two weeks before Hogmanay.

On the afternoon of 31 December the witness had met Soutar in the close and she had asked if Jack (the accused) was in. After midnight the witness had heard quarrelling. About 6 a.m. Soutar came to Mrs Connor's door and lifted the sneck; but she was refused admission.

Margaret Connor recalled that about 6 p.m. on New Year's evening she had heard the accused say, 'Come awa' in Jessie.'

James Connor then took a light into the lobby and saw Soutar lying on the floor with Herdman beside her. Soutar did not speak and Herdman dragged her into the house.

Widow Mrs Budge said that she was wakened about 2 a.m. on 1 January by screaming in the lobby. Between 11 a.m. and noon she was at the common sink and saw Soutar run out of the house pursued by Herdman. Her face was bruised, her mouth swollen, and she was blood-stained. In the mid-afternoon Mrs Budge heard screaming and a noise like a body falling, followed by moaning. It was 9 p.m. before she learned that Jessie Soutar was dead.

An 11-year-old girl, Johan Sorlie, told the court she was playing on the stair with other girls about 4 p.m. when she was sent on an errand. When she returned she saw Jessie Soutar lying in the passage. Herdman kicked her on the head, seized her hair, and said, 'This is another time you have not had my supper ready.' He kicked her 'very sore' five or six times. Herdman then went into the house. A while later Johan saw Jessie still lying on the floor.

Sir Henry Littlejohn and Dr Joseph Bell carried out a postmortem. Jessie Soutar's injuries included a stab wound to the left breast, bruising and wounds to the head, and a mass of bruises covered her body.

The jury took only thirty minutes to reach a 10 to 5 guilty verdict. Immediately, a young girl, believed to be Herdman's daughter, burst into tears. The condemned man left the court, also in tears.

Herdman was hanged at the Calton Jail on 14 March. He wore a rough, brown tweed suit, loose white muffler – and he carried a tweed cap! A newspaper reporter who was present at the execution described Herdman as 'a pitiable figure with a face swollen and lined with debauchery'.

Patrick Higgins

For ploughmen Thomas Duncan and James Thomson, 8 June 1913 started off as just another routine day, as they walked towards a field near Hopetoun Quarry, Linlithgow, West Lothian, to look at some horses.

But as they passed close to the quarry they spotted 'something' floating in the water. Closer inspection revealed the bodies of two young boys.

The following day Constable James Adam interviewed Patrick Higgins, a local man, in Broxburn, regarding his sons who had not been seen for some time. Higgins could give no satisfactory explanation about their whereabouts and he was arrested.

Higgins (38) appeared at the High Court, Edinburgh, on 10 September, charged that he, between 25 October 1911 and 1 January 1912, at a disused quarry known as Hopetoun Quarry, in the Parish of Abercorn, Linlithgow, in which there was then a large quantity of water, assaulted William Higgins and John Higgins, his children, and tied them together with a cord and threw them into the quarry and murdered them.

Higgins pleaded not guilty, submitting a special defence that at the time he was alleged to have committed the crime he was insane and not responsible for his actions.

Mrs C. Cohill, mother of the accused, and a widow living at Niddrie Farm Cottages, near Winchburgh, said that her son had served in the army in India but had been discharged because of epileptic fits. She had last seen her grandchildren in November 1911, although she had contact later with her son.

When asked what had become of the boys, Higgins had told his mother that he had given them to two ladies in a railway carriage. Mrs Cohill said that she had told Patrick that ladies in trains were not that charitable and that she did not believe him.

Elizabeth Hynes, from Tarbrax, told the court that she had known the accused since he was a boy, and she had taken care of his sons (their mother had died at Methil in 1910), although she received no money. The boys 'went off' in October 1911, and she had not seen them since.

In June or July 1912, the accused had visited her and she had asked him about the children. Higgins told her that they were 'all right', but when pressed, the accused replied that they were dead. Asked if they had died of some children's disease, Higgins said that they were drowned.

Archibald Fairnie, a brick-turner, of Station Road, Winchburgh, recalled that on a night in October or November 1911 the accused had come into the brickworks looking for somewhere to sleep. He was wet and dirty and remarked that he had got the children away. A lady in a train had taken them, he was alleged to have said. He claimed that he had got off the train at Ratho and had walked back.

Winchburgh miner James Daly said that he had known the accused for a long time. One wet, stormy evening between seven and eight, early in November 1911, he had seen Higgins and the two boys walking towards Winchburgh. Later that evening he had met Higgins in a public house. When asked about the boys, he said that he had a good home for them. They had taken the 8.30 a.m. train to Edinburgh and two women in the compartment offered to take the boys. Higgins told Daly that he then left the train at Ratho.

Medical evidence regarding the deaths of the children was given by Dr Harvey Littlejohn, who said that the two bodies recovered were boys aged between four and five, and seven and eight. They had been in the water for about two years, and he was unable to state the cause of death.

Dr Keay of the Edinburgh and District Asylum, Bangour, was of the opinion that the accused was neither insane nor an epileptic. Any fits or convulsions could have been caused by alcohol.

On leaving the army Higgins found employment at the brickworks, and it was there that he met his wife. In June 1911, Higgins had served a two-month jail sentence for child neglect. On release from prison on 24 August he removed the boys from the institution where they were resident in Dysart and returned to Winchburgh.

Before summing up, Lord Johnston publicly expressed his concern that the two unfortunate boys were allowed to disappear within the parish and no questions asked – no thought given by the parochial authorities to them for a couple of years.

Higgins was found guilty on a unanimous verdict and was hanged at the Calton Jail on 2 October 1913, confessing that the sentence was just and that drink had been his downfall.

John Henry Savage

The murder of 42-year-old Mrs Jemima Grierson was straight-forward as far as the police inquiries were concerned. They knew the identity of the culprit and it was simply a case of picking him up.

John Henry Savage, aged fifty, was arrested in Bonnington Road, just five-and-a-half hours after the murder. Later a razor was recovered from the Water of Leith at Fishquay Bridge.

Jemima Grierson was the estranged wife of Joseph Grierson, a coalminer from Coaltown of Wemyss. They married in 1905 but she left him in 1914. The dead woman, who was addicted to drink, co-habited with Richard Tillett, and it was in the house they shared at 25 Bridge Street (renamed Sandport Place on 1 February 1968) that Mrs Grierson met her death in the early hours of 14 March 1923.

On 21 May of that year Savage's trial opened at the High Court in the city. Tillett confirmed that he and the deceased had lived together for several years. The night before she died, he had left for work at 9.50 p.m. and subsequently received a message that 'Savage had cut Minnie's throat'. Tillett immediately went to the hospital but Jemima was already dead. He returned home and found the floor covered in blood.

Eighteen-year-old Michael Reilly revealed that he had been told by Tillett not to let anyone into the house. But Savage arrived and gained entry. He got Reilly out of the way by sending him to buy a box of matches. When he returned, Savage and Mrs Grierson were talking and this continued for about an hour. Savage then told Reilly to leave, as he wanted to talk to his wife alone. When the lad returned, some considerable time later, the woman was lying on the floor and neighbours were present.

Mrs Ann Jane McLeod, a widow, said she was roused about 1 a.m. on 14 March by the deceased. 'That brute Savage is here again', she was told, and Mrs McLeod went to find a policeman. She was unsuccessful. This was the third occasion on which she had been asked to help get the accused out of the house.

Mrs McLeod told the court that she understood that Savage was seeking information about a woman, and that Mrs Grierson had refused to help. Savage was sitting on a sofa, his head between his hands, and smoking a pipe. Shortly afterwards, Savage allegedly said to Mrs Grierson, 'If you don't hold your tongue I'll cut the head off your body.'

At that, Mrs McLeod left to put on more clothing and the accused closed the door. Immediately Mrs Grierson was heard to squeal, and called out for help. Mrs McLeod, her son, and her daughter attempted to get into the house and after about five minutes the screaming stopped.

Professor Harvey Littlejohn told the court that death was due to haemorrhage from a wound to the left jugular vein.

The jury of eleven men and four women returned their unanimous verdict of guilty after thirty-five minutes. Savage was sentenced to death, the execution to take place at the Calton on 11 June, his remains to be buried within the prison.

But how did a convicted person meet death even as late as 1923? The facilities were graphically described in one newspaper at the time John Henry Savage paid the penalty:

> In the Calton Prison there is no place of execution in the regular scheme of things, and so it is that the expedient was adopted, as before, of utilising the well of a stair in the prison over which to erect the scaffold. It was the same place – which is the most suitable – that served on some other melancholy occasions.

Of course the construction of the scaffold was supervised by the City Architect and tested by the hangman!

Philip Murray

If, in the early 1920s, an Edinburgh policeman was asked to name the town's most notorious criminal, 'Mad Phil' Murray would have been high on the list. Murray was also a well-known newspaper vendor with a 'pitch' outside Register House in Princes Street.

Despite coming from a respectable background, Murray spent more than half of his relatively short life in crime. But it came to an end on Tuesday 30 October 1923, when he was hanged at the Calton Jail for murder. This 31-year-old Edinburgh man had a criminal record going back eighteen years, with forty appearances before the courts.

Murray was born in 1892, and his father died young, leaving a widow to raise Murray and his sister in their Rose Street flat. By the age of thirteen he was already known to the police. Despite the efforts of his mother and sister, Murray made no attempt to reform or look for a trades apprenticeship, choosing instead occasional work and becoming involved with criminal elements.

When he was prepared to work, Murray was a familiar figure selling newspapers. Any other vendor who dared to invade his 'patch' was warned off with the threat of violence. For spells, however, Murray would disappear from the town, and it was believed that he was visiting the racetracks.

Murray was frequently involved in street fights, on one occasion returning home with a severely damaged eye and blood streaming down his face. Mrs Murray realised the seriousness of her son's injury and rushed him to the Infirmary, where the doctors decided that to save the sight of the left eye, the damaged right would have to be removed.

Despite pressure from the police and his family, Murray refused to divulge how he had sustained the injury. It was generally assumed, however, that it was the result of a drunken brawl.

As he grew older, Murray became more violent, and he was known among the vendors as 'Mad Phil'. Alcohol played a big part in his life and he was never short of money.

Although he had lost an eye, Murray joined the army late in the 1914–18 conflict. He was sent to France, but his 'active service' was restricted to road-building. After the war, Murray lived in Jamaica Street with Catherine Donoghue. His drinking became steadily worse. He was feared by his neighbours in that condition, which was frequent.

Philip Murray's first court appearance was in 1905; he was charged with malicious mischief, namely, damaging property by throwing stones. He was admonished, but at the same court he was convicted of breach of the peace and locked up for six hours!

He evaded the police for three years, before appearing in the Police Court where he was fined one shilling (5p) for breach of the peace. Two years later he was again before the court, and thereafter very much on the slippery slope.

From assault in 1911, the offences became more serious. With twenty-three convictions on his record, Murray was charged in 1914 with assaulting a man and a number of police constables. For this he was sentenced to three months' imprisonment, his longest sentence to date. The convictions came thick and fast, mainly for disorderly behaviour. In May 1916 he was sentenced to six months' imprisonment following a conviction under the Immoral Traffic Act.

Murray's record continued to grow, with six appearances before the court in 1922. The following year he was fined £3 for disorderly conduct. This was a relatively lenient sentence, considering his record, but he had pleaded with the bench to give him a chance!

Time finally ran out for 'Mad Phil' in 1923, when he was arrested for murder. On this occasion there was no second opportunity; he paid the ultimate penalty and was hanged for the offence – the last person to stand on the scaffold at the notorious Calton Jail.

It had all been too much for his mother, however; the year before his capital conviction she had left Edinburgh to live with her married daughter in London.

On 25 June 1923 the *Edinburgh Evening News* reported: 'The working class tenement at 40 Jamaica Street was on Saturday evening the scene of a tragedy of a sordid character, resulting in the death of a man named William Cree, who resided at 47 Inglis Street, Dunfermline. Immediately after the affair, the police took into custody Philip Murray (31) and Catherine Walker or Donoghue (33).'

It was about 10 p.m. when Donoghue and Cree entered the single-room, second-floor flat. Fifteen minutes later shouting and arguing could be heard and a crowd gathered. Suddenly a man came crashing through the closed window to the ground 30 feet below. The victim was rushed to the Infirmary, but he died just before midnight.

The police were quickly on the scene but, finding the door to the flat locked, they had to make a forced entry. Murray and Donoghue were inside.

But who was the victim? The only clue was a return train ticket to Dunfermline. It was a railway 'privilege' ticket, available to employees only. This stroke of luck enabled the police to make a quick identification.

On Monday 8 October, Murray appeared at the High Court charged with Cree's murder.

The dead man's brother David said that William was an unmarried railway surfaceman who had served in the Black Watch from 1914 to 1919 and been wounded three times. He had left Dunfermline between 4 and 5 p.m. and was expected back on the last train.

William Mitchell, a waiter in a Rose Street public house, identified the accused. There was a gasp in the court when Catherine

Donoghue was brought in and was also identified by Mitchell. Shown a photograph of the murdered man, the witness confirmed that Cree and Donoghue had left the public house about 10 p.m. on the night of the alleged murder.

Neighbour William McDonald, who lived directly opposite the flat where the murder took place, told of hearing the noise of breaking wood, followed by the sound of moaning and a man's voice (not Murray's) calling 'Oh don't'. McDonald had said to his wife, 'There's somebody over the window.' He immediately went for the police. When partly down the stair, he heard glass breaking, followed by a thud. McDonald then found the deceased on the pavement.

The upstairs tenant, Catherine Laing, said that she heard a scuffle, went to the window, and saw below a man coming through 'hands, shoulder, head'. Earlier she had heard Donoghue cry, 'Dinna hit him nae mair, Phil.'

Constable John McTaggart confirmed that he had been on duty in nearby Howe Street about 11 p.m. when he was informed that a man had fallen from a window in Jamaica Street. With difficulty, access was gained to the flat, which was in darkness. Donoghue was behind the door; Murray wore trousers only and stood beside the bed. Murray was eventually arrested, but only with the assistance of neighbours, and taken to Stockbridge Police Station. Later Donoghue was taken into full custody.

The flat where the murder had taken place measured only 14 feet by 8 feet and was home for Murray, Donoghue and her 15-year-old daughter.

When charged, Murray replied, 'I'm making no comment.' Donoghue was also charged with murder.

Then, in response to a message from the woman, Inspector George Hall went to see her in Calton Jail on 27 June. She told the Inspector that she was not guilty of murder and thought that Murray would have told the truth. Hall was told that after the man had been pushed out of the window, she had said to Murray, 'The police will be here soon.' He replied, 'It serves the – right. If he had given me his money, he wouldn't have been a dead man tonight.'

Murray also allegedly said, 'Tell the police that you were in the house first and that he was trying to take advantage of you and that when I came into the house he jumped out of the window in fright.'

Donoghue told the court that she was also known as Kitty Rose and admitted that she earned about £7 a week from prostitution. Catherine Donoghue, alias Kitty Rose, had turned King's evidence, the murder charge against her being dropped.

The trial ended on the second day with the accused telling the court that on the forenoon of Saturday 23 June he had been singing in St Andrew Square and had collected about eight shillings. He gave Mrs Donoghue six shillings, went out at 4.40 p.m., and returned home very drunk. He fell asleep and was wakened by the sound of voices. Finding Cree in the house, he ordered him to leave. A fight ensued and Murray admitted hitting Cree.

Murray said, 'If any woman has committed perjury in a court, that woman (Donoghue) committed it yesterday.' She did not say, 'Don't Phil, don't.' Her words were 'Go on Phil, Phil go on, gie him some mair', claimed Murray. 'She may have escaped her rightful punishment here by what she said but God will punish her', Murray concluded.

It took the jury only twenty-seven minutes to return with their verdict of guilty by a majority of 11 to 4 but with a unanimous recommendation to mercy.

The immediate silence following Lord Constable passing the death sentence was broken by the condemned man, who in a low but firm voice said: 'I must thank my counsel for the defence he has put up on my behalf. I do not think that it was very fair for the jury to accept Mrs Donoghue's evidence against me. I am fully prepared to meet my God. I never put that man through the window as is alleged against me.'

There was a great deal of sympathy for Murray and a petition of 22,000 signatures was raised in his support. It was forwarded to the Secretary of State for Scotland, Lord Novar, who decided not to interfere with the sentence. Telegrams were then sent to the king and to the secretary of state, praying for reconsideration of the verdict. Lord Novar replied that he was unable to advise His Majesty to interfere with the due course of the law.

On Tuesday 30 October a crowd, estimated at five hundred, gathered in Regent Road and on Calton Hill.

At 8 a.m. there was considerable excitement when the black flag had not been raised to signify that the sentence had been carried out. Had a last-minute reprieve arrived? No. The authorities were merely following recent custom to discontinue this tradition.

There was a rush for information when Bailies Sleigh and Couston appeared at the prison gates, but it was left to the newspaper reporters to confirm the news that the sentence had been carried out.

The Calton Jail was demolished in the 1930s to make way for St Andrew's House, although the governor's house survived. Jamaica Street, which runs between India Street and Howe Street, has been rebuilt, but the memories of that gruesome Saturday in old Jamaica Street may still haunt some Edinburgh citizens.

The loss of a fine building

Number One Regent Road closed in March 1925 when the last of the inmates were transferred to Saughton Prison. Immediately, consideration turned to possible uses for this architecturally fine building; but it was obvious that it would be demolished.

In 1926 the *Edinburgh Evening News* reported that 'slight' dismantling work had begun. The following year it was suggested as a possible headquarters for Scottish Command, but this was abandoned because of cost. Next, it was to be converted into offices for the Civil Service, which was spread throughout the town.

They were still talking in 1928 when the latest proposal was to use one block for the National Library, and also to locate a municipal health clinic there. In the same year the old prison was being suggested as a possible City Chambers and this proposal reached the subcommittee of the Lord Provost's Committee on 12 December.

Perhaps a Sheriff Courthouse? This was rejected by the Town Council on 24 January 1929 in favour of a more central site. In the end a decision was taken to demolish.

The Calton Jail, a prestigious address – but not for the inmates

Little remains of the old Calton building, apart from the governor's old home. But how many of the diners who drop into the popular Beehive Inn, Grassmarket, for a meal realise that the door through which they pass into the dining room was taken from the condemned cell at the Calton Jail? Through that very door some of Edinburgh's most notorious murderers took their final steps to the gallows.

The Calton was a fine stone-built building, and no doubt much of the material was salvaged. Imagine the scene. An elderly stonemason picks up a piece of stone to 'dress' before re-use. He steps back, pushes his cap to the back of his head, takes the pipe from his mouth and smiles as he reads the message scratched on the material. Perhaps 'R.F.V. 31.3.84'.

The work of a bored prisoner, perhaps, is the thought that might have passed through the head of that old tradesman. How wrong he would have been! Each murderer hanged at Calton Jail was buried within the grounds, with initials and dates of execution crudely scratched on the wall to identify where the body lay, each grave six feet apart.

19

SAUGHTON PRISON, AND THE MEN WHO WALKED TO THE GALLOWS

When the decision was taken that the Calton Jail had outlived its usefulness, the authorities chose a site at Saughton, on the west side of the town, on which to build a replacement prison.

The land had been bought in 1913, and the centre was first used in 1919, but it was not until 1925 that the last of the prisoners were transferred from the Calton.

No doubt, the new establishment at Saughton was fitted with the most sophisticated equipment then available, but the security could be breached . . . and it was! One prisoner walked out forty-two days after he had been sent down. Needless to say, this incident caused considerable embarrassment to the prison authorities.

The escapee was Cedric Norval, who had been sentenced to 18 months' imprisonment on 16 February 1925 at the High Court in Edinburgh for breaking into a house in Cluny Gardens in the city. It was about midday on Saturday 29 March when Norval, who was a member of a prison working party, gave the warders the slip.

The alarm was raised and the police were confident that Norval would be picked up quickly. Why? Because he was dressed in the distinctive uniform of blue- and red-striped jacket and corduroy trousers. But when Norval was arrested in Arthur Street at 7 p.m., seven hours after his escape, he was wearing a tweed jacket and vest, overalls and a cap!

One newspaper reported, 'How he obtained these and where he had effected the change is a mystery.'

No doubt this incident would have been the subject of further police investigation and hopefully a report was submitted to the Procurator Fiscal!

When Saughton Prison was built, the development included a specially constructed cell for condemned prisoners. Adjacent was the iron-beamed scaffold which was the first permanent structure of its kind in Scotland.

This was an area of the prison which everyone hoped would never be required, but on 23 July 1928, that cell received its first occupant, one of four men to be hanged at Saughton for murder.

Allan Wales

Why should a clock that has stood silent and apparently broken for several years suddenly restart? In 1928 such an incident reportedly happened in a Leith house and the following day the mother of Allan Wales, who was under sentence of death for the murder of his young, slightly-built wife, was informed that the Secretary of State had found no evidence to justify the reprieve of her condemned son.

Mrs Wales said that she and her daughter had been sitting in the house in Seafield Avenue, when the alarm clock went off. It stopped only after her daughter moved the hands on the timepiece. The distraught woman was convinced that this was a warning of the news that was to follow.

On 23 July that summer Allan Wales appeared before Lord Anderson and a jury at the High Court, Edinburgh. He was charged that, in the basement area of a house in Pirniefield Place, he assaulted Isabella Wales, his wife, cut her throat with a knife or other sharp instrument, and murdered her, and further that he evinced malice and ill-will against her by repeatedly threatening, beating and assaulting her.

The trial had attracted considerable interest and, long before the court opened, a lengthy queue of citizens had formed in Parliament Square in the hope of gaining admission.

The accused was twenty-two-years old, sturdily built with fair hair. He had worked as a miner with the Niddrie and Benhar Coal Company but at the time of his wife's death he was unemployed.

Florence Hain, the dead woman's mother, told the court that Isabella had married Wales on 2 December 1926, and admitted that she did not approve of the marriage. The couple had lived in a single room, first in Bonnington Road, and later at Thorntree Street. Mrs Hain said that Wales had frequently assaulted Isabella. On 24 October 1927, their son had been born at the Edinburgh Maternity Hospital.

Continuing her evidence, Mrs Hain said that on Saturday 2 June 1928 she and her daughter had met the accused in the Kirkgate,

Leith, and he had asked his wife for sixpence. He then accused Mrs Hain of having 'miscalled' him. His outburst had caused a crowd to gather; this upset her daughter, who burst into tears.

Isabella spent the weekend with relatives in St Anthony Street and on the Monday afternoon she had asked her cousin to take the baby and wedding ring to her mother-in-law's house.

'Did your daughter tell you why?'

'She said that she was not going back to him again. She was going to look for work in service.'

On Tuesday 5 June Isabella and her cousin Jessie Berry arrived about 11 a.m. in Pirniefield Place, where they met Wales. He again asked his wife to go back with him but she refused. Later Wales went back to Pirniefield Place to try to persuade Isabella to change her mind, but again she declined. He then said that his mother wanted to see her and Isabella had told him that she could call at Pirniefield Place.

The accused came back with his mother, who lived in Seafield Avenue, but they were still unable to convince Isabella that she should give the marriage another chance and that she should return to the matrimonial home in Orchardfield Lane.

Asked to explain what happened next, Mrs Hain said that she was peeling potatoes at the sink and did not see Wales coming downstairs. He opened the door and came in, then gripped Isabella by the shoulder. He had a knife. He dragged her into the outside area and threw her to the ground. Mrs Hain fled upstairs to try to get help and when she returned her daughter was dead.

Andrew Hain, a stonemason and father of the dead woman, admitted telling his wife not to interfere in the marriage.

'Why did you tell her that?'

'He was married to her and should have kept her.'

Jessie Berry, Isabella's cousin, said in evidence that Isa had asked her to take the baby to her husband at Seafield Avenue. He was not there, but she left the child with the grandmother, explaining that Isa was going into service at Newington.

The witness went on to say that on the Tuesday she and Isa had taken a tram to the corner of Pirniefield Place, where they had met Wales. Isa and Wales had spoken briefly and privately before parting. Regarding the later return of Wales to the house in Pirniefield Place, Jessie said that when the accused came into the kitchen she ran out because she was afraid of him. He had a fierce look on his face and she thought that he was going to do something. The witness was followed from the house by her aunt (Mrs Hain) and Jessie shouted for help. A man accompanied her back to the house. Five to ten minutes later the accused left, his hands and clothes covered in blood.

William King, 88 Henderson Street, said that he was on Leith Links, heard screaming, and ran over. He then went to the scene of the tragedy. The victim was receiving attention, so he followed the accused to Seafield Avenue. Mr King asked the accused what he had done and Wales allegedly replied, 'She deserved it. I will not beat about the bush. There are some people who can't mind their own business.'

Wales then took a ring from his pocket and said, 'She sent me my ring back and left the kiddie for two nights.'

After their wedding (which Mrs Hain, mother of the deceased, had refused to attend) Allan and Isabella Wales set up home in a single room at 87 Bonnington Road. Their landlord admitted that the couple were not on good terms.

The uncle of the deceased, John Berry, who lived at 1 St Anthony Street, told the court that, because of her fear for the accused, he had advised his niece always to keep to crowded thoroughfares.

Detective Sergeant Alexander Drummond explained that in response to a telephone message he went to a house in Pirniefield Place, where he found the body of a young woman. Drummond then went to Seafield Avenue, where the accused was pointed out to him. Wales was speaking to his sister and his hands and clothes were covered in blood.

Wales was told that he was being arrested in connection with the death of his wife and to say nothing about the matter. He replied, 'I am the man.'

The accused was taken to a police station, and when he was being searched he said, 'I have something for you.' Wales then produced a blood-stained cobbler's knife from inside a jacket pocket.

'He was perfectly calm and cool,' the policeman told the court. On being charged, Wales replied, 'That's right.'

Dr Arthur Murray Wood said that at the request of a policeman he had gone to the scene of the crime, where he examined the body of a young woman and confirmed death.

Police Surgeon Douglas Kerr said that when he saw the accused he was perfectly rational but perhaps a little backward.

William Edington, an employee of an organisation connected with child welfare, told how Wales, whom he had never seen before, called at his office on 4 June (the day before the murder) and explained that his wife and child had left him and asked for assistance in persuading them to come home. Wales returned to the office next day to say that his wife had sent the child and wedding ring to his mother's address.

'Will you be seeing her today?' he had asked. Mr Edington told Wales that he would do his best. The witness added that the accused was sensible and clear in his manner.

The trial continued late into the day, and Wales was found guilty by a majority of 14 to 1; but the jury added a strong recommendation for mercy on account of the convicted man's youth.

Lord Anderson sentenced Wales to death, the execution to be carried out on 13 August. A subsequent appeal was dismissed.

As befitting the sombre occasion, the execution day dawned with a steady drizzle falling over the city, but the weather did not deter a group of approximately three hundred people gathering outside the prison.

Those present, however, were prevented by the police from gaining access to the drive leading to the prison doors. The windows of nearby houses were used as vantage points, but what could they expect to see?

The prison clock finally showed 8 a.m. and simultaneously the horn from the neighbouring works sounded, as if bidding a last farewell. Immediately the formal notice, signed by the Governor, Brigadier R.M. Dudgeon, and other officials, had been displayed, there was a stampede to read it and the police were forced to intervene.

But there was one final twist to this tragic affair. A well-meaning Leith businessman announced that a committee would be set up to raise funds to pay the murdered woman's funeral expenses and erect a stone. It was also hoped that there would be enough money to bring up the 9-month-old orphan.

This proposal was firmly opposed by both families. The day following the execution, Florence Hain, the murdered woman's mother, told newspapers that she 'wished no memorial stone and asks for no charity'.

The clock still stands above the entrance to
Saughton Prison. On execution days vigils
were held and tension rose as 8 a.m. approached.

The Wales family revealed that Allan Wales had 'signed a paper'
for an insurance society to pay his wife's funeral expenses. The balance of the money was to be given to Mr and Mrs Wales senior, on
behalf of their grandson. 'No public fund is therefore required for
funeral expenses,' explained Mrs Wales.

She added that they would not accept any public subscription
towards the upkeep of their grandson; the family were quite willing
and able to support him themselves.

Tragedy may have divided the two families, but they were certainly united in grief, pride and independence.

Robert Dobie Smith

On Saturday 15 September 1951, Robert Dobie Smith, a Dumfries
electrician, was hanged at Saughton Jail for the murder of police
Sergeant William Gibson earlier in the year.

There were about twenty people, three of them women, outside the prison as the appointed time for execution approached. At 8.01 a.m. the statutory notice certifying that the sentence had been carried out was posted on the outside of the building. Signatories to this document included the Rev. C. McArthur Chalmers, the prison chaplain, who was minister of Carrick Knowe Church.

For some inexplicable reason, members of the public were prevented from reading the notice until forty-five minutes after it had been displayed, and several, tired of waiting, left after half an hour. Eventually, the police relented and allowed those remaining to go forward in groups of six to examine the notice and satisfy their morbid curiosity.

It was 2.50 a.m. on 22 May that year when the telephone rang in Dumfries Police Station. The call was taken by Constable James Little, and the message was to the effect that there was a madman in Holm Avenue. In the background the policeman could hear the sound of whimpering.

He alerted all men on the beat, asking anyone who was in the vicinity to investigate. Sergeant William Gibson immediately returned to the station to co-ordinate plans. A later message confirmed that the suspect was Robert Dobie Smith and that he was carrying a shotgun.

Shortly after 4 a.m. it was reported that the wanted man had been seen in Irish Street, and Sergeant Gibson set off in a patrol car with Constables Hope and Campbell to investigate. As the vehicle turned into Bank Street, the policemen spotted a man standing erect with his back to the wall, hiding his hands.

As Constable Campbell was later to tell the High Court in Dumfries, Sergeant Gibson remarked that he thought he was the man they were seeking. He stopped the car and asked the suspect what he was doing. Without warning Smith produced a gun and fired, hitting the sergeant and Constable Hope, who were in the front seats of the car.

Constable Campbell, who was sitting immediately behind the sergeant, jumped out of the vehicle and overpowered the man before he could reload the gun. Told by Campbell that he had shot Sergeant Gibson, he allegedly replied, 'It's a pity it wasn't that – Duncan.' This outburst was to be explained later in court.

Despite his serious injuries, Constable Hope struggled to the

County Hotel, where he was helped by the night staff.

At 4.20 a.m. Constable Campbell returned to the police station with the suspect, accompanied by one of the County Hotel staff, carrying a knife and shotgun.

Meanwhile, several people had gathered at the scene and an employee of a firm of wholesale newsagents drove Gibson and Hope to the Infirmary. The sergeant was dead on arrival; Constable Hope had serious injuries to both arms.

Sergeant Gibson left a widow, an 18-year-old son and a 10-year-old daughter. The son was due to sail from Tilbury that day as an apprentice deck officer. After a frantic search, the port officials found the lad as he walked through the dock area. The 44-year-old sergeant had twenty years police service and his brother was also a police officer.

Constable Hope was twenty-six years old, married, with a young child. The two men were near-neighbours in the police houses.

Later in the day, 31-year-old Robert Dobie Smith appeared at Dumfries Burgh Court, charged with murder and attempted murder.

The trial opened at the High Court, Dumfries, on 24 July, Lord Mackay presiding. It was the first murder trial in that court for eighteen years.

Smith faced three charges: (1) stealing twenty-five cartridges from his father's house; (2) in Bank Street, Dumfries, near the junction with High Street, shooting William Gibson, Sergeant of the Dumfries and Galloway Constabulary, with a shotgun in the head; (3) shooting Constable Andrew Hope in both arms.

Constable James Little told the court of the telephone call and the deployment of men in an attempt to arrest the accused.

Andrew Smith, the accused's brother, said that he had gone to bed about 11 p.m. At approximately 1 a.m. Robert came into the room. He had a shotgun and he told the witness to get up as he had something for him to do. Andrew was then told to go to the kitchen where his brother produced the shank of a hammer from his pocket. Robert was pointing a gun at him. The accused then told his brother to go into the living room and to sit at the table.

Robert had a school jotter and told Andrew to write to his instruction. He dictated: 'To Andy, All the best in the world. I hope that you will live till you are sixty and that by the time you are sixty you have stopped snoring. If you come over to this side of the table I will hit you between the eyes with this hammer.'

Dictation continued for about two hours and included, 'When I get out of this door tonight I will shoot the first policeman I see. The right hammer is faulty but the barrel is clean.'

His ramblings continued, 'I, Robert Smith, know how to use weapons because I had six years of killing men.' The accused had spent six years in the navy. His dictation went on, 'There was one girl. She was nineteen. She was too young. If I had married her I would have made an honest and useful citizen, but alas, I am thirty and no further use to the world.'

When the dictation was eventually finished, Andrew was told to dress and the brothers left the house. They went to a telephone box and Andrew was instructed to phone the police with the message that there was a madman in Holm Avenue. That done, the younger man was told to go home.

James Kenneth MacDonald said that Smith had burst into his house in Irish Street at about 3.30 a.m. He had a shotgun and was very upset, apparently at the death of one of MacDonald's young relatives. Smith told MacDonald, 'They're after me. I got one and I'll get another.' Next he mumbled something about having started something and he would have to finish it.

The accused then asked for a pencil and paper. But as MacDonald moved to get them, he was ordered back to bed and to keep his hands under the bedclothes. Eventually Smith produced paper and instructed MacDonald to write, 'I wrote this under duress. I, Robert Smith, killed a man tonight. I held up K. MacDonald and his wife and forced them to write this.'

Smith added his signature and immediately afterwards wrote: 'Dear Ken and Nan, you have been expecting this for some time. You are two of the finest people I know.'

The accused then left the house but returned a few minutes later. He told the occupants that 'they are all around me so don't make any wrong moves'. He had a hammer and bread knife in his possession.

Asked if he had any reason to believe that Smith had any animosity towards the police, MacDonald said that he had been taken to the police station regarding an incident but had been released.

Mrs Annie MacDonald told the court that she had a 19-year-old sister, Joan Gillespie, who had been engaged to Smith, but it had been broken off. He took it hard; it preyed on his mind, she said.

Constable R.J. Richardson explained that on 26 March, with Sergeant Andrew Duncan, he had taken Smith to the police station for loitering in suspicious circumstances and he was later released.

Advocate-Depute Harald R. Leslie KC, in moving sentence, said that he wished to restrict his motion to the charge of murder. In his closing speech he told the court that Sergeant Gibson, inoffensive and defenceless, had been shot by Smith at a range of two feet and PC Hope's arms were seriously injured by a second shot. On the special defence that Smith was insane at the time and was not responsible for his actions, he said that it must be approached with caution.

At the end of the four-day trial the Judge, Lord Mackay, in summing up, told the jury of ten women and five men that a man had been killed by a shotgun and another had been shot at to kill. It had been proved that Smith discharged the gun and the only question was one of responsibility.

The jury were out for thirty-two minutes before returning unanimous verdicts of murder and wounding. The charge of theft had been abandoned.

The sentence was that Smith would be executed at Saughton Prison on 17 August, between 8 and 10 a.m.

On 28 August the Criminal Appeal Court unanimously dismissed Smith's appeal, and the new date for execution was fixed for 15 September.

Three days before the sentence was due to be carried out, it was confirmed that the Secretary of State for Scotland, after careful consideration of the case, had been unable to find sufficient grounds to advise His Majesty to interfere with the due course of the law.

John Lynch

Greenside Row in the 1950s had some of the poorest housing in Edinburgh. Lying in the valley between Leith Street and the Calton Hill, it stretched for approximately 300 yards and consisted of tenements with cul-de-sacs, closes and alleys running off it. The site today is unrecognisable, with major redevelopment having taken place. But it was the scene of one of the most horrific crimes perpetrated in the town – a double child murder.

The time was approaching 5 p.m. on 11 December 1953, when the police were informed that two small girls, Margaret Johnston, aged three, and 4½-year-old Lesley Sinclair were missing. They had last been seen two hours previously. Margaret lived at 9 Queen's Place and Lesley's address was 5 Marshall's Court, Greenside Row.

Neighbours joined the police in searching the congested closes and passageways which abounded in the area. Torches were used in the hunt, which extended to the bushes on the slopes of the Calton Hill. One man thought that he heard the cries of a child and climbed over a fence, but found nothing.

Ironically, it was directly opposite 5 Marshall's Court that the bodies of the children were found about 11 p.m.

The discovery of the dead girls shocked the neighbourhood and residents who had been in bed rose and dressed. They stood in hushed groups, many of them extremely distressed. In the little conversation that took place, it was revealed that several residents had attempted to get into the communal lavatory where the bodies had been found, but the door always seemed to be locked.

Police reinforcements were soon on the scene and constables were posted at the entrance to 5 Marshall's Court, while others guarded the entrance to the lavatory. By a curious twist of fate, Jean Sinclair, mother of one of the dead girls, had twice passed that door.

Quietly and efficiently the routine procedure of taking statements got under way, and at an early stage a bizarre incident took place. Was it conscience, tension, or guilt that caused 45-year-old John Lynch to lunge forward and launch into a loud, almost hysterical, outburst? Lynch was a labourer, who lived in a flat at the address where the bodies had been found.

'Take my name; I'll tell you how it was done,' he reportedly shouted.

Lynch was not at this stage a suspect and he was quietly taken back to his flat. But no doubt his actions had been noted by the police; in the early hours of the following morning Lynch was arrested and charged with murder. He appeared at the Burgh Court and was remitted to the Sheriff.

Mr and Mrs David Curran, mother and stepfather of Margaret Johnston, told newspaper reporters that Mrs Curran had been in her mother-in-law's house at 5 Marshall's Court when Margaret came in and asked for a 'piece'. As she left, the youngster had been told to play on an area of open space, where she could be seen. At about

3.20 p.m., when Mrs Curran's daughters Jeanette (10) and Irene (8) arrived from school, they had gone looking for Margaret. Almost eight agonising hours were to pass before the body of Margaret and her friend Lesley were found.

Residents in small communities are renowned for rallying round in times of disasters and emergencies and the people of Greenside were no exception.

The neighbours immediately set up a fund for the bereaved families and it was hoped to raise £100. When it closed a few days later, £125 had been collected. At Lady Glenorchy's Church, where the girls attended Sunday School, children gave their pocket money to buy a wreath.

On the morning of 16 December, mourners attended the funeral of Lesley Sinclair at Liberton Cemetery. Earlier, four hundred people stood, heads bowed, as Lesley's pathetically small, white coffin was taken from the undertakers at Greenside Place.

Later that day Margaret Johnston was laid to rest at the Eastern Cemetery. Two hundred people were present.

The trial of stockily-built, grey-haired, John Lynch opened at the High Court on 23 March, 1954. It was to last for three days.

Mrs Jean Sinclair told the court that she had reported her daughter missing about 4.45 p.m. At 5.30 p.m. she located her husband in a Leith Street pub where he had called for a drink on his way home from work. He was in the company of John Lynch.

She called her husband over and, curiously, Lynch came with him. Mrs Sinclair explained the situation and, in an attempt to comfort his wife, the husband told her not to worry. Lynch had allegedly retorted, 'Can't you see that Mrs Sinclair is worried?' Turning to Mrs Sinclair the accused said, 'I'll buy you a drink to pick you up.'

While Mr Sinclair went to buy a newspaper Lynch accompanied Mrs Sinclair home. On the way Lynch had told Mrs Sinclair that he had seen the two girls earlier in the afternoon.

'They all knew him,' Mrs Sinclair told the court. 'They called him Uncle Paddy. He was a friendly man.'

Continuing her evidence, Mrs Sinclair said that about 11 p.m. the shout had gone up that the children had been found. Someone put Lesley's body into her arms. She immediately passed the dead child to her husband, then collapsed.

John Robieson, a newsvendor, took the other child, Margaret

Johnston, to the home of her grandmother, who lived on the same top landing where the bodies had been found.

Margaret McKail, whose daughter discovered the girls, said that about teatime she had heard Lynch's voice and loud banging, which could have been the lavatory door. Later that night the daughter told her mother that the lavatory door was locked. This, the witness explained, happened frequently because of a defective lock. She gave her daughter a knife to pick the lock. The girl returned almost immediately to tell her mother that there was somebody lying in the toilet.

Annie Hall, who shared a flat with Lynch, said that when she left for work, a pair of her stockings were hanging in a prominent place. When she returned, one was missing. She identified a stocking in court and confirmed hearing Lynch's outburst about his involvement in the crime.

A piece of floral cloth, taken from the neck of one girl, matched material found in the flat where the accused was living.

The jury took only fifty-five minutes to reach their unanimous verdict of guilty, and John Lynch was sentenced to be hanged at Saughton Prison on 15 April.

As Lord Thomson passed judgement he lifted the black three-cornered cap, and, holding it over his head, added the words, 'which is pronounced for doom'. A subsequent appeal, which put back the execution date, was dismissed.

The morning of 23 April was sunless, and a cold wind was blowing outside Saughton Prison as 8 a.m. approached. A lone policeman patrolled the drive and a few spectators, newspaper reporters and photographers gathered outside the main gate.

At 8.03 p.m. a man in civilian clothes emerged through a small door and pinned up the notice certifying that the due course of the law had been carried out. John Lynch, the double child murderer, was dead, the third person to be hanged at Saughton in twenty-six years.

George Alexander Robertson

George Alexander Robertson must have been familiar with the location of Edinburgh's High Court, immediately behind St Giles' Cathedral. After all, his future wife lived in Tron Square, a short distance away, and in his courting days he surely walked down the High Street on his way to meet her.

But could Robertson ever have believed that one day he would stand in the dock of that very court, charged with the murder of his then former wife (they were divorced in 1950), their son George, and the attempted murder of daughter Jean in Tron Square on 28 February 1954?

As murder investigations go, it was an uncomplicated case and Robertson was arrested within minutes. But it shocked the close-knit community, not only because they knew everyone involved, but also because of the ferocious, frenzied nature of the attacks.

At the time of the crime, newspaper reporters working on the story could find no one living in this small enclave just off the High Street who was prepared to speak. Approximately forty windows overlooked the square, but apparently no resident saw or heard anything. One neighbour, who lived immediately opposite to where the murder had taken place, reluctantly admitted that about 2 a.m. he was awakened by screaming and smashing glass but chose to ignore it.

The dead mother had been one of the organisers of the Tron Square Coronation celebrations, and above her flat was the now faded picture of the queen. Sadly, the mother (and grandmother) of the two victims also lived in Tron Square but several hours were to

A quiet corner in Tron Square

pass before the 78-year-old woman was told of the tragedy. Meanwhile, police photographers were busy at the scene, while groups of children played close by. Hanging from a window were two knotted blood-stained bed spreads, evidence of a pathetic attempt to escape the carnage.

On 1 March, 40-year-old George Alexander Robertson appeared before the Burgh Court and was remitted to the Sheriff without plea. At the Sheriff Court, Robertson indicated that he wanted to plead guilty, but he was not allowed to do so; this point was to be raised again at his trial.

The two-day trial opened at the High Court on 1 June before Lord Thomson, the Lord Justice-Clerk. Robertson faced three charges: (1) the murder of his 39-year-old former wife Elizabeth; (2) the murder of his 18-year-old son, George, a coal porter who was awaiting his call-up for National Service; (3) the attempted murder of his 16-year-old daughter, Jean, who worked for a firm of paper manufacturers.

The trial had caught the imagination of the public, and hours before the case was due to start, a queue of would-be spectators had formed in Parliament Square.

Jean Robertson, the first witness, told the court that her parents had divorced. At the time of her death her mother was Mrs McGarry but her father had been living with them in Tron Square. Following a dispute with her mother, Robertson had left and had not returned before that fateful 28 February.

'Were you afraid of him coming back?' she was asked.

'Yes,' she replied.

'Did you take any steps to prevent him coming back?'

'Yes, we bolted the door. We put a poker in the window. We put a chair behind the door.'

But on the night of the murder they had forgotten to put the chair behind the door. Jean Robertson was awakened by the voice of her father telling her mother in a whisper to 'go ben the kitchen'. The witness said that she then wakened her brother and they went into the lobby.

'What did you see in the lobby?' was the next question. Shaking her head and crying, Jean described how she saw her father use a knife on George, who fell. He then turned on her, pushing her onto a bed and began stabbing her.

Miss Robertson explained to the court that she had injuries to the left side of her stomach and her arm. 'I was screaming. I then heard the outside door being opened. My father rushed out and went downstairs. George was sitting on a chair and he asked me to get a doctor.'

She said she had tied two bedspreads together and hung them out of the window to climb down, but she was unable to use her left arm. Next was the sound of a window being smashed and Jean 'ran ben the kitchen and went out'. There she saw her father carrying her mother over his shoulder and putting her down beside the cooker. Her mother did not move.

Robertson later returned with George and told Jean to get some hot water. Her father said that he would revive him with whisky and water.

A neighbour, Catherine Hay, said that Mrs McGarry (the deceased) had told her several times that Robertson had threatened to kill the family with a hatchet.

On the night of the murder Mrs Hay had been in bed and had heard the kitchen window being broken. George Robertson appeared in the house shouting, 'Larry, Larry'. He was followed by the accused, who had a knife in each hand.

Her husband Lawrence had attempted to pull Robertson back but had been warned to keep out of it or he would get it too. The accused took his son away but returned soon afterwards asking for bandages. He warned the Hays that if they went for the police, they would find his former wife and himself dead.

Detective Sergeant Walter Middlemist said that at 2.37 a.m. Mr and Mrs Hay had arrived at the Central Police Office in the High Street. They were excited, almost hysterical. Accompanied by three policemen, he had gone to Tron Square and found heavy blood staining on the concrete footway. At one point there were naked footprints in the blood.

The policemen then went to Mrs McGarry's door but got no reply, although they heard movement inside. They entered the flat and found the body of Mrs McGarry. Jean was in the flat and George was sitting on a chair. He had a wound in the region of the heart. The accused was lying on the floor with his head in the oven; he was unconscious and there was a strong smell of gas.

Medical evidence confirmed that Mrs McGarry had fifteen

wounds and George fourteen, one through the heart.

The jury took one hour to reach their unanimous verdict of guilty.

After Lord Thomson had passed the death sentence, Robertson asked permission to speak. In a steady voice he said:

> It could have saved a lot of misery if, under the Scottish Act, Section 31, which gives a prisoner the opportunity to plead guilty to crimes, I took advantage of this when I heard that I was charged with murder.
>
> I took advantage of this to forward a letter to the Department asking them to accept this plea to save any more grief to her family and my own and my mother. I think that it is only right if you can in any way help a man in my position again; he may have an opportunity to plead guilty. That is all. I beg to thank Mr Sloan (defence counsel).

Robertson, who was of medium height with dark, wavy hair, was hanged at Saughton on 23 June, the last man to take that short walk to his end in Edinburgh's jail before the repeal of capital punishment.

The formal notice of execution was pinned up in a glass-fronted noticeboard, a few minutes after 8 a.m. It read: 'We the undersigned, declare that the sentence of death was this day executed on George Alexander Robertson in the Prison of Edinburgh in our presence. Dated this 23rd day of June 1954.'

The document was signed by two bailies, the prison governor and chaplain. Beneath was a certificate of death, signed by the prison medical officer. As a precaution, a policeman and prison officer were on duty outside the prison, but few spectators were present.

Where is their final resting place?

Allan Wales, Robert Dobie Smith, John Lynch and George Alexander Robertson are buried in unmarked graves within the grounds of Saughton Prison, but where is the precise location? The answer to that sensitive question is known to a small number of officials and they guard this information with the utmost secrecy.

20

THE SEASON HEARTS ALMOST WENT WEST

Controversy flared among Hearts fans when it was suggested in 2004 that their team should leave Tynecastle Park and play at the home of Scottish Rugby at Murrayfield. The majority resisted the idea of the Scottish Premier League football club ever leaving their beloved Gorgie ground, so long associated with the Maroons.

But as far back as 1939 the Heart of Midlothian were poised to turn their back on their Gorgie base and move westwards to a greenfield site at Sighthill.

At the Hearts' AGM at Tynecastle on 27 June 1938, club chairman Alex Irvine had stated that on the matter of ground extension the club had been negotiating with Edinburgh Corporation, but had failed to agree either cost or conditions.

George Robertson, a shareholder, then moved that a committee, consisting of directors and shareholders, be appointed to report on the feasibility of moving from Tynecastle, and suggested Sighthill as a possible site to build a stadium 'equal to Ibrox, even if it cost £200,000'. The shareholders appointed to the special committee were Sir James Leishman, George Robertson, R.S.K. Galloway, William Wallace, and D. Wilkie. The directors' representatives were A. Irvine and H. Anderson.

Their remit was: (1) to consider the advisability of moving from Tynecastle Park, Edinburgh; (2) to identify possible sites; (3) to estimate the cost to the club of any sites which might appear suitable, should a removal be decided on.

Their findings were released on 3 March 1939. It was revealed that the directors and special committee had met the previous July when full discussions took place about Tynecastle Park, which extended to about five acres. From time to time the club had carried out alterations, but these had been minimal because of the cramped nature of the ground. The committee conceded that facilities were not ideal.

Various improvements had been considered by the club, which would have required the purchase of land from the Corporation, but the cost proved to be prohibitive.

Tynecastle Park had four major disadvantages: (1) it was almost completely hemmed in by buildings, thus preventing major extension; (2) the ground was too small, with no space available for training facilities; (3) the crowd capacity was limited to 53,000, and then only when spectators were packed tightly together; (4) although only rarely had the ground been closed, fear of a large crowd and consequent crushing kept spectators away.

There was no doubt in the opinion of the committee that a ground with a greater stand capacity and covered accommodation for other spectators would draw larger gates. Nevertheless, the Gorgie Road ground had several advantages. It was conveniently located and served by a reasonable transport system from different parts of the city. The biggest gate was 53,000 and the average attendance during the 1937–38 season was 20,000. The population of the city and areas in close proximity was well over 500,000 and Gorgie was within easy reach of a very much larger population in Fife, the Lothians, and Glasgow. It was important to remember, continued the report, that the city was extending to the west. There were six wards in the vicinity with a population of approximately 170,000 – equal to the number of residents in Aberdeen or Dundee.

The special committee had kept in mind the question of cost, convenience and location of any new stadium. The importance of a comfortable stand was recognised, but they also felt that serious consideration should be given to providing roof covering for the cheaper areas of the ground. And any site would require to have adequate tram, bus, and, hopefully, rail transport, in addition to ample parking.

One novel proposal put forward was the possible provision of road or track facilities exclusively for cyclists attending games, with suitable locations where bikes could be left securely. An admirable and cheap form of transport – although it was acknowledged that it would be unsuitable for the bigger games.

To speed up the survey of possible sites, a small subcommittee had been formed and locations visited at Corstorphine, Willowbrae, Stenhouse, and Sighthill. The first three were immediately eliminated as unsuitable, for reasons which included insufficient land to meet the club's requirements, site levels which would be difficult to develop, unsuitable access and public transport facilities.

An investigation of these sites had convinced the committee that it was impossible to obtain in Edinburgh, on almost any terms, anything like sufficient land for a modern first-class ground without paying such a price as to make such a development prohibitive. The cost of building work and layout would have to be considered.

The committee came to the conclusion that the idea of a centrally-located ground should be abandoned; if the club was to move, it would have to be to the suburbs. Fans would have further to travel, and the important question was: would the support given to the club continue even with adequate tram, bus, and rail facilities? A new stadium might also attract additional support.

These were questions the club would have to address quickly, although the committee realised that it might be two or three years before Hearts would be ready to move. The secretary had written to the Scottish Rugby Union requesting a meeting to discuss the possibility of Hearts having the use of Murrayfield on 'big match' days. But the SRU were blunt and to the point: they informed Hearts that they would not consider letting the ground for soccer matches.

The committee report came to the conclusion that if Hearts were seriously considering leaving Tynecastle, Sighthill was the only area that was capable of providing the facilities required. Although the site was two miles west of Tynecastle, 400 acres of Corporation-owned land were available at Sighthill, and so there was a choice of sites. There was reason to believe that the Council would be prepared to feu sufficient land to provide a pitch, stand, track, and practice areas. There would also be adequate parking facilities.

By coincidence, Edinburgh Corporation were also considering the construction of a municipal sports stadium at Sighthill and had reached the sketch-plan stage. There was the possibility of a long-term arrangement by which the Council and Hearts could use the stadium on a joint basis. Hearts could have exclusive use of the ground for league, cup, and other matches, while the stadium would be available to the Corporation during the close season and in the evenings as required.

Sir James Leishman and Mr Irvine, the Hearts' chairman, had met Lord Provost Henry Steele, the City Treasurer, and other senior city officials on 22 December 1938 for discussions on the project. The

Corporation were sympathetic and had promised that full consideration would be given to Hearts' requirements, with particular
reference to the question of transport. It was emphasised that the
construction of a sports ground would take a considerable time and
the Corporation were pressing for details. It was essential, therefore,
that the club gave the project serious and urgent consideration. They
would have to decide whether to remain at Tynecastle or move to a
new location. And if they were to leave Gorgie, would they press on
with their own exclusive stadium or enter into a joint venture with
Edinburgh Corporation?

Hearts were talking 'big', with facilities for 100,000 spectators.
This would include seating for between 15,000 and 20,000, covered
accommodation for 30,000, and room for a further 25,000 behind
each goal area.

Costs were unknown, but it was believed that the stand at Ibrox
had cost £85,000 and Sunderland FC had spent £100,000 on a similar venture. Hearts recognised that expenditure would be very heavy.
Fortunately the club were financially sound. They had no debt, a
substantial credit bank balance, and no burden of any kind on the
ground or stand. It was confidently believed that backing from the
banks or other money sources would be no problem.

The report concluded with the recommendation that the shareholders authorise the directors of the company and the Special
Ground Committee to enter into negotiations with Edinburgh
Corporation with a view to selling Tynecastle Park to the city on
equitable terms. This would be subject to the condition that suitable
facilities would be made available at Sighthill, for the whole operation of the company, including ground, track, stands, covered
accommodation, and complete equipment for a first-class football
ground, with a practice area and adequate parking facilities. The new
stadium would be capable of holding 100,000 spectators. The land
would be acquired on a long term lease or otherwise on terms to be
agreed.

A full report of any proposals would be submitted to the shareholders for their consideration.

Meanwhile, the *Edinburgh Evening News* had joined in the debate
and for three days before the shareholders' meeting had carried out a
poll among Hearts supporters. It resulted: to leave Tynecastle, 133; to
remain, 1078.

On Friday 10 March 1939 the Heart of Midlothian shareholders met in the Oddfellows Hall, Forrest Road, to discuss the Special Ground Committee's report.

Alex Irvine, who chaired the meeting, was asked what accommodation the club wanted, as Tynecastle was capable of holding crowds in excess of 50,000. Irvine replied that, if possible, they wanted nothing less than double the present capacity.

Dr Fraser Lee told the meeting that the report did not lead them very far. They were still in the air as regards possible costs of the Sighthill scheme, and equally so about the effects such a move would have on the great majority of the club's supporters. His experience, particularly among the working classes, was that the move would be distinctly disadvantageous. Amid applause, he concluded: 'Could the club, when exploring the cost of the Sighthill scheme, not find out the cost of improving the stand, acquiring land at McLeod Street, covering part of the ground and constructing new and more space for the training of players?'

The Chairman replied that the kind of Tynecastle he would like to see was based on Everton FC ground. 'It is my ideal ground. There is covered accommodation for all the shilling spectators,' he said.

R.S.K. Galloway, one of the authors of the report, said that anything the committee was proposing was not for the benefit of Hearts but mainly for the comfort of the supporters.

No football club could succeed without the man round the ropes who paid his shilling, and the 'bob' man was not well looked after at Tynecastle, he told the meeting. 'I will say this: that it was the unanimous decision and findings of the whole committee that Tynecastle, judging by modern standards, is out of date. Time is marching on. Give us freedom to make far-reaching investigations on your behalf. The longer you wait, the further you will have to go out. In a few years time, Sighthill will be in the town.'

Committee man Sir James Leishman commented that the club would have to move sooner or later. Tynecastle was too small for Hearts, the leading club in the capital of Scotland. He was in favour of covered accommodation for all, if it could be got, but as regards a 'Greater Tynecastle', it could be achieved only at tremendous cost.

The meeting lasted one-and-a-half hours and the shareholders resolved unanimously that the Special Ground Committee be authorised to enter into negotiations with Edinburgh Corporation for either a new and separate site for the club's purpose, or the association of the club with the corporation's proposed sports stadium at Sighthill. The committee were also authorised to investigate the practicability and cost of up-grading Tynecastle. But all that talk and planning in 1939 came to nothing. Just six months after the decision had been taken, the country was at war.

Fifty-two years on, however, the question of a move from Gorgie was raised again. This stemmed from the publication of the Taylor Report on ground safety, which had been produced after the Hillsborough disaster in 1989. The report recommended that all grounds should be all-seater by August 1994.

Hearts had two options – to rebuild Tynecastle or to construct a stadium on a greenfield site. Either venture would be very costly. The Gorgie club preferred to go for a new site, preferably in the vicinity of the city by-pass.

After months of speculation, Hearts called a press conference on 25 February 1991 when it was announced that Hearts were to seek planning permission to build a stadium at Millerhill, on the east side of the city. The site covered 167 acres adjacent to both the city and Musselburgh by-passes and the development would include office accommodation, retail outlets, a food superstore, 3-star-plus hotel, motel, fast food outlets and a rural craft centre. It was anticipated that 5,000 jobs would be created.

Hearts believed that Millerhill was an ideal location for supporters from Midlothian, East Lothian, and the Borders. There would also be advantages for supporters travelling from the west or Fife, with easy access to the ground and adequate parking within the complex.

It all seemed an ideal solution for Hearts but the former Lothian Regional Council thought differently, rejecting the scheme on the basis that the commercial aspects of the proposed development would impinge on the Green Belt strategy.

Undaunted, Hearts investigated other possibilities and by November 1991 the club announced that a planning application had been lodged for a 100-acre site at Hermiston, on the west side of Edinburgh. This location, the club explained, was adjacent to the by-pass and the proposed junction for the M8 link road. The Edinburgh–Glasgow railway line was less than 200 metres distant with the possibility of a halt being provided.

It was envisaged that the development would be for a stadium capable of accommodating 25,000 spectators, with provision for a future extension. The site could also contain leisure and recreational facilities.

These proposals appeared to be a perfect solution, bearing in mind also that Hearts fans had a nostalgic liking for the west side of the town and the new ground would not be far from Tynecastle.

But local authorities did not make decisions on sentiment and this second application was rejected by Lothian Regional Council on the basis that the proposed development would again be in conflict with Green Belt policy.

A further controversial proposal – that a stadium should be built that Hearts and Edinburgh's other senior football club, Hibernian, could share – also bit the dust.

In February 1993 the club announced that they would remain at Tynecastle. Planning permission was obtained and a timetable for redevelopment was drawn up. At the conclusion of the 1993–94 season, work began in earnest with the flattening of the School End and the excavations needed at the main stand to allow the pitch to be moved 15 feet.

Many of the older Hearts supporters were relieved that a question which has been under consideration off and on for more than fifty years had once and for all been resolved – Hearts would remain at Gorgie, or so it seemed.

But with new moves afoot, what will the twenty-first century bring?

21

THE COMMON PILLAR-BOX
THAT CAUSED A BLOW-UP

When Queen Elizabeth came to the throne on the death of her father George VI in 1952, many Scots expected her to be crowned Queen Elizabeth I. After all, Good Queen Bess was an English monarch only and the new young Queen Elizabeth was the first British sovereign with that name. But it was confirmed she would be Elizabeth II, much to the disgust of a section of the Scottish public.

Against this background of strong feeling and protest over the Queen Elizabeth II decision, the Post Office, in agreement with Edinburgh Corporation, decided to mark the approaching coronation by erecting one of their new pillar-boxes, specially designed to mark the start of the new reign, in the Scottish capital.

They chose a site at The Inch, the Council's newest housing estate, for the box, which would be unique in Scotland as it would bear the royal cypher EIIR.

But uneasiness was growing and on 25 November 1952, just three days before the official ceremony, a pressure group wrote to Scotland's Post Office headquarters in Edinburgh, the Town Clerk, and the Postmaster-General, suggesting that the unveiling should be postponed until the queen's numeral had been legalised.

In reply, Colonel J. Gardiner, Director of the Post Office in Scotland, pointed out that it was not within his province to comment on the argument brought forward in the letter.

And so, on 28 November, top Post Office officials, Edinburgh's senior bailie James Campbell, and others assembled at the junction of Gilmerton Road and Walter Scott Avenue. In front of them, hidden from public gaze by the Union flag, was Edinburgh's newest and Scotland's most controversial pillar-box, bearing the disputed cypher.

As he removed the flag, Bailie Campbell said that the Corporation regarded the site of the pillar-box as a matter of some importance in

The Inch housing scheme, which had been designed in the best possible manner. It was appropriate that the box should be placed just where a new housing development had occurred.

Colonel Gardiner pointed out that the occasion was unique, and from a Post Office point of view, of considerable historical importance. One hundred years had passed since the first pillar-boxes had been introduced to the public service. The first had been erected in Guernsey, Channel Islands, on 23 November 1852. Edinburgh's first box was at Holyrood Road, then the Dumbiedykes, in 1868.

Colonel Gardiner's reference to 1868 is interesting. *The Scotsman*, Saturday 31 May 1856, reported:

> We understand that it has been determined to introduce pillar-boxes into Edinburgh and that six will be immediately erected in convenient locations. The present receiving houses will be retained and it is intended to put up 'indicators' in conspicuous places stating where the nearest receiving house is situated.

At the conclusion of the ceremony, Bailie Campbell posted the first letter, an airmail, to Lord Provost James Miller, who was in Chicago. The letter was 'lifted' immediately by Postman W. Munro and it was anticipated that the message of greetings would reach the Lord Provost two days later, on St Andrew's Day. The brief ceremony had passed without incident, but the police had taken no chances; five men (one an inspector) were present.

Despite the box receiving special police attention, within thirty-six hours the objectors had struck. At approximately 9.20 on the Saturday evening it was reported that the EIIR cypher had been smeared with a black, tarry substance. There was one clue. About the time of the incident a taxi had pulled up in the vicinity and the driver had asked where the new pillar-box was. There were several people in the taxi. Who were they? Pranksters on a Saturday night out, or were there other motives? It was an embarrassment for the police, who had been keeping watch in the area. The vandals had struck minutes before the 'beat man' arrived.

Post office maintenance staff were unable to remove the substance and the box had to be resprayed. Following this incident, the Secretary of State for Scotland, James Stuart, asked the Postmaster-General, Earl de la Warr, to reconsider the policy on pillar-boxes bearing the EIIR cypher in Scotland.

The pillar-box, unique in Scotland,
bore the Royal cypher EIIR

But matters took a more sinister twist exactly a week later when an anonymous caller telephoned an Edinburgh newspaper office and said, 'An unprimed charge has just been put in the new pillar-box. Tell the police.' The police and post office officials were soon on the scene and the box was found to contain a large brown envelope with the message: 'Danger to the P.M.G. We trust that you will pay attention to Mr Stuart.'

From a corner of the envelope there was a six-inch long fuse. Inside the envelope investigators found a lump of gelignite 'about the size of a duck egg', bound with insulating tape. A detonator was placed against the tape.

The safety aspect was played down by the police, but the incident was condemned by Colonel Gardiner, who said that it was regretted that such incidents should place postmen's lives in danger.

On 12 December came reports that there had been an anonymous call to a Glasgow newspaper office, claiming that Mr P. Ure of Carron Ironworks, Falkirk, and Bailie James Campbell of Edinburgh Corporation had received warning phone calls 'from us' in connection with the part they had played in the unveiling ceremony of the Elizabeth II pillar-box. (Boxes which I have examined have the manufacturer's name 'Carron Company Stirlingshire' on the rear.) 'They have been threatened with reprisals that will follow within thirty-six hours if they ever take part in another such ceremony or if Carron Ironworks ever make another pillar-box with the numeral "second"', the message said.

Bailie Campbell denied that any such message had been received, but Mr Ure said the only thing he knew about it was that a man had telephoned him, and, in what was an apparently disguised voice, muttered something about 36-hours' warning. When Mr Ure asked what he was talking about the caller rang off.

On 2 January 1953, following the New Year holiday, a postman emptying the box found another explosive charge. It consisted of gelignite and a detonator. The fuse had been lit, but had gone out. One letter was slightly charred, suggesting that this was a genuine attempt to cause serious damage.

All was quiet for a spell. Then, on 7 February, about 2.40 p.m., two bricklayers working nearby heard the noise of metal striking metal, and on investigation saw a man swinging blows at the box with something wrapped in sacking. He was described as aged about fifty, 5 ft 4 inches tall, thick-set, of sallow complexion and dressed in a brown pin-striped suit. The attacker ran off, leaving behind a 7lb hammer in a sack – and a badly damaged door, which was removed, repaired, and back by the following Tuesday, only four days later.

The bombers came in for their final assault on 12 February. At approximately 10 p.m., two hours after the last collection, the peace of the neighbourhood was rocked by an explosion heard a mile away. All that remained of Scotland's only EIIR pillar-box was the bottom third, with the ragged edges indicating where it had been blown apart. The controversial structure, the pride of the Post Office, was no more. This red box which had had so much national news coverage had survived for only seventy-seven days.

A couple who had been standing at the nearby bus stop saw a young man, about 5 feet 9 inches tall, with curly dark hair and wearing a long dark overcoat, place 'something' in the box, then leave quickly. Shortly afterwards there was a terrible flash and explosion – and the box was gone.

Our family home at that time was in Redgauntlet Terrace, just a street away from the explosion. I missed the excitement, having been invited by the government to help out in the Royal Air Force for a couple of years, but my brother David and sister Anne were in the house.

As David recalled years later: 'We heard a dull thud in the distance. We looked at each other and said, "That's the pillar-box," because there had been threats to do just that and demolish it. We rushed round, and true enough the box was in bits. Pieces were lying all over the place as far as twenty yards away.'

Meanwhile, some residents had pursued a suspect down Walter Scott Avenue, but he escaped.

Chief Inspector Edward Ferrier of the CID said that he believed that the man who had placed the bomb had a good knowledge of explosives. Gelignite had been used.

At lunchtime the following day, a small lion rampant was found on a pile of bricks and rubble where the pillar-box had stood. It remained for about an hour before being removed by the police. Within two days the box had been replaced by a standard red-topped, black-bottomed structure, but with no cypher.

'I cannot say whether or not this pillar-box will be permanent. Our main concern was to restore the facility to the public', explained a Post Office spokesman.

The matter was far from over and in the House of Commons the Postmaster-General, in response to a question regarding the necessity of the EIIR cypher, said that there had been precedents for omitting numerals.

The controversy had quite understandably caused considerable alarm among local residents, and the management committee of the community association made it clear that, unless the authorities could guarantee absolute safety to the public, and in particular to the residents in the immediate vicinity, the erection of another pillar-box with the identification EIIR would not be in the interests of the community.

That message was sent to Sir William Y. Darling, the local MP, the Secretary of State for Scotland, and to the Controller, Post Office Scotland. There is still a post box at the junction of Gilmerton Road and Walter Scott Avenue, and yes, it displays a royal cypher – GVIR!

It was on 25 May 1950 that Edinburgh Corporation took the decision that the street names at The Inch would be taken from the works of Sir Walter Scott. What, I often ponder, would the great

The post box at the junction of
Gilmerton Road and Walter Scott Avenue,
with the royal cypher GVIR

author have made of the great pillar-box dispute had he been alive today? A novel perhaps? 'At dawn, Queen Elizabeth, sitting on a white charger and surrounded by her faithful retainers, set forth from Holyrood, southwards to The Inch housing scheme, where . . .'

22

THE DAY LEITH WENT INTO MOURNING

The First World War brought a surge of patriotic fervour to Britain. Thousands of men rushed to join the services and in many instances they wanted to serve in their local army regiments. Hundreds of Edinburgh and Leith recruits volunteered for the various battalions of The Royal Scots (The Royal Regiment). But with men from the same tenement or street serving together, if any major disaster occurred it could mean a terrible catastrophe for such close-knit communities.

The tragic story of what happened to the men of Leith, Edinburgh's port, shows this only too graphically.

Leith was in a complete state of shock on that never-to-be-forgotten 22 May 1915. It was a Saturday, and older men sat silently in the pubs, their pints before them, but flat, frothless, and forgotten.

Small groups of women had gathered in Leith Walk and the surrounding streets. Some nervously tightened the shawls which were wrapped round their shoulders to protect young babies, while older children clung to their ma's long skirt. A number of the women were weeping quietly and the bairns had tears running down their cheeks because they did not know what was upsetting their mothers.

Rumours had been circulating in the town for some hours. How the stories started was unclear. But it was believed that the 7th (Leith) Battalion, The Royal Scots, had been involved in a disaster – location and circumstances unknown. The obvious place for information was the battalion headquarters at Dalmeny Street Drill Hall but no news was available there

After many hours of anxious waiting, a newsvendor appeared breathlessly at the foot of the Walk with a very large bundle of papers. It was a first extra edition of the *Edinburgh Evening News* carrying early sketchy details of the Gretna railway disaster.

The townsfolk thrust a halfpenny into the vendor's sweaty hand

and snatched a newspaper. Impatiently they turned the pages (the *News* in those days carried the stories on its inside pages), and there on page 5 was the report they all dreaded. The headlines read:

DISASTER TO LEITH TERRITORIALS
TERRIBLE RAILWAY SMASH AT GRETNA
HUNDREDS KILLED AND INJURED
OUR OWN REPORTER'S STORY
SURVIVORS' GRAPHIC NARRATIVES
'A' COMPANY WIPED OUT
PARTIAL LIST OF INJURED

Briefly, the story explained that the crash had occurred at Gretna Junction, eight miles north of Carlisle. Four trains were involved: the troop train, a local train, the London to Glasgow express, and a goods train. Two trains had caught fire. The death toll was believed to have reached a hundred with several hundred more injured:

> A special troop train containing 500 members of the 7th Battalion Royal Scots which was proceeding to Carlisle collided with the 6.10 a.m. this morning from Carlisle as it was being shunted to Quintinshill. Many passengers are reported killed and about 300 soldiers injured.
>
> Both main lines are blocked . . .

Through the long weekend more news filtered through, and by Sunday evening it was reported that the death total had reached 185

The funeral procession passes in front of thousands of silent spectators

and was expected to exceed 200. Crowds in ever increasing numbers gathered outside the Dalmeny Street Drill Hall. Eventually, all they were told was that the first of those who had perished would be brought home that evening. A thousand people lined the route from Dalmeny Street down the Walk to Leith Central Station. They stood in complete silence.

How different from the Saturday just a few weeks previously when the citizens of Leith gave The Royal Scots a rousing send-off from that very station as they left for active service.

That Sunday evening the coffins were reverently carried into the battalion headquarters, where, on the suggestion of Leith Provost Malcolm Smith, palm trees had been brought in to disguise the barn-like appearance of the hall.

Next day the first of the victims were laid to rest in Rosebank Cemetery at the junction of Pilrig Street and Broughton Road. A short private service was held in the drill hall where the coffins lay, each covered with a Union flag. Family wreaths and flowers had been laid on the coffins of those who had been identified.

The service was conducted by the Rev. William Swan, South Leith Parish Church, and the Rev. W. Harvey, Lady Glenorchy's Church. Both ministers were chaplains to the 7th Royal Scots. Afterwards relatives were admitted to the drill hall.

It is only a 12-minute steady walk from Dalmeny Street to

With full military honours the men of
The Royal Scots were taken to their last resting place

Rosebank Cemetery, and 3,150 soldiers, heads bowed and rifles reversed, lined the route. At 3 p.m. all traffic stopped, and thousands of citizens from both Leith and Edinburgh stood tightly packed and shoulder-to-shoulder on the pavements. Shops closed and blinds were drawn as a mark of respect.

Leith Town Council in their robes, led by Provost Smith, were present to pay their last respects to the men of Leith. Edinburgh was represented by many notable citizens, including Lord Provost Robert Kirk Inches, who, ironically, was to be knighted in the year of Gretna. Leith's Member of Parliament, G.W. Currie, was also present.

First to be buried were the remains of forty-eight unidentified soldiers, carried in Red Cross motor vehicles, four coffins in each ambulance. In the funeral procession were the pipes and muffled drums of the 16th Royal Scots and the Argyll and Sutherland Highlanders. Soldiers from the 16th Royal Scots formed the bearer party, but the public were excluded from the cemetery.

All day soldiers had been preparing the mass grave which measured 24 yards long by 3 yards wide and deep. Three coffins were lowered into each lair, and while the ceremony was in progress, work continued, preparing resting places for more soldiers.

It was 5 p.m. before the last of the forty-eight coffins had been interred and one hour later the tragic ceremony continued, as more and more young soldiers were laid to rest.

A message was sent on behalf of the king and queen to General Sir John Spenser Ewart. It read:

> Please express to the Royal Scots heartfelt sympathy of the King and Queen with all ranks in the loss of gallant comrades through this terrible railway accident and assure the bereaved families how much their Majesties feel for them in their overwhelming sorrow.

The graves and the memorial to the 7th (Leith) Battalion, The Royal Scots, are located at the far right corner of Rosebank Cemetery. But what were the circumstances leading up to this major catastrophe which, after more than eighty years, ranks as Britain's worst railway disaster, with 227 killed, 214 of them Royal Scots, and a further 246 injured?

Many of the Gretna victims were little more than youngsters from Leith and thereabouts; they had just completed their training at Peebles before volunteering to join the 7th Battalion for overseas

The Gretna Memorial in
Rosebank Cemetery, Pilgrig Street

duties. Shortly afterwards, the townsfolk turned out in their hundreds at Leith Central Station to bid the battalion farewell. Never was the word 'farewell' more appropriate. After a short spell at Stenhousemuir, when, time after time rumour spread through the camp, the word finally went out: 'It's the Dardanelles.'

Reveille was very early on that fateful day, and by 3.45 a.m. all were aboard the first of two troop trains at Larbert station. It carried 470 men from 'A' and 'D' companies, and consisted of fifteen carriages, eight men with full kit to a compartment, and the doors were locked. But the men were in safe hands. After all, engine driver Francis Scott in his long career had been entrusted with transporting no fewer that three successive monarchs: Victoria, Edward VII, and George V.

The train was pulled by a coal-burning engine, carriages were constructed of wood, and were gas-lit from tanks located beneath the carriages. At the rear was a waggon containing ammunition. It was all a recipe for disaster.

A simple stone for The Royal Scots

There was a short stop at Carstairs, where light-hearted banter took place between the troops and some women on their way to work. Gradually silence descended as the men drifted off into sleep, for many their last sleep . . . and the train sped closer to disaster.

Quintinshill signal box, the scene of the catastrophe, stood close to Gretna and about eight miles north of Carlisle. The tracks consisted of main 'up' and 'down' lines, supplemented by 'loops' at each side. On the morning of the accident both 'loops' were occupied by goods trains, leaving the two main lines free – but there were three passenger trains converging on the signal box.

The London–Glasgow express was heading north and running late. A decision was taken to allow the north-bound local 'passenger' to leave Carlisle and go forward to Quintinshill, where it was moved onto the 'down' line to allow the Glasgow express through. Meanwhile, the troop-train was thundering south, but the signalmen forgot about the 'local' which was on the same line and standing only yards from their box. They forgot, yet one of them had hitched a lift to work on it!

Suddenly, with the screeching of brakes the troop train smashed into the 'local', sending carriages sprawling over the 'up' line. Then,

The poignant tribute on the base of the Gretna Memorial

to add to the carnage, the Glasgow-bound express ploughed through the wreckage. The troop train, more than 200 yards long, was reduced to a fraction of its original length.

What happened next is best told by one of the survivors, my father, 2567 Private Alexander Thomson, then only seventeen years and eight months old, and on his way to the bloody Dardenelles.

> The carriage which my comrades and I shared seemed to rise up and sink down again in the space of a few seconds, then list dangerously over a steep embankment. Cries and screams rent the air and the hiss of escaping steam was deafening. One by one we climbed through a compartment window and on to the line. What a sight met our eyes!
>
> The wreckage was piled at least 30 feet high and terror-stricken men and women were staggering about amid the confusion. No battlefield could compare with this.
>
> There was no advance or retreat; it had to be faced. Many were already dead; many more horribly injured. Worse still was the lot of the men trapped in the wreckage, never to leave that heap of twisted metal alive, for fire broke out and robbed them of their last chance of being rescued.

Immediately, those who could assist were involved in rescue work, soon to be joined by the women from Gretna, who brought their very bed linen. The dead and injured were carried down the steep

embankment to an adjoining field. Worse was to follow. The gas
tanks began to explode, sending debris high into the air, some of it
falling on the injured men, who had to be evacuated.

By early afternoon all possible rescue work had been completed. A
roll call revealed that only seven officers and fifty-seven other ranks
answered. The Royal Scots survivors were put into goods waggons
and taken to Carlisle for a wash, meal and rest. By 10 p.m., however,
the survivors were back at the railway station and on their way to
Liverpool. But these men were destined not to sail on the *Empress of
Britain*. A War Office instruction ordered them back to Edinburgh.

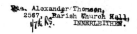

Pte. Alexander Thomson,
2567, Parish Church Hall,
17th R.S.   INNERLEITHEN.

THOMAS J. CONNOLLY,   20, LEITH WALK,
SOLICITOR.
TELEPHONE N? 663 LEITH.   LEITH, 18th February 1916.

Dear Sir,

                    QUINTINSHILL ACCIDENT.
            Claim against the Caledonian Railway Company.

        I have to thank you for your post-card of 16th inst noting
your present address.

        After I saw you on Wednesday, I sent the Company full particu-
lars of your claim. Their Solicitor has now written me as follows:-

        "I am in receipt of yours of the 16th inst.

        "The position of the Company in regard to this claim is
"similar to that in the case of the other claims in your hands
"arising out of this accident.

        "It is unfortunate that your client did not sooner intimate
"his claim. The Company have been prejudiced by the delay and
"that may be founded on.

        "The matter has my attention"

In spite of what is stated in that letter I hope to be able to recover
something for you, as I have done in other cases placed in my hands.
You will keep in mind to let me have any further change of address
immediately it occurs until your claim has been disposed of. Whenever
I have an offer in settlement of your claim, I shall submit same to
you.

                    I am,

                    Yours faithfully,

A letter received by Private Alexander Thomson of
The Royal Scots in connection with his claim for
compensation following the Gretna railway disaster.
Private Thomson was the author's father.

As they marched from the docks to Lime Street station, they were stoned by some youngsters who, because of the bedraggled appearance of the soldiers, assumed that they were German prisoners!

By 10 p.m. on 23 May, the seven officers and fifty-seven men were back in Leith, all that remained as a fighting force. The previous morning 470 had left from Larbert, carrying the men on the first part of the journey to the front.

There was a Board of Trade inquiry and, because of the rumours in circulation that the line had been sabotaged, the proceedings were held in public.

As a result of the findings, George Hutchinson (guard) and signalmen James Tinsley and George Meakin appeared at the High Court in Edinburgh on 15 September on charges arising from the crash. Hutchinson was found not guilty, but Tinsley and Meakin were sentenced to three years' penal servitude and eighteen months' imprisonment respectively. Compensation was paid to the victims. My father received £14 (value today: about £417) for surviving that blazing inferno.

One year on, the people of Leith remembered those who perished in the catastrophe. On 22 May 1916, the *Edinburgh Evening News* published messages of condolence – there were 218 of them, filling a full page. Across the seven columns was the headline:

ANNIVERSARY OF GRETNA DISASTER – IN MEMORIAM

And surely unique in British journalism, the newspaper published this brief message of introduction:

> Seven newspaper columns of In Memoriam notices form a remarkable tribute to the memory of the brave lads who met their death in the Gretna holocaust. The facts of the train disaster, the greatest that ever took place in the history of British railways, are still poignantly fresh in public memory. The troop train, in which there were two companies of the 7th Royal Scots, was travelling from Larbert and ran into a local passenger train on the Caledonian line at Quintinshill and the Scottish express from Euston immediately afterwards crashed into them both. The number of killed or missing was officially stated to be 214. The supreme tragedy is contained in the word 'missing'. Over seventy bodies were unidentified, consumed entirely in the flames or burned beyond recognition. Edinburgh and Leith will never outlive the memory of the disaster – the outcome, simply, of a man's momentary forgetfulness.

One particularly sad message read:

> CUMMING. In loving memory of our dear son, Private John
> Cumming (No. 1515), 7th Royal Scots who died at Carlisle on 22d
> May, 1915, from injuries received in Gretna troop train disaster of
> same date, aged 17 years.
> > O for the touch of a missing hand
> > And the sound of a voice that is still.
> (Inserted by his sorrowing mother and father, 32 Albert Street)

As the years passed, memories faded and the notices became fewer
and fewer. On the fiftieth anniversary, in 1965, the In Memoriam column of the *News* included only two references to Gretna. John
Cumming was still fresh in the memory of his brothers and sisters.
The second message said:

> 1st/7th Royal Scots. In memory of men of No. 13 Platoon who lost
> their lives in Gretna train disaster, May 22, 1915. 'LEST YE FORGET'

At the entrance to Rosebank Cemetery there is a plaque which reads:
'Gretna Memorial. Celtic Cross inside marks the mass grave of 210
men killed in Britain's worst rail disaster, May 1916.'

The number of soldiers who died as a result of the Gretna disaster
was 214 and the year was 1915. Not every Royal Scot was buried at
Rosebank. At least twelve were interred privately in the days following the accident at the Eastern, Warriston, Piershill and Seafield
Cemeteries, with another two at Musselburgh.

A small reminder at the entrance to Rosebank Cemetery.
The year and the number of the men killed are wrong.

23

THE NIGHT THE
ZEPPELIN BOMBERS STRUCK

Leith had a brutal baptism to the horrors of war through the Gretna tragedy, but only a few months later the residents of both the port and Edinburgh itself were to face an unforgettable night of terror and destruction when German Zeppelins raided.

When the Lord Provost's subcommittee 'A' met at the City Chambers on 18 February 1916, they were acutely aware that air attacks on Edinburgh and Leith were strong possibilities; Zeppelins had already bombed areas of England, causing death and damage.

The meeting, chaired by Lord Provost Robert K. Inches, had been convened to consider two items: (1) The Lights (Scotland) No. 1 Order which had been issued by the Secretary of State for Scotland on 9 February that year, under the Provisions of the Defence of the Realm Regulations; (2) a motion by Councillor Lorne Macleod in the following terms: 'To consider anew the arrangements for the city in connection with aircraft invasion.'

The committee was advised and noted that in the event of the police being informed that hostile aircraft were within a certain distance of the city, the electric light in the streets would be turned down to a dull glow, not visible from the aircraft, and likewise would be turned down in private houses where electricity was used. This, if the intimation was received after dark, would be a warning to people in the street and to those in the houses where there was electric light, that an attack was imminent.

As no gas lamps in the streets were lit, nothing needed to be done with them. It was not practicable to turn off quickly the supply of gas to houses with gas lighting, so they would not get a corresponding warning to that given to electric light users. It was pointed out that if an attack was launched late at night the lights might not be on and the residents would be in bed.

Consequently, the first warning of enemy raiders would be when bombs were dropped.

The committee went on to consider the question of providing audible warning, possibly using hooters, buzzers or sirens, but the Councillors decided that any of those methods were unnecessary and undesirable. There had been a Zeppelin raid at Southend and, as the siren sounded, crowds rushed into the streets to watch the attacker.

Evidence given at coroners' inquests in England proved that most casualties were in the street. It had also been proved that the use of a sound warning could be beneficial to the enemy. At Southend a Zeppelin passed over the darkened city, unaware of the town below. The raider returned when the crew picked up the sound of the siren which had been installed at the electric light works to warn the inhabitants. Bombs were then dropped on the town.

There had also been instances of warnings being sounded, causing alarm among the citizens, but with no attack taking place. And in big communities, it was reported, 'There are always many persons who have weak hearts or are in dangerous stages of illness, to whom great excitement might prove injurious or fatal.'

It was interesting that the Secretary of State had not taken the responsibility of recommending or ordering warning sirens to be used, but had left local authorities to make their own decisions. Edinburgh's Chief Constable Roderick Ross was strongly against the use of audible warning.

After lengthy discussion, the subcommittee approved unanimously: (1) that it was not expedient to give the public warning of a possible air attack by sound signals; (2) that the Chief Constable be authorised to advise the public accordingly; (3) that the contents of the notices which he proposed to insert in the newspapers and circulate by means of handbills be delivered to every house and by way of posters be exhibited at certain places.

The citizens of Edinburgh and Leith did not have long to wait, and the authorities' worst fears were realised when, at approximately 11.25 p.m. on Sunday 2 April 1916, a Zeppelin was sighted crossing the Firth of Forth west of Inchkeith and travelling towards Leith Docks. Shortly afterwards, a bomb was dropped at the west end of the Edinburgh Dock, sinking two rowing boats and breaking skylights in two Danish sailing vessels.

The Albert Dock was the next target; incendiary bombs fell on the quay and a nearby yard. Both fires were quickly extinguished. Soon afterwards, an explosive hit Watt & Jackson's grain warehouse at Timber Bush. The roof and part of the wall were damaged, causing masonry to fall onto adjoining properties, with considerable further destruction. A wall at the edge of the harbour quay and close to the Customs House was struck and the blast blew in many house, shop and office windows.

The enemy then turned their attention to the civilian population and a bomb fell at 2 Commercial Street, destroying part of the tenement roof and wall. Robert Love (66) was killed by shrapnel as he lay in bed. An incendiary pierced the roof of the tenement at 14 Commercial Street, went through a room occupied by an elderly woman and into the flat below, where it exploded in flames. According to the contemporary police report, the woman calmly got out of bed, poured water through the hole made by the bomb 'and thus prevented a serious fire'.

Minor damage was also done at 45 Sandport Street, and a bomb which landed on the pavement at 9 Sandport Street did no harm.

Not so lucky was the Innes & Grieve whisky bond; an explosive hit the building, which was destroyed. The estimated loss (including contents) was £44,000 and there was no cover for this type of damage. Nearby premises were affected by the blast.

And still the rampage continued. An incendiary struck the dwellings at 15 Church Street, damaging a house occupied by a soldier, his wife and three children. It then penetrated the floor into the downstairs flat where a man, his wife and five children were at home. Although both premises were set alight and considerable damage done, no one was injured.

Not so lucky was the minister who lived at St Thomas Church manse in Mill Lane, where the thirteenth bomb to be dropped in Leith almost completely wrecked the house, causing an estimated £1,000 damage. The minister, his wife and servant had retired for the night and had a 'miraculous' escape! Unfortunately, the manse was not insured against enemy action.

Leith Hospital in Mill Lane had a close call with a bomb falling on the gravel at the front of the building, but there was no damage; nor was there any problem with a similar incident in the playgound of the adjacent St Thomas School.

A short time later explosive bombs were dropped at 200 Bonnington Road. One fell in the court, breaking windows and damaging doors. Alas, the one-year-old son of Robert Robb was killed as he lay in bed. He was struck by a piece of shell, which came through the bedroom window.

An explosive landed on the railway line near Bonnington tannery and failed to explode, but a second damaged the leather manufacturing tank.

On 7 April the Leith Chief Constable, reporting to the Scottish Office, said:

> The only warning given to the population of this town of an approach by enemy aircraft was the lowering of the electric light and as the electric light is not general only a small percentage of the inhabitants received the warning. The public feeling is that the users of gas should be put on the same footing with the users of electricity. If it were practicable to manipulate the gas supply in the same manner as electricity it would ease the public mind as it is quite evident that the people consider it more secure in the open than in their dwellings. Personally I think the less people know about the presence of enemy aircraft, the better.

The Chief Constable also drew attention to the large number of ships lying in Leith Roads, fully lighted and visible from a long distance. He wrote:

> A better guide for a Zeppelin could not be got. On the night of the raid the Zeppelin came to Leith across the line of the shipping and not till the bombs were falling on Leith were the lights on the ships extinguished. It seems so ridiculous to have the town of Leith in darkness while the sea in front of it is illuminated. This illumination in the Firth of Forth is causing great uneasiness among the inhabitants of this town. Something should be done before this state of uneasiness breaks out into indignation.

The Scottish Office response was swift, and on 10 April they wrote to the Chief Constable stating that the Secretary of State had contacted the Admiralty regarding the lighting of shipping off Leith. Orders had been issued 'prohibiting the docking and undocking of merchant ships at Leith during the hours of official night . . . No lights of any description visible from outboard will be permitted in mercantile shipping anchored in the Leith and Granton roadsteads.'

In a report dated 12 April by the Leith Chief Constable to the Scottish Office at Whitehall, he said:

From the position in which the bombs were dropped it is evident that those in charge of the Zeppelin were following the course of the Water of Leith from Leith Docks to Edinburgh as the bombs dropped were not more than 100 yards from the said Water of Leith at any point except the one dropped in the Edinburgh Dock.

There were a great number of premises rendered insecure through the breaking of glass in windows, doors etc., by the explosion of the bombs and although goods in many cases were exposed, not one case of pilfering has been reported to the police. Though the inhabitants rushed into the streets their conduct was on the whole very good. The authorised police force was assisted by 250 special constables who gave valuable assistance.

The Chief Constable of Midlothian reported that a bomb had been dropped at Longstone, Slateford, Parish of Colinton, when the windows of twenty-three dwelling-houses were broken. The cost of the damage was estimated at £5.

A bomb was dropped the same night at Cameron Bank Dairy, Peffermill Road, in the Parish of Liberton. The windows of two houses were broken and the cost of replacing them was £1.

At 7 p.m. on 2 April the telephone rang in the Edinburgh City Police HQ. It was a message from the Post Office instructing them 'to be prepared to take action'. The wording would have been meaningless to the general public, but it was immediately recognised by the police as a pre-arranged signal from the military authorities, warning of a possible air-raid.

Two hours and five minutes later came the second part of the message: 'Take air-raid action.' Immediately, the police put their plan into operation. The electric light department were instructed to lower all lights, which would warn the public of an impending air attack.

All traffic was stopped, and lights on vehicles were extinguished. The Central Fire Station and Red Cross were alerted. Police stations were informed, and all men then off duty were ordered to report. The Special Force were also called out.

At 11.50 p.m. bombs were reported to be exploding in the Leith area, and from that time until about 12.25 a.m. on Monday 3 April, 24 bombs, 18 high explosives and 6 incendiaries fell on Edinburgh.

The first indication that the city was under direct attack was when a high explosive bomb fell on vacant land at Bellevue Terrace.

External damage, George Watson's College, Archibald Place
(reproduced by kind permission of the Blair-Morrison Library,
George Watson's College)

Although there were no reported injuries, front and rear windows were blown out in twenty houses. Windows in the tenement at 48 and 50 Rodney Street and in nine shops in the street in Heriot Hill Terrace, Cornwallis Place, Summer Place, Canonmills School and at Neil's Printing works were also cracked. Bellevue Parish Church had seven windows broken.

An incendiary landed on the Mound, 400 yards from the castle, but caused no damage.

There was a serious incident at Lauriston Place when a high explosive bomb hit the house at no. 39, occupied by Dr John McLaren, wrecking the roof and the wall which divided the house from no. 41. Although both premises were occupied, no one was injured. Unfortunately 27-year-old David Robertson, a discharged soldier who lived at 4 Graham (now Keir) Street, who was walking in the street, was struck in the stomach by a piece of shrapnel and subsequently died in the Infirmary.

George Watson's College, which at that time was located in

A wrecked classroom in George Watson's
(reproduced by kind permission of the Blair-Morrison Library,
George Watson's College)

Archibald Place, Lauriston, was also a casualty of the raid; a bomb landed in the playground and the school had to be closed for a week while repairs were made. The incident had its lighter moments, none more so than when the pupils discovered that they were to have an unexpected holiday.

Subsequently a plaque was placed on the outside wall, close to where the bomb had fallen. It read: 'This city was raided by a German airship on the night of April 2, 1916. Near this spot a bomb exploded, causing serious damage to the college buildings.' When the school was later demolished the plaque was taken to the new building in Colinton Road, where it is displayed on a classroom wall.

Many windows were shattered at the Royal Infirmary and in nearby Chalmers Street. Then at approximately 11.55 p.m. the raider crossed the Meadows, the open ground south of the Infirmary, dropping a bomb which caused no damage. Not so fortunate, however, was part of a tenement building in Marchmont Crescent, where a high explosive landed and went off on impact. A large section of

The plaque on the Castle Rock which marks the Zeppelin bomb

bomb careered through three flats and came to rest on the floor of the bottom flat next door.

An old tenement at 183 Causewayside, which consisted of single and double-room houses on five floors was practically wrecked, with the front wall taking the brunt of the blast. Remarkably, only six people were injured, including three of the Porteous family. Rose Porteous and Private Thomas Porteous (17), who was home on leave, were detained in the Infirmary, along with Jessie Halkett. Two-month-old Beatrice Pinkerton was described as suffering from 'slight shock'.

Incendiaries were dropped in the rear gardens at Hatton Place and Blacket Place but no damage was caused.

The White Hart Hotel, 34 Grassmarket, suffered considerable damage from a bomb which landed on the pavement. Windows were blown out on both sides of the Grassmarket, West Bow and West Port. Four people were injured, including William Breakey, a 45-year-old carter who lived at the Corn Exchange Buildings. He was struck by shrapnel and died later from his wounds.

There was also an attempt to destroy the castle. The high explosive fell harmlessly on the south-west rock, although again house windows in Castle Terrace, Spittal Street and Grindlay Street were blown in.

At the spot where the bomb exploded there is a plaque which over

The White Hart building in the Grassmarket, damaged by a
Zeppelin bomb

the years has blended with the rock and foliage. It reads: 'On this
spot a bomb fell during the German air raid – 2nd April, 1916.'

Round the corner at 21 Lothian Road, the County Hotel took the
full force of the attack. Although only one person was injured, the
hotel roof was destroyed, while the rear wall and eighteen rooms
were damaged. The hotel at 31 Lothian Road was also affected by the
bombing.

In the valley of the Water of Leith, near Coltbridge Gardens, a
dovecot was demolished and the embankment washed away.
Windows were damaged at Coltbridge Gardens, Belford Place and
Park, Douglas Crescent and Magdala Crescent. Twenty-eight windows were blasted out at Donaldson's Hospital School.

Marshall Street on the south side of the city, however, was the area
that took the brunt of the attack and suffered the greatest number of
casualties. A bomb fell opposite no. 16, destroying the houses on the
first floor, staircase and cellar. Other properties suffered damage to a
lesser degree.

Casulties were high, with six immediately reported dead and seven
injured. Those who perished were: William Smith (15), waiter; John
Smith (45), tinsmith; Henry George Rumble (17), occupation
unknown; Victor McFarlane (age unknown), hotel waiter; 5-year-old
David Thomas Graham, who all lived at 16 Marshall Street; and

William Ewing (23), of 33 Marshall Street. Those who suffered injuries were aged between three and seventy years of age, and included Private Thomas Donoghue (24), 3/4 The Royal Scots, who was stationed at Loanhead. He died at the Royal Infirmary on 10 April.

Still the havoc continued. In nearby Haddow's Court, Nicolson Street, an explosive damaged property. Three people were injured, one severely, and six days after the attack, 74-year-old James Farquhar died. The premises of D. & J. McCallum, Spirit Merchants, were demolished, while windows in Haddow's Court, Nicolson Street and Simon Square suffered extensive damage.

It is only a short distance to the St Leonard's area and at 69 St Leonard's Hill the staircase was wrecked and the building badly damaged. But worse, four-year-old Cora Edmond Bell was killed. Her mother Isabella (36) and sister Alice (2½) were injured and detained in the Royal Infirmary.

Next the bombers turned their attention to the King's (Holyrood) Park, but, not surprisingly, the damage was minimal. A section of boundary wall was hit as was the roof of a bonded warehouse. The bond also lost 341 panes of glass!

A comprehensive police report on the incidents of that night concluded that it had not been possible to obtain the exact time at which the various bombs had been dropped, and it was therefore difficult to say what exact course the attackers had taken.

Mrs Lawson, who lived at Prestonfield Lodge, confirmed that she had seen two airships at 12.15 a.m., one a little higher than the other, in the park at the time the bombs were dropped in the vicinity. The witness also said that a 'strong blinding' light had been displayed by one of the airships, which then turned towards the city centre. Pieces of the bombs which had been collected at various parts of the town were handed over to the military authorities for examination.

The police confirmed that twenty-four incidents had been logged. Eleven people died on that night of destruction, but the number who were injured is uncertain; many who were injured did not seek medical attention.

In a letter to the Secretary of State for Scotland, dated 5 April, the Chief Constable wrote:

It is really remarkable, having regard to the damage done, that the fatalities have been so small and had it not been that several persons in the case of the Marshall Street explosion came out of their houses and entered the common stair, the loss of life would have been reduced to three persons.

The night of 2/3 April had caused considerable concern in Edinburgh and on 6 April the Lord Provost's Committee, as the War Emergency Committee, met at the City Chambers to consider the air-raid.

The Town Clerk read a letter which had been sent to Viscount French, Commander-in-Chief Home Forces, seeking details about measures to be taken for the defence of the city. It was also revealed that the Lord Provost was in London and had arranged a meeting with French to discuss the matter.

The Committee also saw correspondence about the dangers arising from a factory in Edinburgh which produced explosives. The Lord Provost, while in London, took the opportunity to meet officials from the Ministry of Munitions to express the Council's concern.

Chief Constable Ross reported on the police involvement during the raid. He also said that, on the authority of the magistrates, he had made arrangements for the funerals of certain of the victims, for the temporary accommodation of families who had been rendered homeless, and for the relief of victims who were in need of help.

A subcommittee of six was then appointed to consult the local military on the defence of the city and other matters. This subcommittee reconvened the following day but, and no doubt for security reasons, the minute of that meeting simply reveals that the Councillors met military representatives.

On 8 April the War Emergency Committee again convened at the City Chambers and the first item on the agenda was a letter from the military authorities replying to the Lord Provost who had sought assurances on the defence of the city. It read:

General Headquarters,
Home Forces,
Horse Guards,
London, S.W.

6th April, 1916

Sir,

I am directed by the Field Marshal Commander-in-Chief, Home Forces, to acknowledge the receipt of your letter of the 3rd instant, in which you refer to the fact that guns are not at present mounted for the defence of the City of Edinburgh, and in which you express your astonishment that this has not been done.

I am to say that the City of Edinburgh has not been forgotten, and that, when available, guns will be mounted for its defence; but I am also to point out that there are many other places which are of vital importance to the country, and to the successful prosecution of the war, and that the City of Edinburgh is to be considered with these.

The Field Marshal also hopes you will understand that guns and lights cannot be provided at short notice, and that the fact that the aerial defence of the whole of the United Kingdom is not at present complete is not due to the want of recognition of its importance on the part of the Military Authorities, but to the unprepared state of the country on the outbreak of war.

I have the honour to be,
Sir,
Your obedient
Servant,
(Signed) F. Shaw
Major General, General Staff, Home Forces

There were two other items on the Committee's agenda that day: a deputation was heard from the Rotary Club on the measures which might be taken for warning the public in the event of an air-raid; the Committee had under consideration the question of whether any further arrangement should be made for giving intimation of approaching enemy aircraft.

It was suggested that warning might be given to the users of gas, similar to that given to users of electricity. After discussion, the Committee resolved to recommend to the magistrates and Council that the Gas Commissioners be requested, on the appropriate signal being given by the police, to reduce the pressure if that could be done with safety. The Committee further agreed that should the foregoing recommendation be approved, representation be made to the Leith Corporation suggesting that the same arrangement should be made in Leith.

As the Zeppelins drifted and droned over Leith and Edinburgh and the horrors of war were brought home to the civilian population, few of those who wandered into the streets to stare at the cigar-shaped objects would have been aware of the historical background which culminated in the production of those bombers. The name was derived from the German inventor, Count Ferdinand von Zeppelin, who was born in 1838 and was a career soldier.

He retired from the army in the early 1890s and devoted his time to the study of air travel, producing his first aircraft in 1900. By 1910 there was a Zeppelin service operating between Berlin and Lake Constance. With the advent of the Great War, the Zeppelins were adapted for military purposes and bombing raids were launched on several areas of Britain.

Von Zeppelin died on 8 March 1917, eleven months after his aircraft made their attacks on Leith and Edinburgh. The use of airships was commercially abandoned in the 1930s.

24

LEITH THREATENED BY JOHN PAUL JONES

The man credited with being the founder of the modern American navy was a Scot, John Paul Jones. He made his reputation as a privateer sailing under the American flag, but when he came to attack Edinburgh's port of Leith in 1770 he found things did not go as he had planned. And the £200,000 ransom he was demanding for sparing the harbour town slipped from his hands.

It was Sunday 17 September and the good citizens of Leith worked frantically to prepare defences. The danger came from the 40-gun *Bon Homme Richard* under the command of Paul Jones, together with the support vessels *Vengeance* and *Pallas* lying off Inchkeith Island in the Firth of Forth.

But the danger was averted when a gale blew up and drove the enemy ships out to sea. No doubt the citizens breathed a sigh of relief at their good fortune, but was it nature or Divine Providence (following a prayer offered by the Rev. Robert Shirra, a Kirkcaldy minister) that prevented the attack?

Several stories have been told about that memorable incident – that Mr Shirra took an old chair to the beach, where he sat and prayed, vowing that if God did not answer his prayers and raise a storm to drive the privateers away from the coast he would remain there until the tide came in and he drowned. Or did he go to the water's edge where, accompanied by a large terror-stricken congregation, he fell on his knees and asked for deliverance?

The most likely explanation is that the minister, seeing a crowd watching the ships, called at the home of one of his congregation and asked what was causing all the excitement. On being told that the ships in the distance were American privateers, Mr Shirra allegedly prayed: 'Lord, if they are enemies, put thou a hook in their nose and a bridle in their jaw and take them back to where they came from.'

Shortly afterwards Mr Shirra made his way to the shore to witness the spectacle, where, it is said, he remarked to a friend: 'The Lord wi' His wind could easily blaw them out of the Firth.' Whether by faith or good fortune the gale rose, and Jones and his vessels were blown out the Firth never to return.

The villain of the piece was the son of a Kirkcudbright gardener and was born John Paul on 7 July 1747, in a cottage overlooking the Solway Firth. It was not until 1773 that he adopted the name Paul Jones. Curiously, he had a Leith connection, for it was believed that his grandfather kept a 'mail-garden' or 'public', better known today as a market-garden, in Leith. At the age of twelve he was apprenticed to a shipowner in Whitehaven.

Paul served on the slaver *King George* and by his nineteenth year he was mate on another slaver, *The Two Friends*. During the period 1769–70 he commanded the merchantman *John* and made two trips to the West Indies. While in Tobago on the second voyage he allegedly flogged the carpenter, Mungo Maxwell, for neglect of duty, and several weeks later Maxwell died at sea. Maxwell's father had Paul charged with murder but he was released from prison on bail, and while awaiting trial he obtained sworn statements establishing his innocence.

In 1773 John Paul was again in Tobago as master of the *Betsey* of London. The crew mutinied and, in an incident that followed, the ringleader died from wounds received from a sword held by the master. Paul alleged that the victim died when he ran onto his sword! On this occasion, however, there were witnesses who were prepared to give evidence against Paul and he fled to America.

It was at this time he changed his name, in all probability to conceal his true identity. He was commissioned in the American navy in 1775, where his outstanding seamanship was quickly recognised and promotion was rapid.

In 1777 Jones was posted to Europe and in April of the following year he sailed from Brest for the Irish Sea. He attacked Whitehaven, and, after spiking the town's guns, he attempted to set fire to the shipping. He planned also to take the Earl of Selkirk as a hostage to ensure the proper treatment of American prisoners. His intended victim was not at home, but the crew did not leave empty-handed, taking a quantity of silver. He returned to Brest after twenty-eight days with a sizeable quantity of booty, including seven vessels and a number of prisoners. His activities had caused considerable concern in Britain, where Jones's reputation as corsair was much respected.

The pirate was then given command of the French ship *Duras*, which he promptly renamed *Bon Homage Richard*. On 14 August 1779 Jones again put to sea, this time paying particular attention to the east coast. He was supported by *Vengeance* and *Pallas*.

Jones, who had now attained the rank of commodore, described his exploits in a report dated 3 October of that year to Benjamin Franklin, the American Ambassador to France at the time Jones was active in British waters. He wrote:

> The winds continued to be contrary, so that we did not see the land till the 13th (September) when the hills of Cheviot, in the south-east of Scotland, appeared. The next day we chased sundry vessels, and took a ship and a brigantine, both from the Frith of Edinburgh, laden with coal. Knowing that there lay at anchor in Leith Roads an armed ship of 20 guns, with two or three fine cutters, I formed an expedition against Leith, which I purposed to lay under contribution, or otherwise to reduce it to ashes. Had I been alone, the wind being favourable, I would have proceeded directly up the Frith and must have succeeded, as they lay then in a state of perfect indolence and security, which would have proved their ruin. Unfortunately for me, the *Pallas* and *Vengeance* were both at a considerable distance in the offing, they having chased to the southward. This obliged me to steer out of the Frith again to meet them. The captains of the *Pallas* and *Vengeance* being come on board the *Bon Homme Richard*, I communicated to them my project, to which many difficulties and objections were made by them. At last, however, they appeared to think better of the design, after I had assured them that I hoped to raise a contribution of £200,000 sterling on Leith, and that there was no battery of cannon there to oppose our landing. So much time, however, was unavoidably spent in pointed remarks and sage deliberations that night, that the wind became contrary in the morning.

On 15 September the three privateers were spotted off the Berwickshire coast near Eyemouth, and later in the day, at Dunbar, about seven miles out to sea. Next day the progress was being watched by the citizens of Leith and Edinburgh. By 5 p.m. the ships were clearly visible and the following day they had taken positions opposite Kirkcaldy with the *Bon Homme Richard*'s broadside facing the town.

Meanwhile, the townsfolk of Leith were toiling feverishly to repel the expected attack. A number of old cannons with their carriages, all in a very poor state, were manhandled over the old stone bridge at the Coalhill to be mounted on the ruined citadel. A few brass field-pieces manned by artillerymen were stationed at Newhaven and the Incorporation of Traders petitioned the commander-in-chief at Edinburgh Castle for arms, which were readily supplied. Even sacks of wool were requisitioned to build barricades, and all night long soldiers and seamen patrolled the front.

Such was Jones's confidence that at one time he was almost within cannon range of the town. This was no foolhardy act, for the attacker was well aware of the lack of defences in Leith. This information had been provided by Andrew Robertson of Kirkcaldy, whose vessel, the *Friendship*, had been taken by Jones. In return for this information the pirate had agreed to release Robertson and his ship.

Jones's intention had been to press home an immediate attack on the port, but his two support vessels were still some way to the south. He decided to sail out of the forth to rendezvous with them. Vital time was squandered, however; the wind rose and the initiative was lost.

In anticipation of his success this Scottish-American had prepared the following letter, which he had intended to deliver to Leith Town Council. It was from 'The Honourable J. Paul Jones, Commander-in-Chief of the American Squadron now in Europe, etc., to the Worshipful the Provost of Leith, or, in his absence, to the Chief Magistrate who is now actually present and in authority there.'

> Sir, The British marine force that has been stationed here for the protection of your city and commerce being now taken by the American arms under my command, I have the honour to send you this summons by my officer, Lieutenant-Colonel de Chamillard, who commands the vanguard of my troops. I do not wish to distress the poor inhabitants; my intention is only to demand your contribution towards the reimbursement which Britain owes to the much injured citizens of the United States – for savages would blush at the unmanly violation and rapacity that has marked the tracks of British tyranny in America, from which neither virgin innocence nor hapless age has been a plea for protection or pity. Leith and its port now lies at our mercy; and did not our humanity stay the hand of just retaliation, I should, without advertisement, lay it in ashes.
>
> Before I proceed to that stern duty as an officer, my duty as a man

induces me to propose to you, by the means of a reasonable ransom, to prevent such a scene of horror and distress. For this reason I have authorised Lieutenant-Colonel de Chamillard to conclude and agree with you on the terms of ransom, allowing you exactly half-an-hour's reflection before you finally accept or reject the terms which he shall propose (£200,000). If you accept the terms offered within the time limited, you may rest assured that no further debarkation of troops will be made, but that the re-embarkation of the vanguard will immediately follow, and that the property of the citizens will remain unmolested. I have the honour to be, with sentiments of due respect, Sir, your very obedient and very humble servant, Paul Jones. On board the American ship-of-war the *Bon Homme Richard*, at anchor in the Road of Leith, September the 17th, 1779.

The letter was never dispatched.

25

DID TWO LEITH MEN INVENT
THE CHRISTMAS CARD?

Christmas is the season of peace on earth and goodwill to all men, and for days the postmen struggle through the snow, 'deep and crisp and even' (or more likely the slush), to deliver sackfuls of Christmas cards. But how many of the recipients ever give a thought to the origin of the card or realise that its beginnings may be traced to small premises in the old Kirkgate in Leith?

The Christmas card industry is a highly successful business, and the number of messages of greeting sent throughout the world during the festive season is incalculable. Yet, despite the popularity of the Christmas card, which has been with us for more than 150 years, its origins have been the subject of controversy: was it two Englishmen or two Leithers who were responsible for the production of the first one?

In 1843 an Englishman, Henry Cole, approached a friend, artist John Calcott Horsley, with a proposal: design a card which will convey a Christmas message, yet require nothing more than a signature.

Needless to say, the introduction of the Christmas card in the south met with some opposition, mainly because the design showed a large affluent Victorian family toasting absent friends. In the eyes of the critics this was not in keeping with the Christian message and what Christmas represents. Indeed, claimed the objectors, the card did nothing more than encourage the needless habit of consuming alcohol.

It was ironic that such an accusation should be levelled against Horsley, the designer, whose morals were beyond reproach; he was an active campaigner against the use of nude models by artists and his views allegedly earned him the title of 'Clothes-Horsley'!

A card by William Maw Egley, with an intricate design showing various aspects of Christmas, was thought to have been made in

1843, but it was later established that the year was 1848.

But was a card produced in Leith two years previously? There is certainly strong evidence to suggest that in 1841 (two years before the English claim) Thomas Sturrock and Charles Drummond (who had a printing and publishing business at 133 Kirkgate) had produced a festive card. Much of the controversy surrounding their claim, however, is clouded by the reference to a New Year card; not surprisingly, because of the prominence given to that day in Scotland.

From time to time the merits of the Leithers' case have been aired in the local press, but never more strongly than during a three-week period between 26 December 1934 and 14 January 1935. It was, however, a correspondence that was to shed a great deal of light on the background to the festive card.

The correspondence started quite innocently when, on 26 December 1934, the Port of Leith column in the *Edinburgh Evening News* remarked that at the festive time, when greetings were being exchanged through the medium of the card, it was appropriate to point out that the Christmas card is regarded as owing its origin to a Leith man, Thomas Sturrock.

Was this the first Christmas card? (from an old print)

It was he who first suggested the New Year card, and in 1841 supplied Charles Drummond with the design. Drummond had the sketch, a laughing face, with the motto 'Guid New Year and Mony o' Them' engraved on copper. The printed reproductions found a ready market. Two years later the English Christmas card made its first appearance, but by that time Sturrock's claim to be the originator of the festive card had been established in Edinburgh and London.

On Hogmanay the *News* reported that a correspondent had drawn the paper's attention to a letter which had been contributed by him on 26 February 1907, shortly after Sturrock's tragic death in a car accident in Princes Street. This 1907 letter included the following:

> The card showed the curly head of a boy, open-mouthed (minus a tooth in the upper row) with fat, chubby cheeks, merry twinkling eyes and an expression of such hearty laughter that the happy combination, by the natural infectious process, produced the desired result on the onlooker, who was greeted with the wish of 'many happy years'. I am not aware whether the study was from life, but the whole expression is so vivid that it afterwards appeared as a plate in Vasey's Philosophy of Laughter and Smiling. The card was engraved by Mr A.T. Aikman of Edinburgh and was published by Mr Drummond, bookseller, Leith.

The New Year was only five days old when James Telford wrote to the paper stating that the 'laughing face' referred to was originally engraved for Mr John Aikman, by his father, for use as a cover for a jest book. His grandfather, James Gould, who was employed at the time as an assistant in the Cross Post Office, 231 High Street, asked Alexander Aikman to engrave the words: 'A Happy New Year' and 'Many Happy Returns of the Season'. Hence, claimed Mr Telford, the first New Year card. To support his claim Mr Telford said that he had one of the first impressions from the plate.

Mr J.B. Aikman wrote that he was interested that James Telford also possessed one of the first New Year cards dated (in pencil) 1853, two years before the one that had been reproduced in the *News*:

> As the engravings were made in the days of our grandfathers, about 90 years ago, I cannot say anything about Mr Telford's statement that the 'laughing face' was engraved by Mr Alexander Aikman for his son John, but as the latter was only 11 years old in 1841, it is possible that one of the faces might have been put on the cover of a jest

book for the boy. It was always understood that Mr Sturrock was the originator of the card.

Douglas L. Sturrock told the *News*:

> I have read with interest the correspondence regarding the first New Year card, designed and invented by my grandfather, the late Thomas Sturrock. The copy which was in my grandfather's possession hung in the Leith Town Hall Chambers for many years and was returned to my late father on the amalgamation of Leith with Edinburgh. It is before me now and bears the inscription 'The first New Year's card, designed by Thomas Sturrock, printed by Charles Drummond, Leith, about 1841 or 42'.

At this point the correspondence on the origin of the Christmas card came to an end . . . for the time being.

Then in the 1950s an Edinburgh man, John Chalmers, contacted the *Evening Dispatch* to say he possessed what he believed was a proof copy of one of the first Christmas cards published in 1841. Mr Chalmers had obtained it in an unusual way.

In 1946 his daughter had been working in a shop, and in the course of a conversation with an elderly gentleman had casually mentioned that her father was a printer. The customer left the shop but returned shortly afterwards, carrying a set of metal plates, which he had obtained routinely in his scrap-metal business.

They were examined by Mr Chalmers, who suspected their historical significance and thought that they might be the original 1841 plates. Although they were corroded, he was able to clean them sufficiently to obtain reasonable prints before returning them to the owner.

The reproduction showed a laughing face with a pair of extended hands and a display of fruit and wine. More interestingly, however, the open mouth revealed that an upper tooth was missing, a characteristic of the original Sturrock/Drummond prints. But, even more significantly, it carried the message: 'Wishing you a Merry Christmas and a Happy New Year'.

Many years have elapsed now since the story of the Sturrock/ Drummond plates came to light and, so far as I am aware, all traces of them have vanished. What does remain, however, is the controversy surrounding the invention of the Christmas card; after more than 150 years since the introduction of the first festive card, the chances of solving the mystery diminish by the year.

26

SCOTLAND'S FORGOTTEN MEMORIAL

Strange, is it not, that one of the least-known memorials in Edinburgh, the home of the world-famous International Festival of Music and Drama, is the one that commemorates the contribution made to music by three Scottish singers.

The Singers' Memorial is a plaque on the rock on the right-hand side of the steps facing St Andrew's House in Regent Road and leading to the Calton Hill.

It bears the simple inscription 'In Memoriam' and the wreathed profiles of John Wilson, John Templeton and David Kennedy – vocalists who, in their day, sang to packed audiences in various parts of the world. The three men started their careers similarly, as precentors in Edinburgh churches.

John Wilson was born in the Canongate on Christmas Day 1800.

Edinburgh's forgotten (and half-hidden) memorial,
opposite St Andrew's House.

After his apprenticeship, he joined the staff of James Ballantyne, printer of Sir Walter Scott's works. He developed an interest in music, and, after a spell singing in the choir at Duddingston Kirk, was offered and accepted the post as precentor at a city church.

At the age of twenty-five, Wilson abandoned printing to study music. He made his first stage appearance at the Theatre Royal, Edinburgh, in *Guy Mannering*; among those present on that memorable night was Sir Walter Scott. The Theatre Royal was located in Shakespeare Square and was demolished to make way for the old General Post Office building at the east end of Princes Street – just a short distance from the Singers' Memorial.

The Canongate man's reputation as a tenor continued to rise and shortly afterwards he was invited to Covent Garden. Wilson moved to London, realising that his future lay there. During the following eight years his outstanding ability enabled him to hold his own on the London stage. He also completed a highly successful trip to America. It was a proud John Wilson who, in 1842, received a royal command to sing before Queen Victoria at Taymouth Castle.

Seven years later, however, Wilson's life was to end suddenly and tragically. He was on a tour of north America, performing his repertoire of Scots songs and attracting full houses. During a brief break in his hectic programme he decided to relax with a spot of fishing. He was soaked in an unexpected downpour, caught a chill, and shortly afterwards died of cholera, which had broken out in the area. He passed away on 8 July 1849, a comparatively young man.

John Templeton was born at Riccarton, near Kilmarnock, in 1802, and was a member of an extremely talented musical family. His father and brothers were renowned vocalists.

Templeton arrived in Edinburgh at the age of twelve and served part of his singing apprenticeship as a church precentor. His ability was beyond question, and it came as no surprise when he made it known he he intended to further his career in London. He was well aware of the risks involved, but he had confidence in himself.

Templeton moved cautiously; his first appearance in the south was at Worthing, where it is said that he worked for three weeks without salary – a price he was prepared to pay in the interests of experience. He then moved to Brighton, where he attracted sufficient attention to be offered a reasonably important engagement with the Southampton and Portsmouth Operatic Society. London was taking note, however, and Templeton was invited to Drury Lane.

As so often happens, Templeton's big chance came unexpectedly. The lead in *Don Giovanni* became available. There was only one week to go before the opening night, and the part was offered to the young Scot. He accepted without hesitation, and his performance was hailed by the critics as an outstanding success.

Templeton never forgot his Scottish homeland. He travelled extensively and Scottish songs were always featured in his concerts. He retired when only fifty but was usually available for charity concerts.

He lived for thirty-four years after his retirement, remaining a much respected figure in the musical world. He died in London aged eighty-four, and reportedly left a fortune of £80,000.

The third member of the celebrated trio was David Kennedy, who was born in Perth on 15 April 1825. He too had music in his blood and both his father and his uncle were precentors at the North and South Kirks, Perth. David Kennedy's mother also played a big part in developing her son's talents, and it was she who took the young laddie to the harvest gatherings where he learned the traditional farming community songs.

Kennedy was apprenticed to a house painter, which involved a fair amount of travel. On one occasion, while working about twelve miles from Perth, he decided that he would go to the town where Templeton was singing. But he had no money. It is said that he set out on a dark night in pouring rain and covered the distance in two hours. He listened from the doorway, then made his way back to be ready for work at 6 a.m.

It has also been said that Kennedy and his father walked from Perth to Edinburgh for a performance of Handel's *Messiah* in the Music Hall.

David Kennedy moved to Edinburgh and in 1857 was appointed precentor at Nicolson Street United Presbyterian Church. Competition for the post was fierce, for the salary was £40 per annum. He was selected from forty applicants and for five years he remained with this prosperous south-side congregation.

His heart was set on public singing, however, and in 1859 he was invited to appear at the Burns centenary celebration at St George's Hall, Liverpool. Kennedy was a great success. Concerts at the Buccleuch Halls, Edinburgh, followed by a tour of Scotland, convinced him that he had the ability to make a full-time career on the stage. This he did, and was joined by his family.

After a successful series of concerts in Canada, the Kennedy family embarked on a world tour which included Australia, New Zealand, the United States and Canada. Kennedy died at Stratford, Ontario, 1886, while on a farewell visit. His body was brought home for burial in Edinburgh. The last resting place of David Kennedy and members of his family is marked by an imposing memorial-stone, which backs on to the wall at the south end of the Grange Cemetery.

It was the London-based critic John Forbes-Robertson who said of Kennedy that he was 'by far the most perfect and dramatic exponent of Scots songs that Scotland has produced'.

Successful as he was, Kennedy always remembered the poor in Edinburgh and regularly gave concerts for their benefit.

Although the Kennedy family enjoyed considerable success, they also experienced tragedy. In 1881 three of them – Kate, Lizzie and James – were on their way to study in Italy. They broke their journey at Nice, where they went to a concert at the Théâtre des Italiens on 23 March. Fire broke out during the performance and the trio perished.

Marjory Kennedy-Fraser

Gaelic music and song enjoy considerable popularity today. Much of this material would have been lost but for the work of Marjory Kennedy-Fraser, who spent a considerable part of her life ensuring its survival.

Marjory was David Kennedy's daughter. By the age of twelve she was already travelling with her father as his accompanist, and two years later she joined the family on their four-year-long world tour.

Later Miss Kennedy studied singing at Milan and Paris. In 1887 she married A.Y. Fraser, the headmaster at Allan Glen's School in Glasgow, but tragedy struck once more when he died on 9 November 1890, aged only thirty-three.

The young widow then elected to settle in Edinburgh, where she devoted much of her time to teaching music and lecturing on musical subjects. Her interest in the music of the Gaels went back to before the turn of the century, but it was not until 1905 that she visited the Outer Hebrides.

In her quest for material, Marjory Kennedy-Fraser undertook

many arduous journeys. In one such trip, recorded in *A Life of Song*, she tells of leaving Edinburgh on an August evening and sailing from Oban for Lochboisdale at six the following morning – then on to Eriskay in an open boat. At the time of her death it was reported that several of the Eriskay songs had been gathered at the evening ceilidh which was held at the post office.

Her *Songs of the Hebrides* was published in 1909 and *Sea Tangle* followed four years later. In between her busy collecting schedule, Marjory Kennedy-Fraser found time to give recitals with her sister, Margaret Kennedy, and her daughter, Patuffa Kennedy-Fraser. Her last recital, appropriately enough, was broadcast nationwide on the wireless.

Marjory Kennedy-Fraser died at 6 Castle Street, Edinburgh, on 22 November 1930. She was seventy-three years old. In recognition of her services to music this remarkable lady had been granted a Civil List pension and was awarded the CBE. The University of Edinburgh recognised her achievements with a doctorate of music.

Three days after her death, a memorial service was held at St Giles' Cathedral. As the huge congregation assembled, three pieces from

The flats at 6 Castle Street, where
Marjory Kennedy-Fraser lived and died

Songs of the Hebrides were played, and later a woman member of the choir sang Marjory Kennedy-Fraser's 'Land o' Heart's Desire'. The service was conducted by the Very Revd Charles L. Warr, Dean of the Thistle, and minister of St Giles'. He told those present: 'She has done what no one else has done, and which in fact, no one but herself could do . . . what the great Sir Walter did for Lowland Scotland, what Neil Munro has done for those beyond the Highland line, Marjory Kennedy-Fraser effected for the immortal music of the Hebridean Isles.'

Contemporary newspaper reports state that Marjory Kennedy-Fraser was cremated at a private service in the Edinburgh Crematorium, and her final resting place was to be Iona.

Edinburgh musical festivals

When did the first Edinburgh Musical Festival take place . . . 1947 perhaps? No – you have to go back to the early part of the nineteenth century to find the answer. Over a period of nine years a group of enterprising men got together and organised three highly successful and profitable festivals. They were not subsidised by public money and the profits went to the welfare of the poor in the town.

The first, described as 'a Grand Musical Festival', opened on Tuesday 31 October 1815, and continued for the remainder of the week. Morning performances were held in Parliament Hall and in the evening audiences flocked to Corri's Rooms, which stood at the junction of Broughton Street and Little King Street.

Patrons could purchase six tickets for three guineas and they were transferable. In return, ticket-holders were able to enjoy works by Mozart, Handel, Beethoven, Haydn and others. The capital was crowded with visitors and the performances were well attended by what was described as 'the largest assemblages of beauty and fashion ever seen in the city'.

It was a highly organised occasion and the directors included a certain Mr Walter Scott, Henry Mackenzie (author of *The Man of Feeling*), Sir William Fettes, the Hon. Henry Erskine, Principal Baird of the University, Gilbert Innes of Stow and Lord Grey. The venture was a resounding success, not least financially, and £1,500 was distributed to charity.

There was a second festival in 1819, which attracted 8,526 theatregoers for the six performances. Receipts were £5,256 and expenses amounted to £4,024, leaving more than £1,200 for distribution among Edinburgh's needy. This was a drop of £300 on the previous festival and the writing was already on the wall.

The third and last of these nineteenth-century events was held in 1824, with morning performances in Parliament House and at the theatre in the evening. Interestingly, the cost of the tickets remained at three guineas. Although the performances were again well attended and receipts came to £4,940, expenditure was again up. The profit at the end of the week had dropped to only £543. The reason was given as the 'high demand of the principal singers'. The organisers decided that they could not justify further events.

But, as a result of these festivals, the Edinburgh Institution for the Encouragement of Sacred Music was born. An appeal for choristers attracted 780 hopefuls, about half of whom were selected.

And where can you find a permanent reminder of Edinburgh's first musical festival? At the entrance to number 84 Great King Street. There, cut into the stone is the inscription: 'Felix Yaniewicz, Polish composer and musician, co-founder of First Edinburgh Festival, lived and died here, 1823–48.'

The plaque at 84 Great King Street where Felix Yaniewicz lived

27

A FORTH ROAD BRIDGE FOR £3 MILLION

The Forth Road Bridge was finally opened to the public in the early evening of 4 September 1964. During the first three-and-a-half hours it was estimated that 20,000 toll-payers made the crossing.

The project had cost a massive £19 million and the ceremonial launch was carried out by the queen. But had the authorities paid more attention to an Edinburgh-based journalist, J. Inglis Ker, the bridge could have been in use almost forty years earlier for the relatively low figure of £3 million. This proposal was no fanciful idea, and Inglis Ker had gone into the matter very deeply, working closely with a reputable firm of engineers.

James Inglis Ker's family hailed from the Borders, although he was born in Dunfermline. He was educated at Dunfermline High School and later studied at the University of Edinburgh. Journalism was his chosen career, and over many years Inglis Ker contributed articles on motoring topics to some of the leading journals in Britain. In 1928 he founded the much respected *SMT Magazine* and guided it through the first eight years of its existence.

Throughout his life he worked for the improvement of roads in Scotland and his dream was to have a major road crossing of the Firth of Forth. His proposals, however, were not the first; a scheme had been discussed a century-and-a-half earlier. But it was Inglis Ker's proposal, published in 1923, which culminated in the construction of that great engineering masterpiece which now spans the Forth. He wrote:

> The building of a road bridge across the Forth is admittedly a proposition of the first magnitude and it is not to be lightly considered. It will tax the minds of our greatest road builders and bridge engineers, while in its financial aspects it will demand the most searching examination on the part of the Ministry of Transport and local authorities concerned.
>
> I think it will be generally conceded that there is an urgent need

for such a bridge and that its advantages to the entire community would be incalculable . . . There is no reason why Scotland, the cradleland of many eminent engineers, should be behind other countries in the new movement. It is the natural order of things that the country which gave the world its finest achievements in railway bridges should now lead the way in road bridge engineering.

Inglis Ker's proposals for a Forth road bridge were made public at a press conference at the Hawes Inn, South Queensferry, on 3 November 1923. The meeting was chaired by Bailie William L. Sleigh, an Edinburgh Corporation Councillor, who, exactly a week later, was elected Lord Provost of the city and subsequently knighted.

Inglis Ker explained that the proposals had been given very detailed consideration. A suggestion that the Forth (railway) Bridge might be adapted to take vehicular traffic had been examined. This, he had been assured, was impracticable. Improvements to the ferry service had also been mentioned, but the uncertainty of the weather and varying tides ruled this out. In any case, that could only be looked upon as a compromise.

He emphasised that the road bridge was all that was required to restore Edinburgh to its rightful place as the gateway to the north and that it would materially enhance the usefulness of the new highway between Glasgow, Edinburgh, and Leith. It would bring these three centres into direct and immediate touch with Dunfermline, Kirkcaldy, Perth, and Dundee.

'It would be', Inglis Ker believed, 'the completion in the link of the great highway from Dover to John o' Groats, and would achieve for the new bridges contemplated at Berwick and Tay a still greater usefulness.'

Turning to the construction of the bridge, the Edinburgh journalist dealt with the advantages and problems involved. The project would ensure employment for 5,000 men, who could be accommodated at Rosyth; it would also stimulate the steel, iron, wood, cement, brick, stone, and lime industries. He estimated the construction period to be approximately five years.

Inglis Ker concluded by emphasising that the problem had to be examined by the local authorities concerned, particularly Fife and Midlothian. If they considered that the project was unnecessary or impracticable then the matter would be dropped, but if not, they must approach the government. A strong committee would also require to be set up.

The technical details were explained by Mr Leitch of Messrs Leitch and Sharpe, civil engineers, Glasgow, who revealed that the design was for a suspension bridge, to be constructed east of the railway bridge, featuring two spans, each of 2,400 feet, and sharing a common pier on the island of Inch Garvie.

He told the press conference that the southern approach would start at a point on the public highway leading from Edinburgh to South Queensferry, about 80 yards east of its junction with the road leading to Dalmeny Station. It would begin at the same level as the existing roadway, about 150 feet above the high water level and at the height of the railway bridge. The new roadway would be carried on an embankment for a distance of about 200 yards until the embankment was 20 feet above the existing surface of the ground. An abutment of masonry would then be formed supporting the girders for the first span of the southern approach viaduct, which would then be carried on eight masonry piers for a distance of 560 yards before joining the main bridge.

The northern approach viaduct would also be on eight piers, covering a distance of 660 yards, starting at the Carlingnose whinstone quarry workings. From that point the road would be continued for 50 yards to join the existing public road near North Queensferry at its present level. The approach viaducts at both ends were to consist of steel girder work and decking.

At high tide the south pier would be covered by water and the foundations would have to be put in by using a caisson with compressed air. The Inch Garvie and north piers would have their foundation on dry land at low tide.

The bridge would be one mile long overall, and 58 feet wide, with

Inglis Ker's proposal for a Forth road bridge (from an original sketch)

9-ft pathways on each side and 40 feet between the kerbs for traffic. It would not run parallel to the railway bridge, for, although the north end would converge at North Queensferry, the southern approach would begin at the top of Hawes Brae, several hundred yards east of the railway bridge. The two spans of 2,400 feet were considered by Mr Leitch to be extremely long.

The pioneering efforts of Inglis Ker during the 1920s met with a certain amount of criticism. They were described as 'utopian', 'idealistic', and 'visionary' but he was not disheartened. He declared:

> If such an attitude of mind prevailed, human progress would be arrested and nowhere with such disastrous results as in the world of physical science. Such criticism is useful only in so far as it serves to remind us that it is from the realms of dreams and visions that we have our steamships and telephones, our wireless and our present Forth Bridge. One day from exactly the same source we shall have our road bridge over the Forth.

But the scheme had a great deal of support. In a long and enthusiastic leading article, the *Edinburgh Evening News* said: 'It is hardly likely that the idea of building a road bridge over the Forth, now that it has been mooted, will be speedily dropped. It would be an insult to the energy and acumen of Mr J. Inglis Ker to think it.'

The *News* pointed out that the contemplated new bridges over the Tweed and the Tay made it logically imperative that the Forth be likewise spanned or the dream of a direct highway to the north would be lost. The editorial had a word of advice for Inglis Ker. Had he ever thought of the advantages his bridge would have if tram lines were included? 'The linking of the West Fife and Edinburgh trams is an ideal that ought not to be lost sight of, for it means cheap and commodious travelling to thousands.'

On 18 January 1924 an informal gathering took place in Edinburgh, attended by members and officials from the local authorities of Edinburgh, Linlithgow, Dunfermline, South and North Queensferry, Inverkeithing, Perth, Kirkcaldy, and Dundee. Also present were the motoring organisations and other interested parties. A Ministry of Transport representative told the delegates that the proposal was worthy of the most serious consideration, and that from an engineering point of view the construction was not expected to present any difficulty.

The next meeting was held at the House of Commons on 25 March and was attended by thirty Scottish MPs. After a full discussion, a committee was appointed to press the scheme on the Ministry of Transport. Exactly one month later the minister wrote to Inglis Ker confirming that the Ministry would defray 75 per cent of the cost of a survey, provided the balance was met by the local authorities.

A meeting of local authorities in the Forth area was then held in Edinburgh on 21 January the following year to discuss the government's offer, when it was estimated that the preliminary survey would cost £10,000. This meeting was chaired by Edinburgh's Lord Provost, and after lengthy discussion the following motion was approved:

> This conference agrees in the importance of the proposed bridge across the Forth, near Queensferry, but are of the opinion that no further progress can be made without a full preliminary survey and, as the project will form a link in a national highway, that the full cost of the preliminary survey should be borne by the State and that representations should be made to the Ministry of Transport to this effect.

In 1928 it was noted that for some months boring operations had been carried out on behalf of Basil Mott, Hay & Anderson, the well-known civil engineers, who were acting for the Ministry of Transport. It was believed that the Ministry would report later in the year. A number of sites had been explored and the most likely recommendation from the engineers would be to the east of the railway bridge.

The matter dragged on, however, and James Inglis Ker was not to see his dream realised. He died suddenly on 11 September 1936, and was buried in Edinburgh's Grange Cemetery. His funeral was attended by a large gathering of mourners from every walk of life.

No better tribute could have been paid to the work of this man than that penned by George Eyre-Todd, in the October 1936 issue of the *SMT Magazine*:

> To his initiative and persistent advocacy was largely owed the construction of the wonderful new highway through Glencoe and the idea was his for a great road bridge across the Firth of Forth, which, there can be little doubt, will be one of the most notable developments of the future.

Twenty-eight years later that prediction became a reality.

28

BONNIE PRINCE CHARLIE
CAPTURES EDINBURGH

One of the great romantic figures in Scottish history is Bonnie Prince Charlie. He came to Scotland intent on restoring the Stewarts to the British throne, and his arrival sparked off the 1745 Jacobite rising which was brutally ended on the battlefield of Culloden the following year. One of the tasks his army had to tackle in 1745, however, was the capture of Edinburgh – and it was so easy.

As early as 1743 the Town Council had been warned by the government of the possibility of a Jacobite attack. The advice was taken seriously, and the Council informed the king 'of our detestation of an undertaking no less insolent than wicked; and of our firm determination to defend your Majesty's sacred person, and the settlement of the crown upon your royal family, against the open attempts of foreign enemies, and against all treasonable practices at home'.

News of the Young Pretender's landing reached Edinburgh on 17 August 1745. At that time the town's protection depended largely on the Town Guard, consisting of a little over a hundred (mainly old) men, and the trained bands of approximately 1,000 men. They were poorly armed.

On 27 August the Provost and magistrates met to draw up plans for the defence of the city. The proposals included repairs to the city walls. A trench was to be dug from the northern side of the castle rock to the Nor' Loch; such was the importance of this project that Sunday working was permitted. In addition, the trained bands were put on full alert. Meanwhile, King George's approval was obtained to raise 1,000 volunteers, who would be under the control of the Council. After a week only 200 had enlisted.

On the evening of 31 August there was panic in the town when it was learned that Prince Charles' rebels were in Perthshire. The drum was sounded to call the men to arms, and, following a meeting of the Council, the city keys were entrusted to the captain of the Town

Guard. Sentries were posted at all points of entry to the town and the guard strength was increased. In addition, troops under arms were deployed close to the capital. Security was tightened and instructions were issued to innkeepers, stablers and owners of any establishment taking lodgers, requiring them to inform the captain of the Guard, in writing, of everyone in casual residence. Failure to comply carried a penalty of £5 for every name omitted.

Muskets were issued to the four trained bands in Leith, and arms were provided to the citizens in Potterrow and Portsburgh, then baronies outside the city walls. To complete the defences, cannon were sited strategically on the town wall.

For a time all was quiet. Then on 13 September came news that the prince had crossed the Forth and was heading for Edinburgh. Two days later it was reported, incorrectly, that he had reached Kirkliston. This information once more caused panic in Edinburgh, and activity became frantic.

Money which was being held by the banks, and other valuables, were transferred to the castle, the trained guards were mobilised and deployed to protect the important buildings, and a detachment of troops was ordered to forward positions at Corstorphine.

On the Sunday morning, the fire bell, which was located on the castle wall and used to warn citizens of impending danger, was sounded. Immediately churches emptied and the ministers (who had arrived at their respective kirks with swords at their sides) headed for the Lawnmarket, where the armed citizens joined the regular troops. Groups of mothers, wives and girlfriends tearfully endeavoured to dissuade their menfolk from embarking on this dangerous mission.

The men set off to war by way of the West Bow, which led to the Grassmarket. But before the guardians of the city had reached the West Port at the western end of the Grassmarket their numbers were already badly depleted. As the 'heroes' moved off, deserters quickly and quietly slipped down one or other of the many closes on the route, and eventually only a small contingent marched to Corstorphine. That night a guard was posted while the main body fell back to safer positions.

Next day a small vanguard of rebels approached Corstorphine and surprised the government troops. More in jest than in anger the Jacobites fired a few shots; to their utter amazement the dragoons turned and fled to join the main group at Coltbridge. On being advised that a full-scale attack was imminent, General Hawkes ordered a retreat. Between three and four o'clock that afternoon the citizens of Edinburgh were horrified to see the dragoons skirting the north side of the town, heading at speed for Leith and, eventually, Musselburgh. Meanwhile, the infantry were making their way to Edinburgh.

Once more there was considerable unrest in the town as residents implored Lord Provost Archibald Stewart not to defend the capital, as it would most certainly result in bloodshed. This was a situation that the Provost could not win. To defend would mean casualties; to offer no resistance could have serious consequences. A meeting of the Council was hastily called and it was decided to seek the advice of the law officers – but they had fled!

A letter was dispatched from Prince Charles, who was camped at Gray's Mill, Slateford, only a couple of miles outside the town, requiring the Council to meet him, and dictating terms and conditions for the surrender of Edinburgh.

One historian quoted the letter as follows:

From our Camp, 16th September, 1745.
Being now in a condition to make our way into the capital of his Majesty's ancient Kingdom of Scotland, we hereby summon you to receive us, as you are in duty bound to do; and in order to it, we hereby require you, on receipt of this, to summon the Town Council, and to take proper measures for securing the peace and quiet of the city, which we are very desirous to protect; but if you suffer any of the usurpers troops to enter the town, or any of the cannon, arms, or ammunition now in it (whether belonging to the public or private persons) to be carried off, we shall take it as a breach of duty, and a heinous offence against the king and us, and shall resent it accordingly. We promise to preserve all the rights and liberties of the city, and the particular property of every one of his Majesty's subjects. But if any opposition be made to us, we cannot answer for the consequences, being firmly resolved to enter the city; and in that case, if any of the inhabitants are found in arms against us, they must not expect to be treated as prisoners of war.

(Signed) Charles. P.R.

At eight in the evening the Council sent a message asking for time to consider the matter. Two hours later the Council were given a deadline of 2 a.m.

Meanwhile, the small delegation of council representatives who had been sent to Slateford returned by coach, entering the city through the West Port. There they were dropped off and met by an anxious Lord Provost. The coach continued through the town, heading for the Canongate. This required exit by way of the Netherbow Port, which was locked for the night.

There was a delay while the guards debated whether or not to make an exception and allow the coach to leave. They decided that this was in order, the gate was opened, and the rebels, who were concealed nearby, rushed the gate and were into Edinburgh itself. The site of the gate is marked today by a series of brass bricks on the roadway where the High Street intersects with St Mary's Street and Jeffrey Street.

The Young Pretender, having heard of his vanguard's success, left Slateford at 8 a.m. with the remainder of his forces, and, in order to avoid attack from the castle guns, approached Holyrood Palace by way of Duddingston.

That night a ball was held in the palace and the following day (18 September) a proclamation was issued requiring the citizens to surrender all weapons and ammunition. Failure to do so would result in all offenders being treated as rebels. On the next day a demand was sent to the Council for the supply of 1,000 tents, 2,000 targets, and 6,000 pairs of shoes. The cost of this equipment was estimated at £1,500.

To meet this expenditure, a rate of 2s.6d. (12½p) was imposed on the town, Canongate, and Leith. There was a promise that the money would be repaid – later. The Council, believing that they had no alternative, complied with the order, but it was to have serious consequences for Lord Provost Stewart.

Stewart lived in the West Bow, on the west side, with his upper windows overlooking the Grassmarket. There is a tradition that his was a house of architectural mystery, with secret stairs, hidden trapdoors, closets, and concealed recesses behind the panelling.

Was Stewart a Jacobite? Who knows? But it has been suggested that during his occupation of the city, the Pretender and a number of his supporters were entertained in the house. In a town full of rumour, news reached the castle that the clandestine meetings were taking place and troops were dispatched to investigate. The raid was ill-planned, however; the secret apartments were put to good use, and the visitors made their escape.

Unfortunately for Stewart, he was also Member of Parliament for Edinburgh, and in November 1745 he returned to London to look after his constituents' interests. He was immediately arrested and, after being questioned by the Privy Council, was committed to the Tower of London. There he remained for some time, until he was released on bail of £15,000, to appear before the High Court in Edinburgh.

In due course the rebellion came to its bloody end at Culloden. Immediately, the king in London was showered by loyal addresses, including one from the citizens of Edinburgh.

Part of it read:

> Most Gracious Sovereign, We the citizens who have at any time shared in the government of the city of Edinburgh, now destitute of magistrates and town-council, by our city's having unfortunately fallen under the power of the rebels before the time of our last annual elections, humbly presume, as private subjects, to join in expressing our most sincere and hearty congratulations to your Sacred Majesty, on the late happy and compleat victory gained by his Royal Highness the Duke of Cumberland over the rebels . . .
>
> We cannot however at this time avoid expressing our deepest sorrow and regret, that, from some circumstances, our zeal and activity in defending the ancient metropolis of this part of the united kingdom, may seem to have come short of the insolent boldness with which the rebels presumed to rise in arms against your Majesty. But it is with the highest satisfaction that we can assure your Majesty that by far the greatest part of the most reputable burgesses showed a chearful readiness to hazard their lives and bestow their fortunes in defence of your Majesty's government, and for preserving this city from falling into the hands of the rebels; tho' our endeavours came to be disappointed by a variety of circumstances, which we could not foresee, nor was it in our power to prevent.

King George was obviously not impressed, for Lord Provost Archibald Stewart MP duly appeared in the High Court, charged with 'neglect of duty, misbehaviour in public office and violation of the trust and duty thereof'. There were several delays before the trial got under way, and after five days the jury returned their verdict – not guilty! Soon afterwards Stewart left Edinburgh and settled in London, where he became a successful businessman. He died in Bath in 1780.

Not surprisingly, there was considerable relief among Stewart's friends at the verdict, and they proposed to organise a celebration to welcome his acquittal. But there were those in Edinburgh who had doubts about the verdict, and discussions took place in high circles, not least between Lord Provost George Drummond and the Lord Justice-Clerk. Discretion prevailed and the idea of a celebration was abandoned.

29

THE DOCTOR WHO CONQUERED PAIN

Queen Street has changed little architecturally since it was built as part of the New Town more than 200 years ago. The houses, with their commanding views over the fine gardens towards the distant Firth of Forth, were desirable residences for some of the town's notable citizens. Sadly, no more. Office use predominates.

Nevertheless, it is not difficult to imagine the scene some 150 years ago, with the cabs moving slowly along the dimly lit street before pulling up at one or other of the houses for a social gathering, where the merriment would continue until the early hours of the morning.

At 52 Queen Street the house lights frequently burned late, but for a very different reason. Behind the closed door there were regular meetings involving three doctors. These were nights of experiments and disappointments, until finally came the exciting news – Professor James Y. Simpson and his assistants had discovered the anaesthetic use of chloroform. They had found a method of controlling pain.

Simpson was born in 1811 at Bathgate, and was the eighth child in a family of seven sons and one daughter born to Mary and David Simpson. His father was the local baker in Bathgate, which, at that time, was little more than a large village.

The future doctor was four years old when his education began at the local school, and immediately he impressed his teacher with a remarkable memory and ability to learn.

Simpson was only nine when his mother died and the responsibility of running the household fell on the shoulders of his sister Mary. Money was scarce, but it was recognised that James Simpson had more than average ability and that he would benefit greatly from a university education.

Thus, at the age of fourteen the young lad left the protection of his father's village home for the big friendless city, where he enrolled in the Arts classes at the University of Edinburgh. In 1827, however,

Professor James Y. Simpson

The room at 52 Queen Street where Simpson made his historic discovery
(photo by George D. Smith)

influenced by two medical students living in the same accommodation, Simpson's interests turned to medicine and the start of what
was to become an illustrious career. Distressed at what he witnessed
during operations, Simpson all but abandoned medicine in favour of
law, but the pull was too strong.

Shortly before completing his course, Simpson temporarily gave
up his studies to look after his father, who was in poor health. This
he did faithfully until 1830, when David Simpson died. The young
medical student then returned to Edinburgh and completed his
studies.

Meanwhile, his brother David had opened a baker's shop at
1 Raeburn Place, Stockbridge, and the pair were able to share each
other's company and accommodation. James loved to drive his
brother's cart and enjoyed nothing better than a run out to Pilton.
The fresh air of Stockbridge beside the Water of Leith also appealed
to the young student.

Dr Simpson's daughter states that her father first put up his 'plates'
in fashionable Heriot Row. In 1840 he was at 22 Albany Street, where
he remained until 1845, when he moved to 52 Queen Street.

Simpson was only twenty-one when Professor Thomson of the

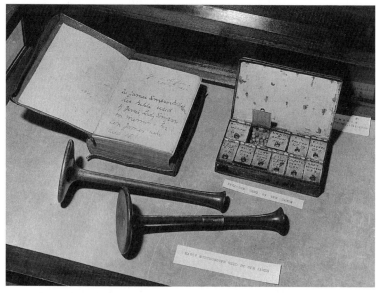

Lady Simpson's bible together with pillbox and an early stethoscope
used by Sir James (photo by George D. Smith)

Pathology Department offered him an assistant's post at £50 a year. In 1839, however, the Chair of Midwifery became vacant. Simpson was determined that it would be his. But the doctor had two major problems to overcome – age (he was still only twenty-eight) and bachelorhood. He could do nothing about his youth, but marriage, he believed, would be no problem. For some time he had been corresponding with Miss Jessie Grindlay of Liverpool, whose forefathers had hailed from Bo'ness. He proposed, and the wedding took place on 26 December 1839. There was no honeymoon; it was straight back to Edinburgh.

The election to the Chair of Midwifery took place on 4 February the following year, and Simpson was appointed by 17 votes to 16. Simpson's lectures were very popular and, despite additional classes, many students had to stand to hear him teach.

It was on his appointment that Professor Simpson moved to Albany Street and subsequently to Queen Street. His fame spread, and while many titled families boasted that Professor Simpson was their doctor no poor patient was ever turned away from his door. In 1847 Simpson was appointed one of Queen Victoria's physicians in Scotland. The village laddie had come a long way.

Simpson's home at 52 Queen Street

News from America that ether had been used in surgery was received by Simpson with great satisfaction, for the suffering he had seen in the operating theatres had disturbed him greatly. All through the summer of 1847, he and his assistants, Dr Keith and Dr Duncan, worked late into the nights searching for a better 'drowsy syrup' than ether. He wrote: 'I have tried upon myself and others the inhalation of different volatile fluids, with the hope that one of them might be found to possess the advantages of ether without its disadvantage.' On more than one occasion Simpson was found unconscious as a result of his experiments.

Summer turned to autumn and, after the routine work of the day had been completed, Simpson and his two assistants worked more long hours searching for the elusive miracle. The night of 4 November 1847 is accepted as being the occasion on which the anaesthetic properties of chloroform were discovered. After several compounds had been used, a small phial of chloroform, which had been suggested by David Waldie, was produced and poured into tumblers. One by one the 'guinea-pigs' came under its influence; eyewitnesses to the experiment recalled seeing Simpson lying insensible, Duncan snoring heavily, and Keith kicking violently.

Writing to Waldie later, Simpson said; 'I had the chloroform for several days in the house before trying it, as, after seeing it such a heavy, unvolatile-like liquid, I despaired of it . . . Doctors Duncan and Keith and I tried it simultaneously and were all under the table in a minute or two.'

There was much opposition to the use of chloroform, particularly from the clergy, but the news that it had been used by Queen Victoria during a confinement helped to overcome these prejudices.

Professor Simpson was not a man who sought honours, and he twice refused a baronetcy before finally accepting the title. He was the first physician practising in Scotland to be so honoured.

A letter, dated 3 January 1866, from the queen's residence at Osborne reads: 'Your professional merits, especially your introduction of chloroform, by which difficult operations in surgery have been rendered painless and which in many cases made that possible which would otherwise have been too hazardous to attempt, deserve some special recognition by the Crown.'

Sir James Simpson died on 6 May 1870; he was only fifty-eight. Westminster Abbey was offered as a last resting place but it was respectfully declined. He was buried at Edinburgh's Warriston Cemetery where five of his nine children already lay, and his wife joined him within four weeks.

On his death Queen Victoria sent a message expressing 'her sorrow on account of the loss which the country has sustained in the death of so great and so good a man'. Speaking in the House of Commons, Prime Minister William Gladstone said: 'Sir James Simpson's death is a grievous loss to the nation; it is truly a national concern.'

How true this statement proved to be; it was estimated that 30,000 citizens lined the route of the great man's funeral.

Professor Simpson always acknowledged that, without the financial support of his oldest brother Sandy, he might never have been a doctor. Some years ago I had the privilege of spending an hour talking to Miss Catherine S. Simpson, Sandy's grand-daughter, at her West End home, just five minutes walk from where the historic discovery war made. Although Sir James had been dead several years before she was born, Miss Simpson learned much about her famous ancestor from her father, Sir Robert Russell Simpson W.S.

'Sir James,' Miss Simpson told me, 'was very much a family man and no matter how busy he was or how hard a day he had had, he always insisted in having his play hour with the children. He had a most beautiful speaking voice with a broad accent, which he never lost, and a great sense of humour.'

Despite the work that Professor Simpson did for mankind, five of his nine children predeceased him.

'Did he ever feel bitter about it?' I asked.

'Sir James was never bitter,' she replied quietly. 'He was a deeply religious man, and while their deaths hurt him terribly, he accepted them as the will of God.'

31

A RIGHT ROYAL FARCE

Royal visits to Edinburgh are routine. There is a well-rehearsed formula involving the 'Establishment', the Scottish Executive, the police, and, no doubt, other lesser-known organisations, and the possibility of anything going wrong is remote. But occasionally there can be 'misunderstandings', as demonstrated by Queen Victoria's first visit to Scotland in 1842, which, without doubt, was the most embarrassing royal occasion to take place in the city.

The incidents prior to and at the time of her arrival suggest that a deliberate attempt may have been made to snub her loyal Scottish subjects. The only other explanation is that an unfortunate series of blunders by certain officials led to the confusion that prevailed.

During the summer of 1842 Queen Victoria directed the Prime Minister, Sir Robert Peel, to arrange an autumn holiday in Scotland. It was believed that Her Majesty would travel by sea, land at Granton in the Firth of Forth and then proceed by road to Dalkeith Palace.

When news of this historic occasion reached the ears of the City Fathers, they decided to get in on the act. Plans were quickly drawn up, including a proposal that the keys of the city should be ceremonially offered to the young queen. As she would be travelling by road from Granton to Dalkeith, an elaborate replica of an old city gate would be erected at Brandon Street. From the start, however, rumour was rife in the capital that the royal party would travel direct to Dalkeith and would by-pass Edinburgh.

At a meeting of the Town Council, and in an attempt to dispel these stories, Bailie Richardson told the assembled Councillors that he and Lord Provost Sir James Forrest had spoken to the Duke of Buccleuch, who had confirmed that the presentation of the keys was a perfectly acceptable arrangement.

In reply, Bailie Thomson expressed considerable surprise 'at the apparent want of respect manifested to the city by her Majesty's advisors.' If her Majesty's arrangements were not altered it would create much disappointment and might be productive of very serious results, he warned.

By three days before what was believed to be the date of the visit vast crowds had gathered in Edinburgh, and it was estimated that there were 100,000 visitors. As they took up positions on the supposed route, rumour again spread through the town that the queen intended to drive through at a quick pace and in a closed carriage.

The queen's vessel, *Royal George*, anchored in the lee of Inchkeith in the Forth about 2 a.m. on 1 September and shortly before 7 a.m. the royal yacht weighed anchor and sailed to Granton. At 8.55 a.m. the queen stepped on Scottish soil for the first time, and shortly afterwards set off with an escort of dragoons. Only a few of the more enthusiastic spectators were about at this relatively early hour, and the first news of the queen's landing was the sight of the procession making its way along Inverleith Row.

With a mad rush citizens seized the nearest vantage points as Queen Victoria's coach approached at a slow pace. No city official was present at Brandon Street, and the royal entourage swept through the ornamental gate and started the long haul up Pitt Street (now the northern end of Dundas Street).

Meanwhile, the Lord Provost and other city officials were assembling in a leisurely way at the City Chambers. There was still no sign of panic, for it was anticipated that the queen would not land before 11 a.m. Suddenly a salute was fired from the castle and church bells began to peal to welcome Victoria to the capital of Scotland!

'Then', reported a contemporary newspaper, 'commenced a scene which perhaps had few parallels in the historical recollections of the High Street of Edinburgh.' Crowds ran down the Canongate, hoping to reach Abbeyhill before the queen passed. They were joined by others from the North and South Bridges to form a crowd which resembled 'nothing as much as a routed army'.

At the City Chambers all thoughts of a formal ceremony were quickly forgotten as Councillors and officials left in various directions in an attempt to overtake the elusive Victoria. One carriage carrying four officials was successful and located the royal party some way ahead. It was a rather surprised queen who acknowledged the respects of these city representatives as they stood by the roadside with their panting, sweating and froth-covered horses.

Within minutes the City Chambers was besieged by a vast angry crowd demanding an explanation. The Council assembled at 11 a.m. and deliberated behind closed doors for two hours. Finally, it was decided that a visit to Dalkeith Palace was required for discussions with the queen's officials. On their return a notice was posted at the City Chambers intimating that the queen had agreed to make a visit to Edinburgh.

Two days later Queen Victoria made her state visit to the capital but the wrath of the citizens had not subsided. An inquiry into the chaos which prevailed on that day of confusion was held at a Council meeting on 8 September, when the following interesting details were revealed:

When, two weeks before what was believed would be the date of the visit, no official notification had been received, the Duke of Buccleuch had been approached for information. It is alleged that he evasively replied that the queen wanted the visit to be 'as quiet as possible'.

The following day the Council decided to write to the appropriate government department for details; it was further claimed that the duke offered to deliver the letter. It may have reached its destination, but certainly the Council had no record of any reply, nor was any satisfactory explanation ever provided to clear up the confusion.

But were Edinburgh Town Council as blameless as they claimed? Leith Town Council had no problem. It was found that shortly after the *Royal George* anchored in Leith Roads a messenger was despatched with instructions to contact the Lord Provost of Edinburgh and the Provost of Leith, and to advise them that it was the queen's intention to disembark at 6 a.m. He arrived at Bailie Hutchison's house in Bernard Street at approximately 2 a.m. and was immediately redirected to the home of Provost James Reoch, near Leith Links. At the same time the magistrates of Leith were awakened from their slumbers to be told the arrangements and carriages were made ready.

As the *Royal George* passed Leith, making her way to Granton, a royal salute was fired from the fort. Slowly, the royal yacht edged towards the pier at Granton on what proved to be a dull, overcast morning. At approximately 8.30 a.m. the vessel tied up, and immediately the Duke of Buccleuch, Lord Liverpool, and Sir Robert Peel went on board. Half-an-hour later Queen Victoria and Prince Albert stepped ashore to be formally welcomed by the Duke of Buccleuch in his capacity as Lord-Lieutenant.

This totally mismanaged disaster had its lighter moments, however, and was a godsend for the satirists. One notable contribution, a parody on the theme 'Hey Johnnie Cope' is reported to have sold by the thousand and it ran:

> Hey, Jamie Forrest, are ye waukin' yet,
> And are yer Bailies snorin' yet?
> If ye are waukin' I wud wit
> Ye'd hae a merry, merry mornin'.
> The Queen she's come to Granton Pier,
> Nae Provost and nae Bailies here;
> They're in their beds, I muckle fear,
> Sae early in the mornin'.
> The frigate guns they loud did roar,
> But louder did the Bailies snore,
> An' thocht it was an unco bore
> To rise sae early in the mornin'.
> An syne the Castle thundered lood,
> But kipper it is savoury food,
> And that the Bailies understood,
> Sae early in the mornin'.
> The Queen she's come to Brandon Street,
> The Provost and the keys to meet,
> An' div ye think that she's to wait
> Yer waukin' in the mornin'?
> My Lord, my Lord, the Queen is here,
> And wow, my Lord he lookit queer;
> An' what sets her so soon asteer?
> It's barely nine in the mornin'.
> Gae bring tae me my robes of State,
> Come, Bailies, we will catch her yet.
> Rin, rin, my Lord, ye're ower late,
> She's been through the toon this mornin'.
> Awa' to Dalkeith ye maun hie,
> To mak' yer best apology.
> The Queen she'll say, Oh fie! oh fie!
> Ye're lazy loons in the mornin'.

A great deal of fence-building had to be done – and quickly. The queen responded by agreeing to alter her itinerary to include a visit to Edinburgh. The 'gate' was removed from Brandon Street and hastily re-erected at the Mercat Cross in the High Street where the traditional offer of the city keys was ceremonially carried out before a large crowd.

But even this visit did not pass without incident. A stand, which had been built at the foot of the Mound for spectators, became over-crowded and collapsed. Two people were killed, and around fifty injured.

For her part, Queen Victoria did return to Edinburgh with no reported 'misunderstandings'.

32

THE MYSTERIOUS VISITOR TO
ROSEBANK CEMETERY

On infrequent occasions during the second half of the nineteenth century, a closed horse-drawn carriage could be seen entering Edinburgh's Rosebank Cemetery at the junction of Pilrig Street and Broughton Road.

The coach was driven slowly and reverently along the pathway, the loose chippings being churned up by the weight of the vehicle and the horses' hooves, the animals struggling to keep the coach moving, encouraged by a considerate and sympathetic coachman.

In a few minutes they reached a point more or less in the centre of the cemetery and halted in front of a pair of comparatively simple gravestones. A coachman dismounted, opened the carriage door and assisted a small, slightly plump woman in dark clothes to alight. This task completed, the servant turned away and joined the other members of the small party, who had retired discreetly a few yards distant.

That lady stood before the two memorials, head bowed on a fine autumn day, alone with her private thoughts. It was still and sunny and the peace was disturbed just occasionally by the snorting of one or other of the horses or the chirping of birds as they flitted among the stones.

What went through the head of that relatively young woman will never be known – memories of a woman only three years the mourner's senior who had died so suddenly in Edinburgh. She was German by birth but the pair had worked closely, sharing much enjoyment and no doubt personal secrets.

The second grave contained the remains of a man who perhaps was more fortunate, having survived seventy-two years, no mean achievement in the nineteenth century.

In due course, her contemplation completed, the lady raised her head, a signal quickly seen by the observant coachman, to announce that the visit was finished. He walked the few steps to the coach, opened the door and assisted the mourner into her seat, soon to be joined by the other members of the group. The coachman then joined the horseman, who had brought the relaxing animals back under his control.

There was a pause of a few seconds; then, following only the slightest sign of a final wave and bow, the vehicle was driven out of Rosebank Cemetery and headed for home.

Nothing unusual in that you might think, except that lady was Queen Victoria. And the purpose of that visit by Her Majesty? She was there to pay her respects to two royal servants whose last resting place is Rosebank.

On 13 October 1854, Queen Victoria left Edinburgh and returned to London, leaving her dresser, Ida Bonanomi, who was ill. Could Victoria have realised just how seriously ill Miss Bonanomi was and that only two days later she was to die at 9 Princes Street? The queen was obviously deeply upset at the loss of a woman who was probably just as much a companion as a member of the staff.

And so in due course Ida Bonanomi was laid to rest at Rosebank. Why Rosebank? That is a mystery, but the explanation might be that Rosebank was a relatively new cemetery, opened only eight years previously, and where, at that time, the land was a vast green field in the middle of town. Such spaciousness could not have been found in any of the older graveyards. So there lies Ida Bonanomi, a servant who had known the palaces of Britain, among the shipowners, businessmen and other folk who had been born, worked and died in Leith.

In time Victoria remembered her dresser in a permanent way by erecting a stone over her grave, with the simple but adequate inscription which reads:

> Sacred to the memory of Miss Ida Bonanomi, the faithful and highly esteemed dresser of Queen Victoria, who departed this life Octr 15th 1854 in the 37th year of her age, beloved and respected by all who knew her. This stone has been placed by Queen Victoria as a mark of her regard.

Immediately to the right there is a second memorial with the following inscription:

> Sacred to the memory of Owen Couch, who died at Holyrood Palace on 9th November 1872 aged 72 years. He was a faithful servant in the household of their majesties George IV, William IV and Victoria for upwards of fifty years. Also of Mary Jupp his wife, who died at Musselburgh on 11th March 1875 aged 73 years.

Was it coincidence or is there another explanation of why two royal servants should be buried in adjoining graves? Perhaps palace officials were aware that the land acquired in 1854 was sufficiently large to allow the burial of two families and, as a mark of respect and in consideration of his long service to the throne, the lair was made available for the interment of Owen Couch and later his wife.

Fifty years is a long time to spend in one job, and in the case of Couch this meant serving three monarchs. What indiscretions did he overhear, remembered but never revealed, as he attended to the needs of two kings and a queen? Although he died at Holyrood, Couch must have spent some of his working life at Buckingham Palace, which was bought by George III in 1762.

He would have remembered George IV as a debtor, as the man who had a liaison with Mrs Fitzherbert and as builder of the Brighton Pavilion. George died in 1830 and was followed by William IV, third son of George III. Owen Couch would have recalled William as a statesman who refused to swamp the majority in the House of Lords which had rejected the Reform Bill in 1832. And, of course, Victoria.

Couch must have heard many stories and rumours in the rooms and corridors of the palaces but this faithful servant kept them secret.

The graves of the two royal servants can be found with no difficulty. From the main entrance in Pilrig Street walk straight ahead for perhaps 200 yards, then take the tarred pathway to the right. Count the stones which face directly onto the access, and the 'royal' memorials are numbers 13 and 14 along the line.

Queen Victoria's visits to Rosebank cemetery were strictly private and therefore the number of times she visited is unknown. On 7 August 1860, however, the queen reviewed army volunteers in the Queen's (Holyrood) Park. A total of 20,000 troops were on parade and accompanying the queen were her husband, Prince Albert, Princesses Alice, Helena and Louise, and Prince Arthur.

And it has been recorded that on 17 September Victoria was seen leaving Rosebank accompanied by Lady Churchill and Lord Charles Fitzroy, 'this visit being neither the first nor the second'.

One journal was to report: 'There is something very touching as well as endearing in the feeling which prompts the Queen of Great Britain to secure an hour, whenever possible, to visit the last resting place of her humble handmaid.'

BIRLINN LTD (incorporating John Donald and Polygon) is one of Scotlandís leading publishers with over four hundred titles in print. Should you wish to be put on our catalogue mailing list **contact**:

Catalogue Request
Birlinn Ltd
West Newington House
10 Newington Road
Edinburgh EH9 1QS
Scotland, UK

Tel: + 44 (0) 131 668 4371
Fax: + 44 (0) 131 668 4466
e-mail: info@birlinn.co.uk

Postage and packing is free within the UK. For overseas orders, postage and packing (airmail) will be charged at 30% of the total order value.

For more information, or to order online, visit our website at **www.birlinn.co.uk**